Table of Contents

Introduction

Advancing Phonics Skills builds on the scope and sequence of *Benchmark Advance*, Kindergarten–Grade 2. *APS* provides an enriched option for teaching essential phonological/phonemic awareness and phonics skills. In Kindergarten, the scope and sequence of phonics skills and high-frequency words is accelerated for use with students who are ready to advance to the next level of phonics instruction. In all three grades, the series introduces the most frequently used word families along with spelling words based on these word families, so that students have additional word-building tools to increase vocabulary. In addition, abundant reading, writing, listening, and speaking activities for every week encourage students to practice and apply their developing phonics and word skills.

Routines

Advancing Phonics Skills features instructional routines for phonological/phonemic awareness, phonics, high-frequency words, spelling, and dictation. These time-saving routines help maintain consistently high instructional standards and offer familiar structures that enable students to focus on content. The routines also provide a built-in formative assessment opportunity. These routines appear once at the beginning of each grade-level book. They use sample target elements and words, which appear with gray shading. As teachers use these routines in the classroom, they replace the shaded sample elements and words with others that correspond to a given week's phonics focus.

APS INSTRUCTIONAL ROUTINES

- Word Awareness
- Sentence Awareness
- Syllable Segmentation
- Syllable Blending
- Rhyme Recognition
- Rhyme Production
- Onset and Rime Segmentation
- Onset and Rime Blending
- Phoneme Recognition
- Phoneme Isolation
- Phoneme Segmentation
- Phoneme Blending
- Phoneme Categorization
- Phoneme Substitution
- Phoneme Addition
- Phoneme Deletion
- Introduce Sound/Spelling Correspondence
- Blend Words
- Build Words
- Introduce High-Frequency Words
- Practice High-Frequency Words
- Introduce Spelling Words
- Spell Words in Context
- Dictation

Routine 8: Onset and Rime Blending

Model

Say: *Today we are going to blend, or put together, the first sound and end part of a word to make a whole word. I'll say the first sound and then the end of a word. Next I'll blend the first sound and the end part together to make the word. Listen: /f/ /an/,* fan. *What is the word? The word is* fan.

Guided Practice

Say: *Now say /fff/ with me. /fff/ What is the sound? (/fff/) Now say /aaannn/ with me. (/aaannn/) If we blend /fff/ and /aaannn/ together we get /fffaaannn/. Say it few times, a little faster each time. What is the word?* (fan)

Apply

Say: *Your turn. Listen to the word parts I say. Repeat the words parts I say aloud and then blend them together to make the word.*

Routine 8 Adaptations
• Adapt the routine using words that begin with a consonant blend.

Routine 9: Phoneme Recognition

Materials: Picture cards: magnet, map, mitten

Model

Say: *Today we are going to listen for the first sound we hear in some words. What do you see in the pictures?* (magnet, map, mitten) *Listen as I say the words again:* magnet, map, mitten. *I hear the /m/ sound at the beginning of all three words.*

Guided Practice

Say: *Now listen to these words:* tiger, top, tub. *Let's say the words together:* tiger, top, tub. *The beginning sound I hear in* tiger, top, *and* tub *is /t/. Repeat the beginning sound with me.* (/t/)

Apply

Say: *Your turn. Repeat these words:* fan, fish, fox. *What sound do you hear at the beginning of these words? (/f/) Repeat the beginning sound with me.* (/f/)

Routine 9 Adaptations
• Adapt the routine for medial and final sounds in words.
• Adapt the routine for initial and final digraphs and blends in words.

Tools for Meaningful Phonics Instruction

These grade-level pages enrich student learning of essential phonics and word skills through listening, speaking, reading, and writing opportunities.

Interactive Writing

Interactive writing features group writing every week to practice newly acquired phonics skills and use of word families in a supportive and fun activity.

Collaborative Conversations

Collaborative conversations offer students opportunities to develop oral language as they discuss and exchange ideas about the passages they read.

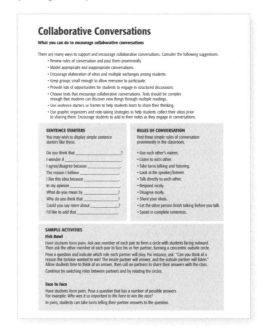

Using the Decodable Readers

Decodable readers provide opportunities for students to apply newly acquired phonics skills and high-frequency words in a new context.

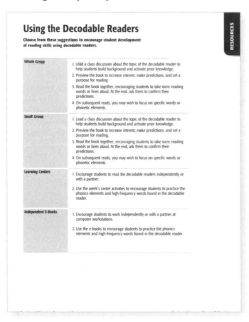

Using Flexible Blackline Masters

The four flexible BLMs (A, B, C, and D) show simple generic formats that can be customized for use in a variety of phonics games and activities.

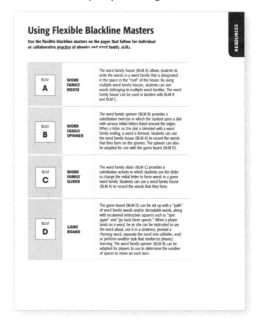

Consistent Daily Instruction

The Advancing Phonics Every Day spread offers a consistent instructional sequence for every day of the week. These activities can be used to reinforce core instruction, to provide additional practice, or to accelerate and deepen instruction.

Phonological/Phonemic Awareness
To foster awareness of the rhythms and sounds of English

Phonics
To build knowledge of sound/symbol correspondence

Word Families
To increase vocabulary through word-building

High-Frequency Words
To teach the most common words we use every day

Writing
To practice encoding of new sounds and symbols

Spelling
To reinforce spelling patterns

Shared Reading
To apply decoding skills in a new context

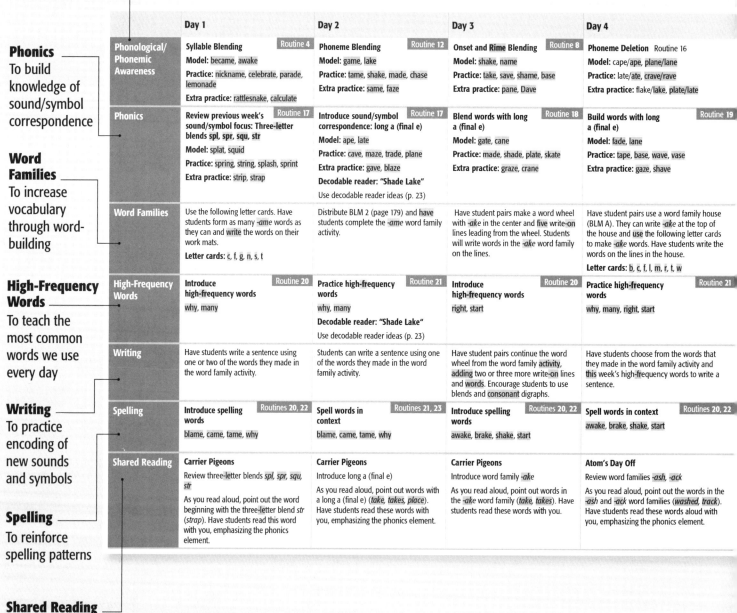

	Day 1	Day 2	Day 3	Day 4
Phonological/ Phonemic Awareness	**Syllable Blending** Routine 4 **Model:** became, awake **Practice:** nickname, celebrate, parade, lemonade **Extra practice:** rattlesnake, calculate	**Phoneme Blending** Routine 12 **Model:** game, lake **Practice:** tame, shake, made, chase **Extra practice:** same, faze	**Onset and Rime Blending** Routine 8 **Model:** shake, name **Practice:** take, save, shame, base **Extra practice:** pane, Dave	**Phoneme Deletion** Routine 16 **Model:** cape/ape, plane/lane **Practice:** late/ate, crave/rave **Extra practice:** flake/lake, plate/late
Phonics	**Review previous week's sound/symbol focus: Three-letter blends spl, spr, squ, str** Routine 17 **Model:** splat, squid **Practice:** spring, string, splash, sprint **Extra practice:** strip, strap	**Introduce sound/symbol correspondence: long a (final e)** Routine 17 **Model:** ape, late **Practice:** cave, maze, trade, plane **Extra practice:** gave, blaze **Decodable reader: "Shade Lake"** Use decodable reader ideas (p. 23)	**Blend words with long a (final e)** Routine 18 **Model:** gate, cane **Practice:** made, shade, plate, skate **Extra practice:** graze, crane	**Build words with long a (final e)** Routine 19 **Model:** fade, lane **Practice:** tape, base, wave, vase **Extra practice:** gaze, shave
Word Families	Use the following letter cards. Have students form as many -ame words as they can and write the words on their work mats. **Letter cards:** c, f, g, n, s, t	Distribute BLM 2 (page 179) and have students complete the -ame word family activity.	Have student pairs make a word wheel with -ake in the center and five write-on lines leading from the wheel. Students will write words in the -ake word family on the lines.	Have student pairs use a word family house (BLM A). They can write -ake at the top of the house and use the following letter cards to make -ake words. Have students write the words on the lines in the house. **Letter cards:** b, c, f, l, m, r, t, w
High-Frequency Words	**Introduce high-frequency words** Routine 20 why, many	**Practice high-frequency words** Routine 21 why, many **Decodable reader: "Shade Lake"** Use decodable reader ideas (p. 23)	**Introduce high-frequency words** Routine 20 right, start	**Practice high-frequency words** Routine 21 why, many, right, start
Writing	Have students write a sentence using one or two of the words they made in the word family activity.	Students can write a sentence using one of the words they made in the word family activity.	Have student pairs continue the word wheel from the word family activity, adding two or three more write-on lines and words. Encourage students to use blends and consonant digraphs.	Have students choose from the words that they made in the word family activity and this week's high-frequency words to write a sentence.
Spelling	**Introduce spelling words** Routines 20, 22 blame, came, tame, why	**Spell words in context** Routines 21, 23 blame, came, tame, why	**Introduce spelling words** Routines 20, 22 awake, brake, shake, start	**Spell words in context** Routines 20, 22 awake, brake, shake, start
Shared Reading	**Carrier Pigeons** Review three-letter blends spl, spr, squ, str As you read aloud, point out the word beginning with the three-letter blend str (strap). Have students read this word with you, emphasizing the phonics element.	**Carrier Pigeons** Introduce long a (final e) As you read aloud, point out words with a long a (final e) (take, takes, place). Have students read these words with you, emphasizing the phonics element.	**Carrier Pigeons** Introduce word family -ake As you read aloud, point out words in the -ake word family (take, takes). Have students read these words with you.	**Atom's Day Off** Review word families -ash, -ack As you read aloud, point out the words in the -ash and -ack word families (washed, track). Have students read these words aloud with you, emphasizing the phonics element.

Collaborative Learning and Independent Practice

Collaborative learning and independent practice activities offer students multiple opportunities to build targeted skills through games that encourage teamwork and reflection, and short texts with speaking, writing, and drawing response options. Many of the activities use the weekly word and picture cards to practice spelling patterns and word families.

Day 5	Collaborative Learning and Independent Practice*
	• Elkonin Boxes: Words with Long a (Final e) Days 1–5
	• Phonemic Concentration: Words with Long a (Final e) Days 3–5
Decodable reader: "Shade Lake" Use decodable reader ideas (p. 23)	• Phonics Picture Word Cards: Words with Long a (Final e) Days 1–5 • Word Rainbows: Words with Long a (Final e) Days 3–5 • Read/Underline/Write: "The Same Name": Words with Long a (Final e) Days 3–5
Review -ame, -ake words Display the *cake, flake, frame, game, rake,* and *same* picture cards. Have students take turns saying the word for one of the pictures and then using the word in an oral sentence.	• Word Family Scramble: -ame Days 1–5 • Word Family Ice Cream Cones: -ame, -ake Days 3–5 • Word Family Tic-Tac-Toe: -ame, -ake Days 3–5
Decodable reader: "Shade Lake" Use decodable reader ideas (p. 23)	• High-Frequency Word Board Game Days 1–5 • High-Frequency Word Yoga Days 3–5
Interactive writing (see p. 22) **Story starter:** Jake likes to bake cakes. **Word bank:** came, name, fame, take, shake, flake, make	• Reading/Writing: Respond to the Story "Nate and Kate Skate" Days 1–5 • Reading/Writing: Continue the Story "The Bake Sale" Days 3–5
Test words in dictation Read aloud each of the week's spelling words for students to write. Then collect and review student work.	• Spelling Homework: BLM 1 Days 1–5
Atom's Day Off Review inflectional ending *-ed* As you read aloud, point out the verbs ending in *-ed* (*washed, cooked, cleaned, beeped*). Have students read these words aloud with you.	

Weekly spelling list with home connection for every day of the week

Reading, drawing, and writing activities with listening and speaking connections

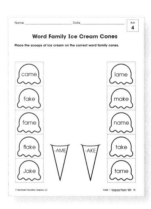

Activities to build phonics, word-building, and fine motor skills simultaneously

Pacing Guide

Teacher's Resource System Unit	Advancing Phonics Skills Week	Phonics Skill	High-Frequency Words	Word Families	Advancing Phonics
Being a Good Community Member	1	Short a; ck/k/	the, see, go, she, and	at, ad, an	pp. 30–31
	2	Short i; plural nouns (-s)	play, little, you, with	in, it, ip	pp. 42–43
	3	Short o; double final consonants	for, no, jump, one, have	op, og, ot	pp. 54–55
Many Kinds of Characters	4	Short e	are, said, two, look, my	et, en, ell	pp. 66–67
	5	Short u; inflectional endings (-s)	come, here, to, of	ug, up, un	pp. 78–79
	6	l-blends	what, put, want, this, saw	ob, ot, ock	pp. 90–91
Plants and Animals Grow and Change	7	r-blends; possessives	now, do, which, went	im, ill, ick	pp. 102–103
	8	s-blends, contractions ('s)	was, there, then, out	ap, am, ag	pp. 114–115
	9	Final consonant blends (nd, nk, nt, mp, st); inflectional endings (-ed, no spelling change)	who, good, by, them	ent, est	pp. 126–127
Stories Have a Narrator	10	Consonant digraphs (th, sh, ng); inflectional endings (-ing, no spelling change)	were, our, could, these	ung, ing, ink	pp. 138–139
	11	Consonant digraphs (ch, tch, wh); closed syllables	once, upon, hurt, that	unk, ump	pp. 150–151
	12	Three-letter blends (spl, spr, squ, str); plurals (-es) compound words	because, from, their, when	ash, ack	pp. 162–163
Technology at Work	13	Long a (final e); vowel-consonant-e syllables	why, many, right, start	ame, ake	pp. 174–175
	14	Long o (final e)	find, how, over, under	ope, ape	pp. 186–187
	15	Soft c, g; contractions with not	try, give, far, too	ace, age	pp. 198–199
Stories Teach Many Lessons	16	Long i (final e)	after, call, large, her	ine, ife, ide	pp. 210–211
	17	Long e (final e), long u (final e); inflectional endings (-ed, -ing, dropping final e)	house, long, off, small	ale, ane, une	pp. 222–223
	18	Long a vowel teams (ai, ay); inflectional endings (-ed, -ing, double final consonant)	brown, work, year, live	ail, ain, ay	pp. 234–235

Teacher's Resource System Unit	Advancing Phonics Skills Week	Phonics Skill	High-Frequency Words	Word Families	Advancing Phonics
Past, Present, and Future	19	Long o vowel teams and single letters (o, oa); long o vowel teams and single letters (ow, oe)	found, your, know, always	ow, oat, old	pp. 246–247
	20	Long e vowel teams and single letters (e, ee, ea, ie); prefixes un-, re-	all, people, where, draw	eat, eet, eed	pp. 258–259
	21	Long i vowel teams and single letters (i, y, igh); open syllables	again, round, they, country	ight, ice, ile	pp. 270–271
Observing the Sky	22	/är/ (farm); vowel-r syllables	four, great, boy, city	ar, all	pp. 282–283
	23	/ôr/ (for, ore); /ôr/ (oar)	laugh, move, change, away	orn, ore, oar	pp. 294–295
	24	/ûr/ (girl, herb, spur)	every, near, school, earth	ern, urn	pp. 306–307
We Use Goods and Services	25	/ou/ (house, clown); comparative inflectional endings (-er, -est)	before, done, about, even	out, ouse, own	pp. 318–319
	26	/oi/ (join, boy); suffix -ly	walk, buy, only, through	oil, oin	pp. 330–331
	27	/ōō/ (broom) vowel team syllables; /ŏŏ/ (book) vowel team syllables (single and multi-syllable words)	does, another, wash, some	oom (boom), ood (good)	pp. 342–343
Exploring Sound and Light	28	Silent letters (wr, kn, gn)	better, carry, learn, very	oon (moon), ool (pool)	pp. 354–355
	29	/ô/ (aw, au, al, augh); suffixes (ful, less)	mother, father, never, below	aw, awn	pp. 366–367
	30	Long e (y, ey); consonant-le syllables	blue, answer, eight, any	eep, ey	pp. 378–379

Routine 1: Word Awareness

Materials: Workmat with Elkonin box, counters

Model

Say: *Today we are going to count words in a sentence.* Listen: Dogs run fast. *Now I'm going to slide a counter into the box for each word in the sentence.*

Repeat each word in the sentence clearly. For each word, slide a counter into a cell of a three-cell Elkonin box. Then touch and count each one.

Say: *Now I'll count. There are one, two, three counters. That means there are three words in the sentence.*

Guided Practice

Say: *Now let's repeat the sentence. This time, we'll say it together. For each word we say, let's slide a counter into a box:* Dogs run fast. *Now repeat the sentence slowly, and touch a counter for each word you hear.*

Say: *How many counters are there?* (three) *How many words are there in the sentence?* (three) *Right. There are three words in the sentence:* Dogs run fast.

Apply

Say: *Your turn. Say a sentence and slide a counter into a box for each word you hear. Now touch each counter and count them. How many counters are there? How many words are in the sentence?*

Routine 1 Adaptations

• Adapt the routine using sentences that have more than three words.

Routine 2: Sentence Awareness

Model

Say: *Today we are going to learn about sentences. Listen to this sentence:* Dad reads stories. *"Dad reads stories." is a sentence. It tells about someone doing something.* Ask a student to come to the front and complete a simple action. Actions might include: hopping, jumping, clapping, humming, walking, stomping, laughing.

Say: *I can make a sentence by saying [_____'s] name and telling what he or she is doing.* Provide more examples of simple oral sentences using the names of other students in the class.

Guided Practice

Ask a different student to perform an action while others watch. **Say:** *What is his/her name? What is he/she doing?* Then work as a class to make a sentence. The sentence should start with the student's name and describe what he or she is doing.

Apply

Say: *Your turn. I will ask a volunteer to perform an action, and you will create a simple sentence to describe it.*

Routine 2 Adaptations

• Adapt the routine by having student start sentences with things rather than people.

Routine 3: Syllable Segmentation

Model

Say: *Today we are going to segment, or take apart, the syllables we hear in a word. A syllable is a word part. Words are formed of syllables. Listen carefully to the words I say. The first word is* magnet. *Be sure to stress each syllable. Repeat the word with me:* magnet. *Listen:* mag-net. *There are two syllables, or chunks, in* magnet. *Let's say them together slowly:* mag-net. *Say the first syllable with me.* (mag) *Now say the second syllable with me.* (net)

Guided Practice

Say: *Say* magnet. *What is the word?* (magnet) *Now say the syllables slowly with me, stressing each one.* (mag-net) *How many syllables do you hear in* magnet? (two) *What is the first syllable?* (mag) *What is the second syllable?* (net)

Apply

Say: *Your turn. The word is* napkin. *Now say the syllables you hear slowly, stressing each one.* (nap-kin). *Tell me how many syllables are in* napkin. (two) *Then tell me what the syllables are.* (nap-kin)

Routine 3 Adaptations

• Adapt the routine using the names of students.

• Adapt the routine using compound words and three-syllable words.

• Use Elkonin boxes and counters to count the number of syllables in each word.

Routine 4: Syllable Blending

Model

Say: *Today we are going to blend, or put together, syllables to make a whole word. I'll say the syllables in a word as I clap on each one. Next I'll blend the syllables together to make the word. Listen:* pump *(clap)* kin *(clap),* pumpkin. *What is the word?* (The word is pumpkin.)

Guided Practice

Say: *Now clap and say each syllable with me:* pump *(clap)* kin *(clap). If we blend* pump *and* kin *together, we get* pumpkin. *Say the syllables together fast. What is the word?* (pumpkin)

Apply

Say: *Your turn. Listen to the syllables. Repeat the syllables I say aloud:* pen *(clap)* cil *(clap). Now blend the syllables together. What's the word?* (pencil)

Routine 4 Adaptations

• Adapt the routine using the names of students.

• Adapt the routine using compound words and three-syllable words.

• Use Elkonin boxes and counters to count the number of syllables in each word.

Routine 5: Rhyme Recognition

Materials: Picture cards for rhyming word pairs like: *cat/hat, hen/ten, frog/log, fox/box, fan/pan, mouse/house, vest/nest*

Model

Say: *Today we are going to identify rhyming words. Let's look at pairs of pictures together. The first two pictures show a* cat *and a* hat*. Listen as I repeat the names of the pictures:* cat, hat*. These words both end with /at/. Listen: /k/ /at/,* cat*; /h/ /at/,* hat*. They end with the same sounds, so that means they rhyme.*

Guided Practice

Say: *Now let's look at two more pairs of pictures. What do you see in the first one?* (hen) *Say* hen *with me.* (hen) *Say the ending sounds in* hen *with me.* (/en/) *What do you see in the second picture?* (the number 10) *Now say* ten *with me.* (ten) *Say the ending sounds in* ten *with me.* (/en/) *Do* hen *and* ten *have the same ending sounds?* (yes) Hen *and* ten *have the same ending sounds, so they rhyme.*

Apply

Say: *Your turn. Say* frog*.* (frog) *Say the ending sounds in* frog*.* (/og/) *Now say* log*.* (log) *Say the ending sounds in* log*.* (/og/) *Do these words rhyme?* (yes)

Routine 5 Adaptations
• Adapt the same routine for groups of three words.
• Adapt the same routine using some pairs that don't rhyme.

Routine 6: Rhyme Production

Materials: Picture cards for words like: *cat, hen, frog, fox, fan, mouse, vest*

Model

Say: *Today we are going to produce rhyming words. Let's look at this picture together. What does the picture show?* (cat) *Let's repeat the word:* cat*. What do you hear at the end of* cat*?* (/at/) *Now I'll think of a word that rhymes with* cat*. How about* hat*?* (yes) *Yes,* hat *rhymes with* cat *because both words end with /at/.*

Guided Practice

Say: *Let's look at another picture. What does the picture show?* (hen) *Now say* hen *with me.* (hen) *Say the ending sound in* hen *with me.* (/en/) *Yes,* hen *ends with /en/. Now let's think of another word that ends with /en/. Does* ten *end with /en/?* (yes) *Let's repeat both words together and listen for their ending sounds. Do* hen *and* ten *have the same ending sounds?* (yes) *That means that they rhyme.*

Apply

Say: *Your turn. Say* frog*.* (frog) *Say the ending sounds in* frog*.* (/og/) *Now say another word that has the same ending sounds. What is the new word? Do these words rhyme?*

Routine 6 Adaptations
• Adapt the routine using words that don't rhyme.
• Adapt the routine using groups of three words, two of which rhyme.

Routine 7: Onset and Rime Segmentation

Model

Say: *Today we are going to segment, or take apart, the sounds we hear in a word. The word is* fit. *Listen:* fit. *I'll say the first sound and then the end of the word. The first sound in* fit *is* /fff/. *The end part of* fit *is* /it/. *Listen:* fit, /fff/ /it/.

Guided Practice

Say: *Now say* fit *with me. Say the first sound in* fit. (/fff/) *What is the first sound?* (/fff/) *Now say the end part.* (/it/) *What is the end part?* (/it/) *Listen:* fit, /fff/ /it/.

Apply

Say: *Your turn. Say* bin. *Tell me the first sound you hear in* bin. (/b/) *Now tell me the end part of the word* bin. (/in/)

Routine 7 Adaptations

• Adapt the routine using words that begin with a consonant blend.

Routine 8: Onset and Rime Blending

Model

Say: *Today we are going to blend, or put together, the first sound and end part of a word to make a whole word. I'll say the first sound and then the end of a word. Next I'll blend the first sound and the end part together to make the word. Listen:* /f/ /an/, fan. *What is the word? The word is* fan.

Guided Practice

Say: *Now say* /fff/ *with me.* /fff/ *What is the sound?* (/fff/) *Now say* /aaannn/ *with me.* (/aaannn/) *If we blend* /fff/ *and* /aaannn/ *together we get* /fffaaannn/. *Say it few times, a little faster each time. What is the word?* (fan)

Apply

Say: *Your turn. Listen to the word parts I say.* /s/ /it/ *Repeat the word parts I say aloud and then blend them together to make the word.* (/s/ /it/, /sss/ /iii/ /t/, sit)

Routine 8 Adaptations

• Adapt the routine using words that begin with a consonant blend.

Routine 9: Phoneme Recognition

Materials: Picture cards: *magnet, map, mitten*

Model

Say: *Today we are going to listen for the first sound we hear in some words. What do you see in the pictures?* (magnet, map, mitten) *Listen as I say the words again:* magnet, map, mitten. *I hear the /m/ sound at the beginning of all three words.*

Guided Practice

Say: *Now listen to these words:* tiger, top, tub. *Let's say the words together:* tiger, top, tub. *The beginning sound I hear in* tiger, top, *and* tub *is /t/. Repeat the beginning sound with me.* (/t/)

Apply

Say: *Your turn. Repeat these words:* fan, fish, fox. *What sound do you hear at the beginning of these words?* (/f/) *Repeat the beginning sound with me.* (/f/)

Routine 9 Adaptations

• Adapt the routine for medial and final sounds in words.

• Adapt the routine for initial and final digraphs and blends in words.

Routine 10: Phoneme Isolation

Materials: Picture cards: *ball, mouse, top*

Model

Say: *Today we are going to identify the first sound we hear in a word. Let's look at the picture. The picture shows a* ball. *Say* ball *with me.* (ball) *The first sound in* ball *is /b/.* Enunciate clearly both the /b/ sound in the word and the /b/ sound in isolation.

Guided Practice

Say: *Let's look at another picture. The picture shows a* mouse. *Say* mouse *with me.* (mouse) *What is the first sound you hear in* mouse? (/m/) *Let's repeat both the word* mouse *and the /m/ sound we hear at the beginning of the word.*

Apply

Display the picture card of a *top* for students.

Say: *Your turn. What is this a picture of?* (a top) *Say the first sound you hear. Repeat both the word and first sound you hear in the word.*

Routine 10 Adaptations

• Adapt the same routine for medial and final sounds.

Routine 11: Phoneme Segmentation

Model

Say: *Today we are going to segment, or take apart, all the sounds in a word. Listen:* cap. *Now listen and watch:* cap, /k/ ... /aaa/ ... /p/. *Say the word slowly and hold up one finger for each sound. I count my fingers 1, 2, 3. . . 3. There are three sounds in* cap.

Guided Practice

Say: *Say* cap. (cap) *Now say* cap *slowly and hold up one finger for each sound.* (/k/ ... /aaa/ ... /p/) *How many fingers are you holding up?* (3) *How many sounds are in* cap? (3) *Yes, there are three sounds in* cap.

Apply

Say: *Your turn. Say* tan. (tan) *Now say* tan *slowly and hold up one finger for each sound.* (/t/ ... /aaa/ ... /nnn/) *How many fingers are you holding up?* (3) *How many sounds are in* tan? (3)

Routine 11 Adaptations

• Adapt the routine by having students push a marker into an Elkonin box for each sound.

Routine 12: Phoneme Blending

Model

Say: *Today we are going to blend sounds together to make a word. Listen:* /mmm/ /aaa/ /p/. *I will blend the sounds together to say the word:* /mmm/ /aaa/ /p/, /mmmaaap/, map.

Guided Practice

Say: *Say* /mmm/ /aaa/ /p/. *Now say the sounds together a few times, a little bit faster each time. That's how you blend the sounds to make a word. What is the word?* (map) *Yes, when you blend the sounds* /mmm/ /aaa/ /p/ *together quickly, you get the word* map.

Apply

Say: *Your turn. Listen as I blend the sounds in a word* /sss/ /aaa/ /p/. *Now you blend the sounds.* (/sss/ /aaa/ /p/, /sssaaap/) *What is the word?* (sap)

Routine 12 Adaptations

• Adapt the routine by having students blend words with four or more sounds.

Routine 13: Phoneme Categorization

Model

Say: *Today we are going to listen for words that have sounds in common. I'm going to say three words. Two of the words will start with the same sound. The third word will start with a different sound. Listen carefully so you can tell me the words that start with the same sound and the word that starts with a different sound. For instance, if I say* moon, mat, *and* pin, *you would tell me that* moon *and* mat *start with the* /m/ *sound, but that* pin *starts with the* /p/ *sound.*

Guided Practice

Say: *Listen carefully as I say these three words:* bat, fed, bump. *What is the first sound you hear in* bat? *(*/b/*) What is the first sound you hear in* fed? *(*/f/*) What is the first sound you hear in* bump? *(*/b/*) Which two words start with the same sound?* (bat, bump) *Yes, these words start with* /b/. *And which word starts with a different sound?* (fed)

Apply

Say: *Your turn. Listen to these sets of three words and tell me which words start with the same sound and which one starts with a different sound:* red, sad, sick.

Routine 13 Adaptations
• Adapt the routine choosing words that have medial and final sounds in common.

Routine 14: Phoneme Substitution

Materials: Picture card: *rug*

Model

Say: *We are going to substitute one sound in a word to make a new word.* Display the rug picture word card.

Say: *This is a* rug. *Listen:* /ru//g/. *If I take away the sound* /g/ *from the end of* rug, *I get the sounds* /ru/. *If I add the sound* /n/ *after the sounds* /ru/, *I make a new word:* /ru//nnn/, run. Display the run picture word card.

Guided Practice

Display the picture on the *rug* picture word card.

Say: *Say* rug *with me.* (rug) *Take away the sound* /r/ *from the beginning of the word. What sounds are left? Say* /ug/ *with me.* (/ug/) *Now add the sound* /b/ *to the beginning of* /ug/ *and say the new word with me:* /b/ /ug/. Bug. *What is the new word?* (bug) Display the *bug* picture word card.

Apply

Say: *Your turn. Listen:* bug. *Take away the* /g/ *sound from the end of the word. What sounds are left?* (/bu/) *Now, add the sound* /n/ *to the end of* /bu/. *What is the new word?* (bun)

Routine 14 Adaptations
• Adapt the same routine for initial and medial sounds.
• Use letter cards to model substituting sounds in words.

Routine 15: Phoneme Addition

Model

Say: *We are going to add sounds to a word to make a new word. Listen:* in. *I will add the sound* /f/ *to the beginning to make a new word:* /f/ /in/, fin. *Fin is the new word.*

Guided Practice

Say: *Listen:* in. *Add the sound* /f/ *to the beginning of* in *to make a new word, and repeat after me:* /f/ /in/. *What is the new word?* (fin) *Yes,* fin *is the new word.*

Apply

Say: *Your turn. Listen:* in. *Add the sound* /p/ *to the beginning of* in *to make a new word. What is the new word?* (pin)

Routine 15 Adaptations

• Use letter cards to model substituting sounds in words. This visual representation will make it easier for students to do the task orally.

Routine 16: Phoneme Deletion

Model

Say: *We are going to take away sounds from a word to make a new word. Listen:* pan, /p /a/ /n/. *I will take away the sound* /p/ *from the beginning to make a new word:* /an/. *An is the new word.*

Guided Practice

Say: *Listen:* pan. *Take away the sound* /p/ *from the beginning of the word to make a new word, and repeat after me:* /an/. *What is the new word?* (an) *Yes,* an *is the new word.*

Apply

Say: *Your turn. Listen:* mat. *Take away the sound* /m/ *from the beginning of* mat *to make a new word. What is the new word?* (at) *Yes,* at *is the new word.*

Routine 16 Adaptations

• Use letter cards to model deleting sounds in words. This visual representation will make it easier for students to do the task orally.

Routine 17: Introduce Sound/Symbol Correspondence

Materials: Frieze card: Short vowel a

Model

Display the Short vowel /a/ frieze card.

Say: *The sound is /a/. The /a/ sound is spelled with a. Point to the spelling that stands for the sound.*

Ask: *What is the sound? (/a/) What letters or spellings stand for the sound?* (a)

Guided Practice

Point to the first picture on the frieze card. Say its name, write it on the board, and underline the letter (or spelling) that stands for the sound.

Say: *Look at the word I wrote:* a-p-p-l-e. *I see /a/ spelled* a.
Listen and watch as I sound out the word: /apple/.

Repeat this procedure for every picture and spelling you are focusing on in the lesson. Model how to sound out each word that you write.

Apply

Say: *Your turn. I am going to say some words with the /a/ sound. You will write each word and underline the spelling that stands for the /a/ sound:* cat, map, sat, map.

Make sure the words are ones students can read and write based on the phonics skills they have been taught so far.

Routine 18: Word Blending

Model

Write the letters *s - i - t* on the board. Pronounce the word *sit* slowly, pointing to each letter as you pronounce its sound.

Say: *I know that the letter* s *makes the /s/ sound. The letter* i *makes the /i/ sound, and the letter* t *makes the /t/ sound. When I pronounce the sounds of the letters together, they form a word. Slowly sound out the word by drawing your hand under each letter as you say its sound: /sss/ - /iii/ - /t/, /sssiiit/.* Sit. *These letters spell the word* sit.

Guided Practice

Point to the letters *s - i - t* on the board.

Say: *Pronounce these sounds with me one at a time. (/s/ - /i/ - /t/) Now let's blend those sounds by saying them together. (/sss - iii - t/, /sssiiit/) What word do these sounds make when they're blended together?* (sit)

Apply

Say: *Your turn. Pronounce each of the letters on the board. (/m/ - /a/ - /t/) Now blend their letter sounds together. (/mmm -aaa - t/, /mmmaaat/) What word do these sounds form?* (mat)

Routine 18 Adaptations

• Adapt the routine using words with blends and digraphs.

Routine 19: Word Building

Materials: Letter cards *a, m, n, p, t*

Model

Say: *The letters* m - a - t *spell the word* mat. *Let's blend all the sounds together to read the word:* /mmmaaat/, mat. *What's the word?* (mat) *Now I want to make the word* map. *Which letter will I change? The word* map *ends with the* /p/ *sound so I will replace the letter* t *in* mat *with the letter* p. *Let's blend all the sounds to read the new word:* /mmmaaap/, map. *Is the new word* map? (yes)

Guided Practice

Say: *Use your letter cards to make the word* mat. *Which letter do you have to change to make the word* map? *That's right, you replace the letter* t *with* p. *Why?* (The ending sound is different.) *Sound out the new word formed. What is the word?* (map)

Apply

Say: *Now it's your turn.* Provide a series of words to guide student practice. Say one word at a time. Ask students to add, remove, or change the letter or letters needed to make the new word. Use this sequence: *map, man, pan, pat.* Have students blend each new word formed to confirm before moving on to the next word.

Routine 19 Adaptations

• For students needing extra support, tell them which letter or letters to change and guide them to blend the new word formed.

• Add words with review skills to the word-building chains to build mastery.

Routine 20: Introduce High-Frequency Words

Materials: High-frequency word card: *for*
Display the word card *for* or write *for* on the board.

Read the Word

Point to the word for.
Say: *This word is* for. *Say it with me:* for. *I eat eggs* for *breakfast.*

Spell the Word

Say: *We spell the word* for f-o-r. *Spell the word* for *with me:* f-o-r.

Write the Word

Say: *Watch as I write the word* for. *I will say each letter name as I write it. Let's write the word* for *in the air as we spell it together:* f-o-r. *Say each letter as you write it.*

Say: *Your turn. Write the word* for *three times. Spell it aloud as you write it.*

Routine 20 Adaptations
• Have student partners say oral sentences using the word. Then have them write the sentences on the workmats.

Routine 21: Practice High-Frequency Words

Materials: High-frequency word card: *no*; pocket chart
Display the word card *no* in a pocket chart.

Read the Word

Point to the word *no*.
Say: *This word is* no. *Say it with me:* no. No, *I don't eat eggs for breakfast.*

Spell the Word

Say: *Spell the word* no *with me:* n-o. *What's the first sound you hear in* no? (/n/) *What letter do we know that makes the* /n/ *sound?* (n) *What letter begins the word* no? (n)

Write the Word

Say: *Let's write the word* no *in the air as we spell it together:* n-o. *Say each letter as you write it.*

Routine 21 Adaptations
• Have students practice reading previous high-frequency words for mastery.

Routine 22: Introduce Spelling Words

Model

Write the words *math* and *thin* on the board.

Say: *Today, let's practice spelling words with the /th/ sound. Let's say it together: /th/. We can spell the /th/ sound with the letters* t-h. *Now listen as I say the word* math. *I will sound out the word and spell it: /m/ - /a/ - /th/,* math. *Write each letter on the board as you say the sound.*

Say: *Now listen as I say the word* thin: */ttthhh/ - /i/ - /n/. I can spell the /th/ sound with the letters* t-h.

Guided Practice

Say: *Let's look at the word* math *and sound it out together: /m/ - /a/ - /th/. Place your finger under each letter or letters as you sound it out. What is this word?* (math) *How do you spell the /th/ sound in the word* math? (th)

Say: *Now let's look at the word* thin *and sound it out together: /th/ - /i/ - /n/. Place your finger under each letter as you sound it out. What is this word?* (thin) *How do you spell the /th/ sound in the word* thin? (th)

Apply

Say: *Your turn.* Cover the word math on the board with your hand. *How do you spell the word* math? (m, a, t, h) *Now read the word aloud.* (math) *Which letters make the /th/ sound?* (th) *Let's try this with the word* thin.

Routine 23: Spell Words in Context

Model

On the board, write the following sentence: *The math book is thin.*

Say: *Today, let's practice reading and spelling words with the /th/ sound. Listen as I read this sentence. The words* thin *and* math *both contain the /th/ sound. Now, I am going to read these words slowly: /th/ /i/ /n/, and /m/ - /a/ - /th/. In each word, the letters* t-h *make the /th/ sound.*

Guided Practice

Say: *Listen as I read the sentence again. What words contain the /th/ sound?* (thin, math) *Yes, and what letters do you use to spell the /th/ sound?* (th) *Now, I am going to point to a word in the sentence.* Point to the word thin. **Say:** *What is this word?* (thin)

Do the same for the word math.

Apply

Say: *Now it is your turn to spell and write words with a /th/ sound. Work with a partner to write a sentence using either of the following words:* thin, math.

Routine 24: Dictation

Materials: Student workmat with Elkonin boxes

Model

Display or draw Elkonin boxes.

Say: *When we spell a word, we listen to each sound in the word, then we write a letter or spelling for that sound. Listen as I say the sounds in* sat*: /sssaaat/. I hear three sounds: /s/ … /a/ … /t/. I will draw a circle in each box on the Elkonin boxes as I say each sound.*

Say: *Now I will replace each circle with a letter. I know that the letter* s *stands for the /s/ sound. I will write an* s *in the first box. The next sound in* sat *is /a/. I'll write the letter* a *in the second box. The last sound in* sat *is /t/. I'll write the letter* t *in the third box. Now I'll blend together the sounds to make sure I wrote* sat*: /sssaaat/.*

Guided Practice

Say: *Now say the sounds in* sat*: /sssaaat/. How many sounds do you hear?* (three) *What are the sounds you hear?* (/s/ … /a/ … /t/) *Draw a circle in one cell of the Elkonin box for each sound.*

Say: *Now let's replace each circle with a letter. What letter stands for the /s/ sound in* sat*?* (s) *So we'll write the letter* s *in the first box. What letter stands for the /a/ sound in* sat*?* (a) *So we'll write the letter* a *in the second box. And what letter stands for the /t/ sound in* sat*?* (t) *So we'll write the letter* t *in the third box. Now let's blend together the sounds to make sure we wrote* sat*: /sssaaat/.*

Apply

Say: *Your turn. Say the sounds in* mat*: /mmmaaat/. Tell how many sounds you hear in* mat *and draw a circle in one cell of the Elkonin boxes for each sound.*

Say: *Think about the letter that stands for each sound. Now replace each circle with the letter. Now blend together the sounds of the letters. What word did you write?* (mat)

Interactive Writing in the Classroom

What Is Interactive Writing?

Interactive writing encourages active learning, builds confidence, and helps students develop the writing skills they'll use throughout their school careers. The modeling and scaffolding you provide make it a powerful learning tool.

Unlike shared writing, students involved in interactive writing share the pen with the teacher and classmates, so the whole group writes the text together. Interactive writing can be used to teach or reinforce print concepts, phonemic awareness, phonics, and language conventions. It can also be used to practice and apply phonics skills, word families, and high-frequency words in both whole-class and small-group settings.

Materials

Have these basic materials ready before starting interactive writing:

• An illustrated alphabet chart or poster (for reference)
• Chart paper
• Markers in assorted colors
• Correction tape (or blank labels)
• A pointer (to track rereading)

Procedure

• Decide on a topic with students.
• Early in the year, you might supply an oral sentence that the class can write together.
• Begin by having students write the text one word at a time. As their proficiency increases, they can write a phrase or a sentence.
• Lead students as they reread each new chunk of text in order to check their understanding.
• After writing, proofread the text together.
• Illustrate the text, particularly for emergent readers. After the illustrator or illustrators complete their picture, be sure to review the text and picture together numerous times, each time for a different purpose: to find a letter, to find a phonics element, to find a word family word, etc.

Interactive Writing Tips

• Before writing, have pairs of students discuss the topic to generate ideas.
• Provide a second piece of chart paper for students to write a first draft as practice.
• Display completed samples of student writing only if the grammar, usage, and mechanics of the text provide correct models for other students.

To increase student involvement, consider the following:

• Distribute small dry-erase boards so all students can write on their boards as one student writes on the class chart.
• Have students trace the letters/words in the air.
• Have students trace the letters/words on another student's back.

You may wish to place the completed text in a learning center. There students can reread it, add to it, or complete other activities you create.

Using the Decodable Readers

Choose from these suggestions to encourage student development of reading skills using decodable readers.

Whole Group	1. Lead a class discussion about the topic of the decodable reader to help students build background and activate prior knowledge.
	2. Preview the book to increase interest, make predictions, and set a purpose for reading.
	3. Read the book together, encouraging students to take turns reading words or lines aloud. At the end, ask them to confirm their predictions.
	4. On subsequent reads, you may wish to focus on specific words or phonetic elements.
Small Group	1. Lead a class discussion about the topic of the decodable reader to help students build background and activate prior knowledge.
	2. Preview the book to increase interest, make predictions, and set a purpose for reading.
	3. Read the book together, encouraging students to take turns reading words or lines aloud. At the end, ask them to confirm their predictions.
	4. On subsequent reads, you may wish to focus on specific words or phonetic elements.
Learning Centers	1. Encourage students to read the decodable readers independently or with a partner.
	2. Use the week's center activities to encourage students to practice the phonics elements and high-frequency words found in the decodable reader.
Independent E-Books	1. Encourage students to work independently or with a partner at computer workstations.
	2. Use the e-books to encourage students to practice the phonics elements and high-frequency words found in the decodable readers.

Collaborative Conversations

What you can do to encourage collaborative conversations

There are many ways to support and encourage collaborative conversations. Consider the following suggestions:

- Review rules of conversation and post them prominently.
- Model appropriate and inappropriate conversations.
- Encourage elaboration of ideas and multiple exchanges among students.
- Keep groups small enough to allow everyone to participate.
- Provide lots of opportunities for students to engage in structured discussions.
- Choose texts that encourage collaborative conversations. Texts should be complex enough that students can discover new things through multiple readings.
- Use sentence starters or frames to help students learn to share their thinking.
- Use graphic organizers and note-taking strategies to help students collect their ideas prior to sharing them. Encourage students to add to their notes as they engage in conversations.

SENTENCE STARTERS

You may wish to display simple sentence starters like these.

Do you think that _____?
I wonder if _____.
I agree/disagree because _____.
The reason I believe _____.
I like this idea because _____.
In my opinion _____.
What do you mean by _____?
Why do you think that _____?
Could you say more about _____?
I'd like to add that _____.

RULES OF CONVERSATION

Post these simple rules of conversation prominently in the classroom.

- Use each other's names.
- Listen to each other.
- Take turns talking and listening.
- Look at the speaker/listener.
- Talk directly to each other.
- Respond nicely.
- Disagree nicely.
- Share your ideas.
- Let the other person finish talking before you talk.
- Speak in complete sentences.

SAMPLE ACTIVITIES

Fish Bowl

Have students form pairs. Ask one member of each pair to form a circle with students facing outward. Then ask the other member of each pair to face his or her partner, forming a concentric outside circle.

Pose a question and indicate which role each partner will play. For instance, ask: "Can you think of a reason the tortoise wanted to win? The inside partner will answer, and the outside partner will listen." Allow students time to think of an answer, then call on partners to share their answers with the class.

Continue by switching roles between partners and by rotating the circles.

Face to Face

Have students form pairs. Pose a question that has a number of possible answers. For example: *Why was it so important to the hare to win the race?*

In pairs, students can take turns telling their partner answers to the question.

Using Flexible Blackline Masters

Use the flexible blackline masters on the pages that follow for individual or collaborative practice of phonics and word family skills.

BLM A	**WORD FAMILY HOUSE**	The word family house (BLM A) allows students to write the words in a word family that is designated in the space in the "roof" of the house. By using multiple word family houses, students can sort words belonging to multiple word families. The word family house can be used in tandem with BLM B and BLM C.
BLM B	**WORD FAMILY SPINNER**	The word family spinner (BLM B) provides a substitution exercise in which the student spins a dial with various initial letters listed around the edges. When a letter on the dial is blended with a word family ending, a word is formed. Students can use the word family house (BLM A) to record the words that they form on the spinner. The spinner can also be adapted for use with the game board (BLM D).
BLM C	**WORD FAMILY SLIDER**	The word family slider (BLM C) provides a substitution activity in which students use the slider to change the initial letter to form words in a given word family. Students can use a word family house (BLM A) to record the words that they form.
BLM D	**GAME BOARD**	The game board (BLM D) can be set up with a "path" of word family words and/or decodable words, along with occasional instruction squares such as "spin again" and "go back three spaces." When a player lands on a word, he or she can be instructed to say the word aloud, use it in a sentence, provide a rhyming word, separate the word into syllables, and/or perform another task that reinforces phonics learning. The word family spinner (BLM B) can be adapted for players to use to determine the number of spaces to move on each turn.

Name _____ Date_____

FINISH!					
START					

Advancing Phonics Every Day

Letters/sounds:
a/a/

	Day 1	Day 2	Day 3
Phonological/ Phonemic Awareness	**Word Awareness** `Routine 1` **Model:** Cats can nap. **Practice:** Jan ran fast. Dad has a plan. **Extra practice:** The fat cat sat.	**Rhyme Recognition** `Routine 5` **Model:** cat/hat **Practice:** clap/tap, can/Jan/pan **Extra Practice:** pad/dad, sat/Pat	**Phoneme Recognition** `Routine 9` **Model:** bad, rack **Practice:** mad, cat, hat, sack **Extra practice:** Nat, pack
Phonics	**Introduce sound/symbol correspondence: a/a/** `Routine 17` **Model:** cat, mad **Practice:** mat, dad **Extra practice:** sat, sad, lad, vat **Decodable reader: "Mr. Dan Has a Plan"** Use decodable reader ideas (p. 23).	**Introduce sound/symbol focus: ck as /k/** `Routine 17` **Model:** pack, back, sat **Practice:** tack, hat, sack **Extra practice:** rack, wag	**Blend words with a/a/** `Routine 18` **Model:** fan, back **Practice:** man, can, nack **Extra practice:** ran, tan, van
Word Families	Use the letter cards below and have students work together in pairs to make as many words as possible on their workmats using the letter cards and the word families –at and –ad. **Letter cards:** b, f, h, m, p, s, a, t, d	Use BLM B to make a spinner for –at and –ad word families. Pair students. One student spins the spinner. The other student identifies a word in the word family.	Have students make their own picture cards for the words can, fan, man, and van. Students should write the words on the cards.
High-Frequency Words	**Introduce high-frequency words** `Routine 20` the, see	**Practice high-frequency words** the, see `Routine 21` **Decodable reader: "Mr. Dan Has a Plan"** Use decodable reader ideas (p. 23).	**Introduce high-frequency words** `Routine 20` go, she, and
Writing	Have pairs of students work together to write a sentence using one or both of the high-frequency words and one or more of the words they wrote for the word families.	Have students choose two of the word family words they made in the phonics routine to write a sentence.	Have students write a sentence about the picture on one of the picture cards that they made using the word on the card.
Spelling	**Introduce spelling words** `Routines 20, 22` go, cat, rat, dad	**Spell words in context** `Routines 21, 23` go, cat, rat, dad	**Introduce spelling words** `Routines 20, 22` she, sad, ran, tan
Shared Reading	**"Katie's Crop"** **Introduce a/a/** As you read aloud, point out words that have /a/ spelled a. Have students read aloud each short a word with you, emphasizing the phonics element.	**"Katie's Crop"** **Introduce final ck/k/** As you read aloud, review phonics element; final ck/k/, pick. Have students read aloud each word with you, emphasizing the phonics element.	**"Katie's Crop"** **Introduce a/a/** As you read aloud, point out the /a/ sound in words. Have students read the words with you, emphasizing the /a/ sound.

High-Frequency Words:	Spelling:	Word Families:
the, see, go, she, and	Words with –at, –ad, –an	–at, –ad, –an

Day 4	Day 5	Collaborative Learning and Independent Practice*
Phoneme Isolation `Routine 10` Model: bat, pat Practice: man, sat, back, Jack Extra practice: bad, back		• Phonemic Picnic: Words with Short a Sounds Days 1–5 • Phoneme Cubes: Words with Short a Sounds Days 3–5
Build words with a/a/ `Routine 19` Model: can, fan, man Practice: bat, cat , rat Extra practice: pat, fat, sad, dad	**Decodable reader: "Mr. Dan Has a Plan"** Use decodable reader ideas (p. 23).	• Phonics Board Game: Words with Short a Sounds Days 1–5 • Phonics Word Builder: Words with Short a and ck/k/ Sounds Days 3–5 • Read/Draw/Label: "Cat and Rat": Words with Short a Sounds Days 3–5
Use the following letter cards and have students form as many real words as they can using the word families –at, –ad, –an. Letter cards: b, c, d, f, h, m, p, r, s, t, a, n	**Review –at, –ad, –an words** Distribute the following letter cards and workmats. Have students choose one letter card and form a word from two of the word families that start with that letter. Students can use those words in a sentence. Letter cards: b, d, f, h, m, p, r, s, a, n, t	• Word Family Tic-Tac-Toe: Word Families –at, –ad Days 1–5 • Word Family Sort: Word Family –an Days 3–5 • Word Family Books: Word Family –an Days 3–5
Practice high-frequency words `Routine 21` the, see, go, she, and	**Decodable reader: "Mr. Dan Has a Plan"** Use decodable reader ideas (p. 23).	• High-Frequency Words Bug Catch Days 1–5 • High-Frequency Words Beanbag Toss Days 3–5
Have students compare their lists from the word family activity, and then write other words including proper names, like *Pat, Nan, Van, Jan,* and *Dan.* Students can write a sentence using the words.	**Interactive writing** (see p. 22) **Story starter:** Nan has a bat. **Word bank:** can, fan, rat, sad, bad, ran, dad, van, hat, mat	• Reading/Writing: Respond to the Story "Pat Ran!" Days 1–5 • Reading/Writing: Continue the Story "The Sack" Days 3–5
Spell words in context `Routines 21, 23` she, sad, ran, tan	**Test words in dictation** Read aloud each of the week's spelling words for students to write. Then collect and review student work.	• Spelling Homework: BLM 1 Days 1–5
"Kind Hearts Are Gardens" **Review a/a/; review ck/k/** As you read aloud, review phonics elements a/a/ and ck/k/. Have students read aloud each word with you, emphasizing the phonics element.	**"Kind Hearts Are Gardens"** **Review a/a/** As you read aloud, review phonics element /a/. Point out words that have this phonics element and have students read the word with you, emphasizing short a spelled *a*.	

* Use this menu to plan extra practice and center activities for use through the week. All the skills needed for an activity have been introduced by the first day of the range shown. See pages 32–33 for full descriptions.

Collaborative Learning and Independent Practice

 Phonological/Phonemic Awareness Activities

Phonemic Picnic:
Words with Short a Sounds
Use on Days 1–5

Fill a picnic basket (or lunch box) with toy foods. Each food should contain the short a sound (for example: *apple, candy, sandwich, hamburger*). Have partners sit on the floor as if ready for a picnic. They should take turns choosing a food, say the name of the food, and pass it to their partner to "eat."

Phoneme Cubes:
Words with Short a Sounds
Use on Days 3–5

Gather multiple pairs of cubes (such as empty cube-shaped tissue boxes). Paste the week's twelve picture cards (page 41) on the boxes, six per box. Students can take turns rolling the cubes, saying the two words that face up and identifying the middle vowel sounds.

ABC)) Phonics Activities

Phonics Board Game:
Words with Short a Sounds
Use on Days 1–5

Place copies of BLM D, a spinner (BLM B), and disks or coins for playing pieces in the center. Students use the spinner to advance on the board. If they land on a space that has a word with the short a sound, they use it in an oral sentence and spin again. If the word does not have the short a sound, the next player spins. Students also follow directions on the squares that have them.

Label the squares with words and directions, making a path from the START square to the FINISH square (words and directions can be repeated, as necessary). Examples of words and directions include:

- **bag, bat, fan, gas, hat, nap, pad, pan, ran, tap, back, pack, the, see, go, she, is**
- **"Move back two spaces"**
- **"Move forward five spaces"**
- **"Spin again"**
- **"Skip your next turn"**
- **"Switch squares with the player to your left"**

Phonics Word Builder:
Words with Short a and ck/k/ Sounds
Use on Days 3–5

Provide students with letter tiles (or cutouts) of letter *a*. Have students use letter tiles to complete the activity on BLM 2 (page 35).

Read/Draw/Label a Poem:
"Cat and Rat":
Words with Short a Sounds
Use on Days 3–5

Provide students with BLM 3 (page 36) and have them complete the activity.

 Word Family Activities

Word Family Tic-Tac-Toe: Word Families –at, –ad
Use on Days 1–5

Provide or have students draw a tic-tac-toe board. Have partners play tic-tac-toe using words belonging to the –at and –ad word families. One partner will use –at words instead of an X to mark his/her spots on the board. The other partner will use –ad words instead of an O.

Optional: Have students use word sliders (BLM C)—one for each word family—to form words to use on the board. Write the word family on the wide rectangular piece and initial letters on the narrow rectangular piece.

Word Family Sort: Word Family –an
Use on Days 3–5

Provide students with BLM 4 (page 37) and have them complete the activity.

Word Family Books: Word Family –an
Use on Days 3–5

For each student, cut two index cards in half. Stack these four pieces of index cards, and then staple them to a single index card to form a "book" with four narrow pages and a final full-width page. Instruct students to write –an on the final index card so that those letters are always visible. Then have students form different word family words by writing a letter on each of the first four pages of their books, such as c, f, m, and t. (Other letters that form real words: d, p, r, v.) When finished, students can flip through the first four pages to form and read aloud different word family words (such as can, fan, man, tan).

High-Frequency Word Activities

Bug Catch
Use on Days 1–5

Write a series of high-frequency words, from this week and the words *a, can, I, is* on index cards, and place the index cards on the floor or on a table. Then provide a pair of students with plastic fly swatters. Instruct students to take turns: One student should read a high-frequency word aloud, and then the other student should "swat" it.

- see / the
- a / can / I / is /

Beanbag Toss
Use on Days 3–5

Make high-frequency word cards for a beanbag toss.

- a / and / can / go / I / is / see / she / the /

Have one student choose a word to read aloud, and another to toss the bag to cover the matching picture card.

Writing Activities

Reading/Writing: Respond to the Story "Pat Ran!"
Use on Days 1–5

Provide copies of BLM 5 (page 38) and have students use the sentence starter to write about the story.

Reading/Writing: Continue the Story "The Sack"
Use on Days 3–5

Provide copies of BLM 6 (page 39) and have students complete the activity.

Spelling Homework

**Read each spelling word aloud with your child. Spell it aloud together.
Then ask your child to write each spelling word and say it in a sentence.**

cat _____

rat _____

dad _____

go _____

sad _____

ran _____

tan _____

she _____

Choose a different activity every day to practice this week's spelling words at home with your child.

Flashlight writing	Trace the word	Write it	Write it again	Remember the word
Turn out the lights. Use a flashlight to spell each word on the wall.	Write the word with dotted lines, and then trace the dots with a different color.	Write the word, saying aloud each letter as you write it.	Have your child write the word three times on a sheet of paper and circle the vowels.	Turn the paper over and write the word from memory.

Phonics Word Builder

**Place a letter tile for short a in each box to make a word.
Read the word aloud.**

r ☐ ck   s ☐ ck

p ☐ n   b ☐ ck

h ☐ t   t ☐ ck

b ☐ d   f ☐ n

Cat and Rat

Read the poem. Circle words with a short a sound.
Then draw a picture to show one thing in the poem.

I see a cat.

The cat is tan.

The cat has a fan.

I see the cat nap.

I see a rat.

The rat is fat.

The rat has a hat.

I see the rat at the back.

Word Family Sort

Cut out the words.
Place each word in the basket belonging to its word family.

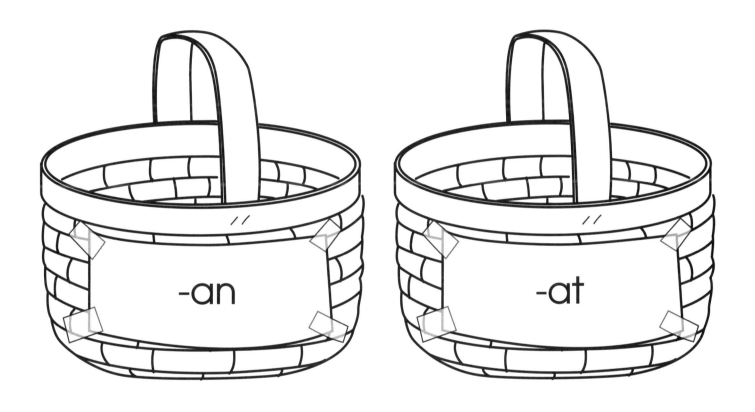

-an   -at

pan	cat	man	fan	hat
Dan	ran	tan	rat	bat

Grade 1 • Advancing Phonics Skills 37

Pat Ran!

Read the story. Then write a sentence about a time you ran.

Pat ran!

Pat ran a lap.

She ran to the van.

She ran to the see Dad.

She ran back.

Pat ran!

Go, Pat!

I ran

The Sack

Read the story.

I can see in the sack.

A tack is in the sack.

A pan is in the sack.

A rag is in the sack.

And a cap is in the sack!

Draw a picture to show what is in the sack.

bat	pack
back	pad
dad	pan
fan	sack
hat	tack
cat	van

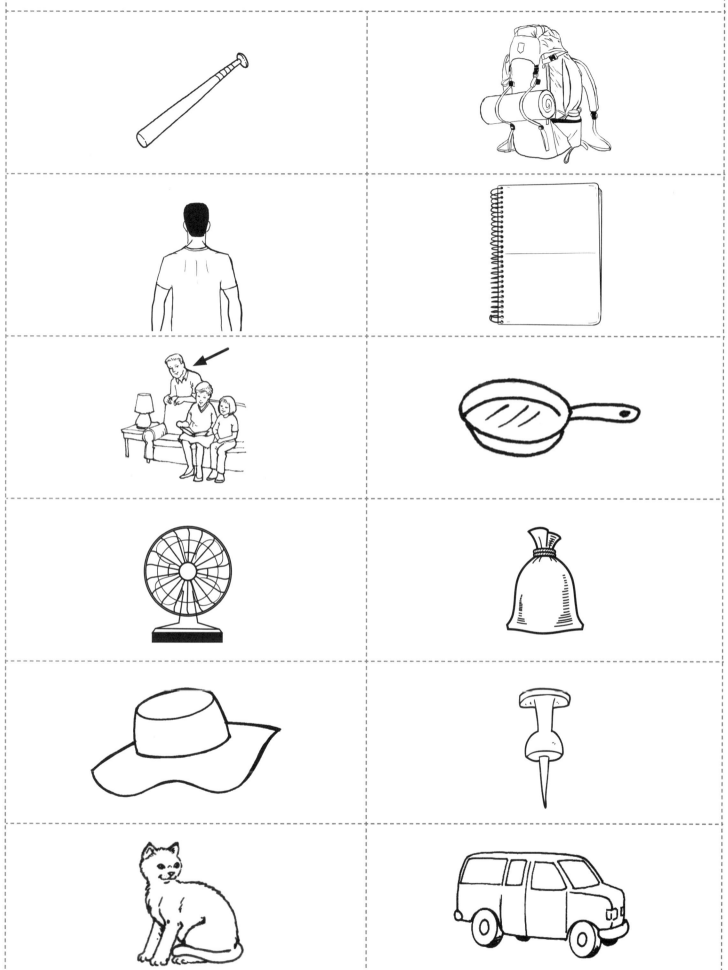

Advancing Phonics Every Day

	Day 1	Day 2	Day 3
Phonological/ Phonemic Awareness	**Sentence Awareness** Routine 2 **Model:** Tim is in the pit. **Practice:** Wow! That fish has thin fins. **Extra practice:** All the kids like to play with him.	**Rhyme Production** Routine 6 **Model:** lip/trip, mitt/pit **Practice:** fit/sit, tin/fin, pin/win **Extra practice:** bit/hit, him/limb	**Phoneme Segmentation** Routine 11 **Model:** lip, kit, fit **Practice:** pin, pins, lip, lips **Extra practice:** fig, figs, fin, fins
Phonics	**Review previous week's** Routine 17 **sound/symbol focus** **Model:** bat, can **Practice:** man, dad, sack **Extra practice:** fat, cat, had, rack **Introduce sound/symbol** Routine 17 **correspondence:** i/i/ **Model:** in, it, lip **Practice:** pin, sit, tick **Extra practice:** win, hit, fin, kit	**Blend words with i/i/** Routine 18 **Model:** bit, lick **Practice:** sit, it, pick **Extra practice:** tin, hit, fit **Build words with i/i/** Routine 19 **Model:** pin, pit, pick **Practice:** win, fin, Lin **Predecodable reader: "We Can Fix It!"** Use decodable reader ideas (p. 23).	**Introduce Plural nouns (-s)** Routine 18 **Model:** kit, kits **Practice:** pin, pins, lip, lips **Extra practice:** fig, figs, fin, fins Display the word card *cats*. Point out the *-s* and tell students that when a noun ends with an *-s*, it is called plural. That means more than one. Reinforce the idea by pointing to a student and saying **"one student."** then point to two students and say **"two students,"** emphasizing the *-s*.
Word Families	Guide students to make a simple five-step word ladder using word family *–in*.	Guide students in making a word wheel with the word family *–it* in the center circle and five lines leading from the circle. Students should write a word on each line in the *–it* word family.	Distribute the following letter cards and have students form words for the *–ip* word family using the letter cards. **Letter cards:** d, h, l, r, s, t, z, i, p
High-Frequency Words	**Introduce high-frequency** Routine 20 **words** play, little	**Practice high-frequency** Routine 21 **words** play, little **Predecodable reader: "We Can Fix It!"** Use decodable reader ideas (p. 23).	**Introduce high-frequency** Routine 20 **words** you, with
Writing	Have students use words from their word ladders and the high-frequency words to write a sentence.	Have students work in pairs to compare their *–it* word wheels and add two more lines to write other *–it* words to their wheels.	Have students work in pairs and use the words from the word family activity to decide if an *-s* can be added to some of the words to form a plural. Have them write the new word.
Spelling	**Introduce spelling** Routines 20, 22 **words** little, bin, win , lit	**Spell words in context** Routines 21, 23 little, win, bin, lit	**Introduce spelling** Routines 20, 22 **words** you, tip, zip, fit
Shared Reading	**"Save Our Planet"** **Review a/a/** As you read aloud, review phonics element /a/ spelled *a*. Point out and have students read aloud with you words that have short a spelled *a*, emphasizing the phonics element.	**"Save Our Planet"** **Introduce i/i/** As you read aloud, point out words with /i/ spelled *i* in words. Have students read the words aloud with you, and invite volunteers to use one of the words in an original sentence.	**"Save Our Planet"** **Introduce plural nouns (–s)** As you read aloud, point out plurals that end in -*s*. Have students read each word aloud with you, emphasizing the phonics element.

High-Frequency Words:	Spelling:	Word Families:
play, little, you, with	Words with –in, –it, –ip	–in, –it, –ip

Day 4	Day 5	Collaborative Learning and Independent Practice*
Phoneme Blending Routine 12 **Model:** zip, rip, pick **Practice:** fins, bit, sit, pits **Extra Practice:** lips, nip		• Elkonin Boxes: Words with Short i Sounds Days 1–5 • Phonemic Word Sort: Words with Short i Sounds and Plural Nouns Days 3–5
Blend plural nouns (-s) Routine 18 **Model:** cats, pigs **Practice:** lids, bats, hats **Extra practice:** vans, fins, pans, pits **Build plural nouns (-s)** Routine 15 **Model:** mat, rat **Practice:** pan, pans, can, cans **Extra practice:** van, vans, kit, kits	**Predecodable reader: "We Can Fix It"** Use decodable reader ideas (p. 23).	• Word Rainbows: Words with Short i Sounds Days 1–5 • Phonics Crossword: Words with Short i Sounds and Plural Nouns Days 3–5 • Read/Draw/Label: "You and I Can Play": Words with Short i Sounds Days 3–5
Have students work in teams. Write the letters –ip on the board. Have teams write as many –ip words as they can think of in three minutes.	**Review –in, –it, and –ip words** Have students work in small groups. Each group uses BLM A to make a word family house with –in, –it, and –ip word families. In their small groups, students take turns writing a word in each of the houses.	• Feed the Creatures: Word Families –ip, –it Days 1–5 • Word Family Towers: Word Family –ip Days 3–5 • Word Family Spinners: Word Families –in, –it, –ip Days 3–5
Practice high-frequency words Routine 21 play, little, you, with	**Predecodable reader: "We Can Fix It"** Use decodable reader ideas (p. 23).	• High-Frequency Words Concentration Days 1–5 • High-Frequency Words Parking Lot Days 3–5
Have students use the high-frequency words to write a simple sentence about playing.	**Interactive writing:** (see p. 22) **Story starter:** Kip and Lin see the pins. **Word bank:** lips, sit, win, fins, rip, hit, lit, dip	• Reading/Writing: Respond to the Story "Kip and Jin Play" Days 1–5 • Reading/Writing: Respond to the Story "Dad and Jin" Days 3–5
Spell words in context Routines 21, 23 you, tip, zip, fit	**Test words in dictation** Read aloud each of the week's spelling words for students to write. Then collect and review student work.	• Spelling Homework: BLM 1 Days 1–5
"What Will Max Do?" **Review plural nouns (–s) and i/i/** As you read aloud, point out words that are plural nouns spelled with –s and words with short i. Have students read these words aloud with you, emphasizing the phonics elements.	**"What Will Max Do?"** **Review i/i/ and plural nouns (–s)** As you read, review the phonics elements /i/ spelled i and plural nouns (–s). Point out words in the story that use these phonics elements and have students read them aloud with you.	

* Use this menu to plan extra practice and center activities for use through the week. All the skills needed for an activity have been introduced by the first day of the range shown. See pages 44–45 for full descriptions.

Collaborative Learning and Independent Practice

 Phonological/Phonemic Awareness Activities

Elkonin Boxes:
Words with Short i Sounds
Use on Days 1–5

Provide the six picture/word cards that contain the short i sound. (page 53). For each card, have students sound out the word, sliding a counter into a cell of an Elkonin box for each individual phoneme. Students can do this individually, or partners can take turns choosing from the picture cards.

Phonemic Word Sort:
Words with Short i Sounds and Plural Nouns
Use on Days 3–5

Distribute copies of the week's picture cards (page 53). Have pairs of students work together to sort the cards by final sound:

- dip / lip
- hit / pit
- cans / cats / pigs
- fin / pan
- rock / tack

ᴬ$_B$꜀)) Phonics Activities

Word Rainbows:
Words with Short i Sounds
Use on Days 1–5

Provide students with the six picture cards that contain the short i sound (page 53). Instruct students to write each word, spelling each sound in the word with an individual color. You might suggest that students choose rainbow colors and use them in that order. Elicit from students that the middle color and vowel in each word is the same.

Phonics Crossword:
Words with Short i Sounds and Plural Nouns
Use on Days 3–5

Provide students with BLM 2 (page 47) and have them complete the crossword activity.

Read/Draw/Label a Story:
"You and I can Play":
Words with Short i Sounds
Use on Days 3–5

Provide students with BLM 3 (page 48) and have them complete the activity.

 Word Family Activities

Feed the Creatures: Word Families –ip, –it
Use on Days 1–5

Provide two small plastic bins. Label each with a word family, –ip or –it. Use a marker to make eyes or a face on each bin to turn the bins into creatures. Provide partners with the following –ip and –it picture cards, and have them take turns "feeding" the creatures the appropriate cards:

- **lip / dip / hit / pit**

Word Family Towers: Word Family –ip
Use on Days 3–5

Provide partners with interlocking blocks. On each block, place a piece of masking tape. Write –ip words on half of the blocks, and other decodable words on the rest of the blocks. Have students find and stack the –ip word blocks into a word family tower, pronouncing each word as they add it to the tower.

(This activity can be adapted for the –in or –it word families.)

Word Family Spinner: Word Families –in, –it, –ip
Use on Days 3–5

Set up a word spinner (BLM B) for each of the week's word families. Write a word family on the long rectangular piece and initial letters around the circle. Provide three copies of the word family house (BLM A) and have students label them –in, –it, and –ip. Ask students to form words using the spinners and to list each word they form in the appropriate house.

High-Frequency Word Activities

Concentration
Use on Days 1–5

Distribute to partners the following Benchmark Advance high-frequency word cards. Each set should contain two copies of each word, for a total of eighteen cards per pair of students.

- **little / play / you / with / see / she / the / go / and**

Instruct partners to arrange the cards face down to form a 3 x 6 grid to play a concentration game. The partners should alternate turning over two cards per turn. When a student uncovers a matching pair, he/she uses the word in an oral sentence and keeps the pair of cards. The student who collects the most pairs wins the game.

Parking Lot
Use on Days 3–5

Provide partners with BLM 4 (page 49) and toy cars, and have them complete the activity. Students should take turns: One student should read a high-frequency word aloud, and the other student should "park" a toy car in that spot and say a sentence using the word.

Writing Activities

Reading/Writing: Respond to the Story "Dad and Jin"
Use on Days 1–5

Provide copies of BLM 5 (page 50) and have students use the sentence starter to write about the story.

Reading/Writing: Respond to the Story "In the Bin"
Use on Days 3–5

Provide copies of BLM 6 (page 51) and have students draw a picture in response to the story.

Spelling Homework

Read each spelling word aloud with your child. Spell it aloud together. Then ask your child to write each spelling word and say it in a sentence.

bin _____   tip _____

win _____   zip _____

lit _____   fit _____

little _____   you _____

Choose a different activity every day to practice this week's spelling words at home with your child.

Flashlight writing	Multi-colored words	Letter tiles	Magnetic letters	Two-toned words
Turn out the lights. Use a flashlight to spell each word on the wall.	Write the spelling words with crayons or colored pencils, using a different color for each letter.	Use letter tiles to spell the words and then write the words on a sheet of paper.	Spell the words on a cookie sheet using magnetic letters and then write the words on a piece of paper.	Write the spelling words with crayons or colored markers. Use one color for consonants and another for vowels.

Phonics Crossword

Complete the crossword puzzle.
Fill in the words for the pictures shown.

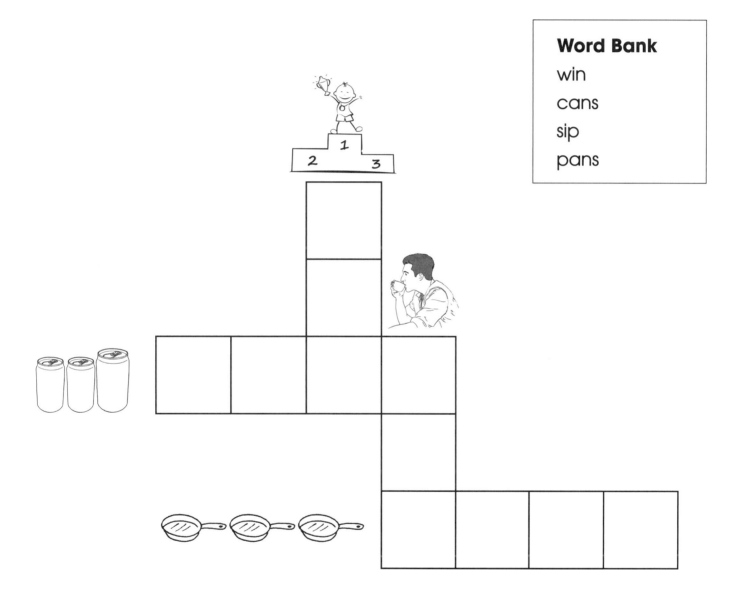

Word Bank

win

cans

sip

pans

You and I Can Play!

**Read the story. Circle words with short i sounds.
Then write one of the words on the lines below.**

Can I play with you?

You and I can play with the kit.

The kit is in the tan sack.

The kit has little bits to play with.

You and I can sit and play!

_____

- -

_____

_____

- -

_____

_____

- -

_____

High-Frequency Words Parking Lot

Listen to the directions from your teacher.

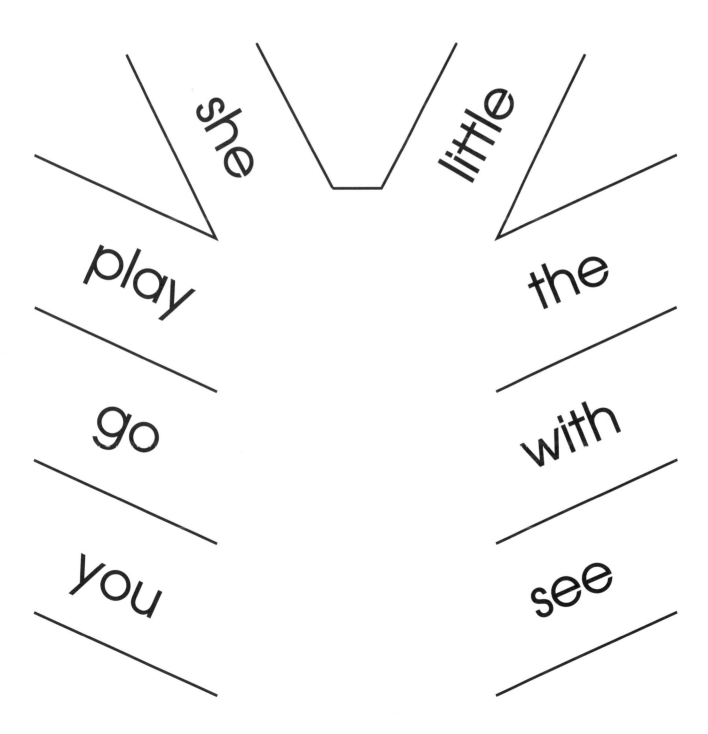

Dad and Jin

Read the story.
Then write a sentence about Dad and Jin.

Jin is little. Dad is big.

Jin can go with Dad.

She can go with him to the play.

Jin and Dad sit in the back.

The play is a hit.

Dad and Jin

In the Bin

Read the story.

I see a big, tan bin.

I see a hat in the bin.

I see little pins in the bin.

I see a big wig in the bin!

Can you see in the bin?

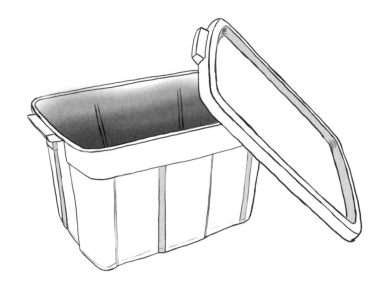

Draw a picture to tell what you see in the bin.

pit	pigs
cans	pad
dip	pan
fin	rock
hit	tack
lip	cats

Advancing Phonics Every Day

	Day 1	Day 2	Day 3
Phonological/ Phonemic Awareness	**Word Awareness** `Routine 1` Model: Hogs can jog. Practice: Dogs have spots. What is on top? Extra practice: It is not hot.	**Rhyme Recognition** `Routine 5` Model: pop/top, shop/drop Practice: chop/stop, log/hog, flop/bop Extra practice: trip/sip, got/knot	**Phoneme Recognition** `Routine 9` Model: hop, pot Practice: mop, log, hog, bop Extra practice: dot, rot
Phonics	**Review previous week's sound/symbol focus** `Routine 17` Model: nip, lips Practice: sips, sit, win, dip, zip Extra practice: hips, pins **Introduce sound/symbol correspondence: o/o/** `Routine 17` Model: hop, bop Practice: got, tot, dog Extra practice: top, pop, dot, hog	**Blend words with o/o/** `Routine 18` Model: fog, pop Practice: top, dog, lock Extra practice: log, bop, hop **Build words with o/o/** `Routine 19` Model: rot, rock Other words: lot, cot, got,	**Introduce sound/symbol correspondence: final double consonants** `Routine 18` Model: kiss, bill Practice: fizz, miss, stiff Extra practice: loss, will, fill, jazz Explain the floss rule, that words with a short vowel ending in -f, -l, -s and -z double the final consonant.
Word Families	Help students make a five-petal flower with –op in the center. Students write –op words on the petals.	Have students use the following letter cards to build words in the –og word family. **Letter cards:** b, d, f, h, j, l, o, g	Guide students in making a five-step ladder with –ot at the top. Students write an –ot word on each rung.
High-Frequency Words	**Introduce high-frequency words** `Routine 20` for, no, jump	**Practice high-frequency words** for, no, jump `Routine 21` **Decodable reader: "A Big Job!"** Use decodable reader ideas (p. 23).	**Introduce high-frequency words** `Routine 20` one, have
Writing	Have pairs of students use the –op words they wrote on the petals and one of the high-frequency words to write a sentence.	Have students use the high-frequency words and the word family words that they made to write a sentence about a dog. Students can illustrate their sentences.	Have students continue with their ladder, adding two more words to the –ot word family.
Spelling	**Introduce spelling words** `Routines 20, 22` for, pop, hop, bog	**Spell words in context** `Routines 21, 23` for, pop, hop, bog	**Introduce spelling words** `Routines 20, 22` one, moss, rot, dog
Shared Reading	**"Jim Henson"** **Review a/a/ and plural nouns (–s)** As you read aloud, point out the words with /a/ and plural nouns (–s). Have students read these words with you, emphasizing the phonics elements.	**"Jim Henson"** **Introduce o/o/; review i/i/** As you read aloud, point out words with /o/ and /i/. Have students read these words with you, emphasizing the phonics elements.	**"Jim Henson"** **Introduce words with final double consonants** As you read aloud, point out words that have final double consonants. Have students read these words aloud with you, emphasizing the phonics element.

High-Frequency Words: for, no, jump, one, have	**Spelling:** Words with –op, –og, –ot	**Word Families:** –op, –og, –ot

Day 4	Day 5	Collaborative Learning and Independent Practice*
Rhyme Production Routine 6 **Model:** stop/cop, tot/pot **Practice:** blot/clot, chop/shop **Extra practice:** Bob/blob		• Phonemic Concentration: Words with Short /o/ Sounds Days 1–5 • Phoneme Cubes: Words with Short /o/ Sounds Days 3–5
Blend words with double final consonants Routine 18 **Model:** pill, kiss **Practice:** pass, puff **Extra practice:** fizz, mess, less, Jill, Bill **Build words with double final consonants** Routine 19 **Model:** fill, hill **Practice:** Jill, bill, till **Extra practice:** boss, loss, moss, toss	**Decodable reader: "A Big Job!"** Use decodable reader ideas (p. 23).	• Letter Cup Substitution: Words with Short /o/ Sounds Days 1–5 • Picture Word Cards: Words with Double Final Consonants: Short /o/ Sounds Days 3–5 • Read/Draw/Label: "Dot and The Little Dog": Words with Short /o/ Sounds Days 3–5
Distribute the following letter cards and have students make new words ending in –ot. **Letter Cards:** c, d, g, h, j, l, n, p, r, t, o	**Review –op, –og, and –ot words** Have students work in small groups, choose one of the word families, and use BLM C to make a word family slider. They can record their answers on BLM A. Each student can choose one word to use in an oral sentence.	• Word Family Board Game: Word Families –og, –op Days 1–5 • Word Family Picture Labels: Word Family –og, –op, –ot Days 3–5
Practice high-frequency words Routine 21 for, no, jump, one, have	**Decodable reader: "A Big Job!"** Use decodable reader ideas (p. 23).	• High-Frequency Words Bug Catch Days 1–5 • High-Frequency Words Chatterbox Days 3–5
Have students work in pairs to write a simple sentence using their words from the –ot family and the high-frequency words.	**Interactive writing** (see p. 22) **Story starter:** Jill and Bill got a pot. **Word bank:** top, pop, log, not, hot, mop, dog	• Reading/Writing: Respond to the Story "Bob and Todd!" Days 1–5 • Reading/Writing: Respond to the Story "The Sick Kid" Days 3–5
Spell words in context Routines 21, 23 one, moss, rot, dog	**Test words in dictation** Read aloud each of the week's spelling words for students to write. Then collect and review student work.	• Spelling Homework: BLM 1 Days 1–5
"The More We Work Together" **High-frequency words: for, no, jump, one, have** As you read aloud, point out this week's high-frequency words. Have students read aloud these words with you.	**"The More We Work Together"** **Review o/o/; double final consonants** As you read aloud, point out the words with o/o/ and words with double final consonants. Have students read these words aloud with you, emphasizing the phonics elements.	

* Use this menu to plan extra practice and center activities for use through the week. All the skills needed for an activity have been introduced by the first day of the range shown. See pages 56–57 for full descriptions.

Collaborative Learning and Independent Practice

 **Phonological/Phonemic Awareness Activities**

Phonemic Concentration: Words with Short /o/ Sounds
Use on Days 1–5

Provide students with a set of the week's picture cards (page 65)—not including the cards for the words *hill* or *mitt*—two of each card, for a total of twenty cards. Instruct partners to arrange the cards face down to form a 4 x 5 grid to play a concentration game. The partners should alternate turning over two cards per turn. When a student uncovers a matching pair, he/she should use the word in an oral sentence and keep the pair of cards. The student who collects the most pairs wins the game.

Phoneme Cubes: Words with Short /o/ Sounds
Use on Days 3–5

Gather multiple pairs of cubes (such as empty cube-shaped tissue boxes). Paste the week's twelve picture cards (page 65) on the boxes, six per box. Students can take turns rolling the cubes, saying the two words that face up, identifying the middle vowel sounds, and noting whether they are the same.

ABC)) Phonics Activities

Letter Cup Substitution:
Use on Days 1–5

Provide plastic cups with a consonant or vowel written on the outside of each. Place upside-down cups in a row to spell a three-letter word. Have partners take turns fitting other cups over one of the original cups, making a new word. Students should read each word aloud and decide if it is a real or nonsense word. If it is a real word, have students record it on a phonics house (BLM A) before continuing. Examples:

- starting word: mop
- substitute initial letter: h, l, m
- substitute final letter: g, p, t
- substitute middle letter: a, i, o

Picture Word Cards: Words with Double Final Consonants: Short /o/ Sounds
Use on Days 3–5

Distribute the following picture/word cards:

- dot, hot, log, mitt, toss, doll, dog
- hop, jog, mop, pot, hill

Have partners take turns. Student 1 holds a card with the picture-only side facing Student 2. Student 1 reads aloud the word on the card. Student 2 spells the word orally. If Student 2 needs a clue, Student 1 provides the first and last letters, and allows Student 2 to indicate the middle letter. (Point out to students that the words will not all have the middle *o*.)

Read/Draw/Label a Poem: "Dot and the Little Dog": Words with Short /o/ Sounds
Use on Days 3–5

Provide students with BLM 3 (page 60) and have them complete the activity.

 # Word Family Activities

 # High-Frequency Word Activities

Writing Activities

Word Family Board Game: Word Families –og, –op
Use on Days 1–5

Label the squares of BLM D with words and directions, making a path from START to FINISH. (Repeat words and directions as necessary.) Words and directions might include:

- bog, fog, hog, jog, log, hop, lop, mop, pop, sop, top, bat, bin, fat, fan, fin, pad, pan, pin, rip, sad, win
- "Move back two spaces"
- "Move forward five spaces"
- "Spin again"
- "Skip your next turn"

Place the prepared BLM D, a spinner (BLM B), and disks or coins for playing pieces in the center. Students play by spinning the spinner to advance. When they land on a -og or -op word, they read the word aloud and use it in an oral sentence. Then the next player spins. Students also follow directions on the squares that have them.

Word Family Picture Labels: –og, –op –ot
Use on Days 3–5

Distribute BLM 2 (page 59) and have students complete each word by adding the missing letter.

Bug Catch
Use on Days 1–5

Write this week's high-frequency words *for* and *no*, as well as high-frequency words from previous weeks, on index cards, and place the index cards on the floor or on a table. Then provide a pair of students with plastic fly swatters. Instruct students to take turns: One student should read a high-frequency word aloud, and then the other student should "swat" it.

Chatterbox
Use on Days 3–5

Fold BLM 4 (page 61) to form a "chatterbox." (See directions on page 390.) Instruct students to play with a partner. One student chooses a word on an outside flap, says the word, and spells it aloud while the other student opens and closes the chatterbox for each letter in the word. Then the other student should pick a word on an inside flap, say the word, and spell it aloud. Finally, the first student should open that flap and form an oral sentence using the word that is found there.

Reading/Writing: Respond to the Story "Bob and Todd"
Use on Days 1–5

Provide copies of BLM 5 (page 62) and have students use the sentence starter to tell what happens in the story.

Reading/Writing Activity: Respond to the Story "The Sick Kid"
Use on Days 3–5

Provide copies of BLM 6 (page 63) and have students use the sentence starter to write their own story.

Spelling Homework

Read each spelling word aloud with your child. Spell it aloud together. Then ask your child to write each spelling word and say it in a sentence.

pop _____

hop _____

bog _____

for _____

boss _____

rot _____

dog _____

one _____

Choose a different activity every day to practice this week's spelling words at home with your child.

Letter tiles	Circle the word	Flashlight writing	Trace your words	Two-toned words
Use letter tiles to spell the words and then write the words on a piece of paper.	Write one sentence for each word and circle the spelling words.	Turn out the lights. Use a flashlight to spell each word on the wall.	Use your finger to write each spelling word in sand, flour, or a similar material.	Write the spelling words with crayons or colored markers. Use one color for consonants and another for vowels.

Word Family Picture Labels

Say the name of the picture aloud.
Write the first letter of the word below each picture.

og

ot

op

og

Dot and the Little Dog

Read the poem.
Write words from the poem that have the short o sound on the lines below.

Dot and the little dog do a lot.

Dot and the little dog can hop.

Dot and the little dog can bop.

Dot and the little dog can mop.

Dot and the little dog do a lot!

BLM
4

High-Frequency Words Chatterbox

Listen to the directions from your teacher.

Bob and Todd

Read the story. Then write a sentence to tell what happens in the story.

Bob and Todd will play.

Bob and Todd will play a lot!

Bob will hop, hop, hop.

Todd will jump, jump, jump.

Bob and Todd will be hot, hot, hot!

Bob and Todd

The Sick Kid

Read the story. Then write a sentence about the story.

I am sick.

I am an ill kid!

I sit on the little cot.

I sit on and on.

I jump on the cot a bit.

I jump on the cot a lot.

Mom can see! She is mad!

I am not sick if I can play!

The kid

doll	log
dot	mitt
dog	mop
hop	pot
hot	hill
jog	toss

Advancing Phonics Every Day

Letters/sounds:
e/e/

	Day 1	Day 2	Day 3
Phonological/ Phonemic Awareness	**Sentence Awareness** `Routine 2` **Model:** Ben has a pet. **Practice:** Ken met the vet. Nell got a bell. **Extra practice:** Jen has a jet.	**Rhyme Production** `Routine 6` **Model:** press/dress, wet/set **Practice:** hen/ten, well/tell, let/get **Extra practice:** less/mess	**Phoneme Categorization** `Routine 13` **Model:** get/ten/pot, bell/net/will **Practice:** tan/pen/met, jet/Jill/bet **Extra practice:** yes/yet/van
Phonics	**Review previous week's sound/symbol focus** `Routine 17` **Model:** dog, fill, pot **Practice:** miss, hot, fizz, pass **Extra practice:** got, fog, mop, top **Introduce words with e/e/** `Routine 17` **Model:** bell, set **Practice:** met, tell, pet **Extra practice:** peck, wet	**Blend words with e/e/** `Routine 17` **Model:** wet, tell **Practice:** net, met, ten **Extra practice:** Ben, fell, well, set, let **Decodable reader: "Get Well Red Hen!"** Use decodable reader ideas (p. 23).	**Blend words with e/e/** `Routine 17` **Model:** yet, net **Practice:** hen, bet, tell **Extra practice:** bell, ten, vet
Word Families	Have students use the following letter cards to make words in the –et word family. **Letter cards:** b, g, j, l, m, n, p, s, w, y, e, t	Guide students to use BLM C to make a word family slider using –en and the letters d, h, m, p, t. Students can write the words that they make.	Guide students to make a simple five-step ladder with –ell at the top. Have them write a word with –ell on each rung of the ladder.
High-Frequency Words	**Introduce high-frequency words** `Routine 20` are, said	**Practice high-frequency words** are, said `Routine 21` **Decodable reader: "Get Well Red Hen!"** Use decodable reader ideas (p. 23).	**Introduce high-frequency words** `Routine 20` two, look, my
Writing	Have pairs of students work together to write a sentence from the words they made in the –et word family and the high-frequency word are.	Have students write a simple sentence about a boy named Ken and the words they made from their word family slider.	Have students work in pairs to write a sentence using the words from their ladders and the high-frequency words.
Spelling	**Introduce spelling words** `Routines 20, 22` vet, set, men, said	**Spell words in context** `Routines 21, 23` yet, vet, men, said	**Introduce spelling words** `Routines 20, 22` fell, yell, ten, are
Shared Reading	**"A Pet for Meg"** **Review the previously learned high-frequency words** As you read aloud, point out the high-frequency word for in the title. Have students read the word with you, and then find and say other high-frequency words they know as you continue.	**"A Pet for Meg"** **Introduce e/e/** As you read aloud, point out the words in the title with the phonics element, /e/: pet, Meg. Have students read the words aloud with you, emphasizing the phonics element.	**"A Pet for Meg"** **Review e/e/ and high-frequency words** As you read aloud, point out words in the title and story that have the phonics element e/e/ and this week's high-frequency words. Have students say these words aloud with you.

High-Frequency Words:	Spelling:	Word Families:
are, said, two, look, my	Words with –et, –en, –ell	–et, –en, –ell

Day 4	Day 5	Collaborative Learning and Independent Practice*
Phoneme Substitution Routine 14 **Model:** men/met **Practice:** ten/tell, yell/yet, set/sell, well/wet **Extra practice:** Ben/bet, den/deck		• Phonemic Picnic: Words with Short /e/ Sounds Days 1–5 • Elkonin Boxes: Words with Short /e/ Sounds Days 3–5
Build words with e/e/ Routine 19 **Model:** let, leg **Practice:** yet, set, met **Extra practice:** den, hen, men, ten, pen	**Decodable reader: "Get Well Red Hen!"** Use decodable reader ideas (p. 23).	• Phonics Beanbag Toss: Words with Short /e/ Sounds Days 1–5 • Picture Word Matching: Words with Short /e/ Sounds Days 3–5 • Read/Draw/Label: "Ben Plays with His Cat": Words with Short /e/ Sounds Days 3–5
Distribute the following letter cards and have students work in pairs to write words for the –ell word family. **Letter cards:** b, f, s, t, w, y, e, l Routine 21	**Review e/e/ words** In small groups, students use BLM B to make a spinner. On the spinner they should write the word families –et, –en, –ell. Students take turns spinning, saying a word in that word family and using it in a sentence.	• Word Family Ice Cream Cones: Word Families –et, –en Days 1–5 • Word Family Books: Word Family –et Days 1–5 • Word Family Picture Labels: Word Family –ell Days 3–5
Practice high-frequency words are, said, two, look, my	**Decodable reader: "Get Well Red Hen!"** Use decodable reader ideas (p. 23).	• High-Frequency Words Yoga Days 1–5 • High-Frequency Words Board Game Days 3–5
Guide students to use the words they wrote for the –ell word family and the high-frequency words to write a simple sentence.	**Interactive writing** (see p. 22) **Story starter:** Ben and Ken get two pets. **Word bank:** vet, hen, pen, fell, sell, tell, yet, let	• Reading/Writing: Respond to the Story "The Pet Hen" Days 1–5 • Reading/Writing: Respond to the Poem "Nell Fed the Pets" Days 3–5
Spell words in context Routines 21, 23 fell, yell, ten, are	**Test words in dictation** Read aloud each of the week's spelling words for students to write. Then collect and review student work.	• Spelling Homework: BLM 1 Days 1–5
"Read to Me" **Review high-frequency words** As you read aloud, point out the week's high-frequency words or other high-frequency words students have already learned. Have students say the words with you.	**"Read to Me"** **Review e/e/ and high-frequency words** As you read aloud, point out words that have the phonics element e/e/ and the week's high-frequency words. Have students say each word with you.	

* Use this menu to plan extra practice and center activities for use through the week. All the skills needed for an activity have been introduced by the first day of the range shown. See pages 68–69 for full descriptions.

Collaborative Learning and Independent Practice

 Phonological/Phonemic Awareness Activities

Phonemic Picnic:
Words with Short /e/ Sounds
Use on Days 1–5

Fill a picnic basket (or lunch box) with toy foods. Each food should contain the phoneme from this week and, if desired, previous weeks (for example: *eggs, jelly, ketchup, lettuce, pretzels*). Have partners sit on the floor as if ready for a picnic. They should take turns choosing a food, say the name of the food, and pass it to their partner to "eat."

Elkonin Boxes:
Words with Short /e/ Sounds
Use on Days 3–5

Provide the week's twelve picture cards (page 77). For each card, have students sound out the word, sliding a counter into a cell of an Elkonin box for each individual phoneme. Students can do this individually, or partners can take turns choosing from the picture cards.

ᴬᵦ⁾⁾ Phonics Activities

Phonics Beanbag Toss:
Words with Short /e/ Sounds
Use on Days 1–5

Arrange the twelve picture cards (page 77) for a beanbag toss. Provide the word cards, and have students take turns reading a word aloud and tossing the beanbag to the corresponding picture.

Picture Word Matching:
Words with Short /e/ Sounds
Use on Days 3–5

Provide students with the week's twenty-four picture and word cards (pages 76–77). Have students match each picture to its word and then sort all the pairs by rime (*bell/sell/tell/well, hen/men/pen/ten*, etc.).

Read/Draw/Label:
"Ben Plays with His Cat":
Words with Short /e/ Sounds
Use on Days 3–5

Provide students with BLM 3 (page 72) and have them complete the activity.

 # Word Family Activities

Word Family Ice Cream Cones: Word Families –et, –en
Use on Days 1–5

Provide students with BLM 2 (page 71) and have them complete the activity.

Word Family Books: Word Family –et
Use on Days 1–5

For each student, cut two index cards in half. Stack these four pieces of index cards, and then staple them to a single index card to form a "book" with four narrow pages and a final full-width page. Instruct students to write *et* on the final index card so that those letters are always visible. Then have students form different word family words by writing a letter on each of the first four pages of their books, such as *b*, *g*, *j*, and *l*. (If necessary, support students by providing a bank of letters that will form real words: *b*, *g*, *l*, *m*, *n*, *p*, *s*, *w*.) When finished, students can flip through the first four pages to form and read aloud different word family words (such as *bet*, *get*, *let*, *met*).

Word Family Picture Labels: Word Family –ell
Use on Days 3–5

Provide students with BLM 4 (page 73) and a word slider (BLM C) for the *–ell* word family. Have students use the slider to form word family words and complete the activity.

 # High-Frequency Word Activities

High-Frequency Words Yoga
Use on Days 1–5

Form groups of three and four students. Provide groups of three with a three-letter HFW on an index card. Provide groups of four with a four-letter HFW on an index card. Instruct students to sound out each letter and read the word aloud. Then encourage students to pose in order to form the letters in the word with their bodies. Each student can then say his or her letter in order so that the group says the word.

High-Frequency Words Board Game
Use on Days 3–5

Place copies of BLM D, a spinner (BLM B), and disks or coins for playing pieces in the center. Students use the spinner to advance on the board. When they land on a space with a high-frequency word, they read the word aloud and use it in an oral sentence. Students also follow directions on the squares that have them.

Label the squares with words and directions, making a path from the START square to the FINISH square (words and directions can be repeated, as necessary). Examples of words and directions include:

- **are, said, two, look, my, for, no, jump, one, has, have, play, little, you, with, the, see, go, she, and, can**
- **"Move back two spaces"**
- **"Move forward five spaces"**
- **"Spin again"**
- **"Skip your next turn"**
- **"Switch squares with the player across from you"**

Writing Activities

Reading/Writing: Respond to the Story "The Pet Hen"
Use on Days 1–5

Provide copies of BLM 5 (page 74) and have students read and respond to the story by drawing a picture.

Reading/Writing: Respond to the Story "Nell Fed the Pets"
Use on Days 3–5

Provide copies of BLM 6 (page 75) and have students write a sentence about the poem.

Spelling Homework

Read each spelling word aloud with your child. Spell it aloud together. Then ask your child to write each spelling word and say it in a sentence.

vet _____

fell _____

set _____

yell _____

men _____

ten _____

said _____

are _____

Choose a different activity every day to practice this week's spelling words at home with your child.

Write it	Write it again	Two-toned words	Trace your words	Circle the word
Write the word, saying aloud each letter as you write it.	Have your child write the word three times on a sheet of paper and circle the vowels.	Write the spelling words with crayons or colored markers. Use one color for consonants and another for vowels.	Use your finger to write each spelling word in sand, flour, or a similar material.	Write one sentence for each word and circle the spelling words.

Word Family Ice Cream Cones

Place the scoops of ice cream on the correct word family cones.

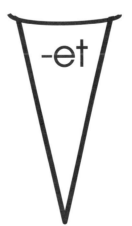

Ben Plays with His Cat

**Read the story. Circle words with the short e sound.
Then write a sentence about a cat.**

Ben has one pet.

It is a red cat.

Ben's cat will play with little bells.

Ben tells his cat, "Look at the bell!"

The cat jumps for one bell.

The cat jumps for two bells!

The cat

© Benchmark Education Company, LLC

Word Family Picture Labels

Say the name of the picture aloud.

Write the first letter of the word below each picture.

e l l

e l l

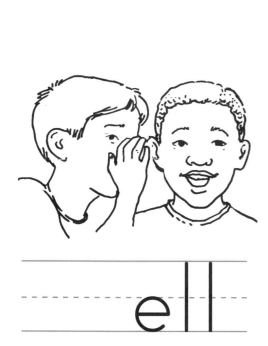

e l l

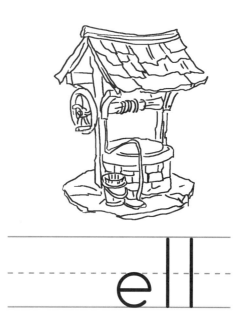

e l l

The Pet Hen

Read the story.

Jen ran to the pen.

The pet hen was in the pen.

"Look! Look!" said Jen.

"My little hen has two eggs!

I will go get Mom to see the eggs," said Jen.

Mom said to the hen, "You did well!"

Draw a picture of what happened to Jen's hen.

Nell Fed the Pets

Read the poem. Then write a sentence about how to take care of a pet.

Nell has a big pet.

She fed the big pet.

Nell has two little pets.

She fed the little pets.

Nell fed the big and little pets!

"I have fed my pets!" said Nell.

bell	Ben
hen	Ted
jet	yell
men	ten
web	well
pen	wet

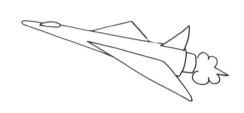

10

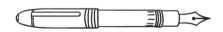

Advancing Phonics Every Day

Letters/sounds:
u/u/; inflected endings (–s)

	Day 1	Day 2	Day 3
Phonological/ Phonemic Awareness	**Syllable Segmentation** `Routine 3` **Model:** under **Practice:** funny, butter, number **Extra practice:** umbrella, bathtub	**Onset and Rime Segmentation** `Routine 7` **Model:** cut, rug **Practice:** puff, bun, luck **Extra practice:** hush, fuss	**Phoneme Recognition** `Routine 9` **Model:** sun/nut/crumb **Practice:** rug/gum/pup, run/luck/bug **Extra practice:** cup/numb/fun
Phonics	**Review previous week's sound/symbol focus** `Routine 17` **Model:** pet, hen **Practice:** jet, yell, bell **Extra practice:** wet, vet, sell, men, ten **Introduce sound/symbol correspondence: u/u/** `Routine 17` **Model:** cup, tub **Practice:** hug, nut, us **Extra practice:** bug, fun, gum	**Blend words with u/u/** `Routine 18` **Model:** hug, duck **Practice:** mud, up, hum **Extra practice:** but, gum, hut, rub, tub **Build words with u/u/** `Routine 19` **Model:** us, bus **Other words:** cub, cut, nut, duck, luck **Decodable reader: "Big Bus"** Use decodable reader ideas (p. 23).	Display the word card *runs*. `Routine 15` Point out the -s and tell students that the -s shows actions for a verb. Demonstrate by running in place and saying, "The teacher runs." Empasize that the –s means the action is happening right now. **Model:** run, runs **Practice:** play, plays **Extra practice:** talk, talks
Word Families	Guide students to make a five-petal flower with –ug in the center. Have students write one word on each petal in the –ug word family.	Guide students to use the picture cards for *cup* and *pup*. Have them write the word *up* at the top of their paper and then say and write the name of the picture cards.	Use the following letter cards and have students write words in the –un word family. **Letter cards:** b, f, r, s, u, n
High-Frequency Words	**Introduce high-frequency words** `Routine 20` come, here	**Practice high-frequency words** come, here `Routine 21` **Decodable reader: "Big Bus"** Use decodable reader ideas (p. 23).	**Introduce high-frequency words** `Routine 20` to, of
Writing	Have students use their –ug flower petals to write a sentence about a bug.	Have students write a sentence using the words up, cup, or pup.	Have students use the words they wrote for the –un word family and the day's high-frequency words to write a sentence.
Spelling	**Introduce spelling words** `Routines 20, 22` bun, dug, up, come	**Spell words in context** `Routines 21, 23` bun, dug, up, come	**Introduce spelling words** `Routines 20, 22` cups, fun, hugs, of
Shared Reading	**"Nan and Blue"** **Review e/e/** As you read aloud, point out words with the phonics element u/u/. Have students read the words aloud with you, emphasizing the phonics element.	**"Nan and Blue"** **Introduce u/u/** As you read aloud, point out words with the phonics element u/u/. Have students read the words aloud with you, emphasizing the phonics element.	**"Nan and Blue"** **Review u/u/; Introduce words with inflection ending (–s)** As you read aloud, point out the words with the phonics element u/u/ and words with inflectional ending (–s). Have students say these words with you.

High-Frequency Words:	Spelling:	Word Families:
come, here, to, of	Words with –ug, –up, –un	–ug, –up, –un

Day 4	Day 5	Collaborative Learning and Independent Practice*
Phoneme Isolation Routine 10 **Model:** rug, nut **Practice:** cup, cut, duck **Extra practice:** fun, tuck		• Phonemic Concentration: Words with Short /u/ Sounds Days 1–5 • Phonemic Classroom Clean-Up: Words with Short /u/ Sounds, Inflectional Ending –s Sounds Days 3–5
Blend words with inflected ending (–s) Routine 18 **Model:** runs, hums **Practice:** bats, rips, tells **Extra practice:** yells, hugs, tugs **Build words with inflected ending (–s)** Routine 19 **Model:** rub, rubs **Practice:** dig, digs, hop, hops **Extra practice:** sell, sells, pick, picks	**Decodable reader: "Big Bus"** Use decodable reader ideas (p. 23).	• Phonics Word Builder: Words with Short /u/ Sounds Days 1–5 • Craft Stick Chains: Words with Short /u/ Sounds, Inflectional Ending –s Sounds Days 3–5 • Read/Draw/Label: "Lots of Bugs Here!": Words with Short /u/ Sounds, Inflectional Ending –s Sounds Days 3–5
Guide students to use BLM B to make a word spinner. Have pairs take turns spinning the spinner and make a word for the –un word family. They can write the words using the BLM A word house.	**Review u/u/ words** Guide students to use BLM C to make a word family slider for each of the word families –ug, –up, and –un. One student moves the slider and says a word in that word family. The other student says a sentence using that word.	• Feed the Creatures: Word Families –ug, –up Days 1–5 • Word Family Spinners/Sliders: Word Families –un, –ug, –up Days 3–5 • Word Family Towers: Word Family –un Days 3–5
Practice high-frequency words Routine 21 come, here, to, of	**Decodable reader: "Big Bus"** Use decodable reader ideas (p. 23).	• High-Frequency Words Beanbag Toss Days 1–5 • High-Frequency Words Graph Days 3–5
Have students use the words they wrote in the word house and the week's high-frequency words to write a sentence.	**Interactive writing** (see p. 22) **Story starter:** Look at the pup jump! **Word bank:** dug, tug, up, fun, run, hug, pup, sun	• Reading/Writing: Respond to the Poem "Little Cub!" Days 1–5 • Reading/Writing: Continue the Story "My Pup" Days 3–5
Spell words in context Routines 21, 23 cups, fun, hugs, of	**Test words in dictation** Read aloud each of the week's spelling words for students to write. Then collect and review student work.	• Spelling Homework: BLM 1 Days 1–5
"The Tortoise and the Hare" **Review u/u/; Review inflected ending (–s)** As you read aloud, point out the words with the phonics element u/u/ and words with inflected ending (–s). Have students read these words aloud with you.	**"The Tortoise and the Hare"** **Review high-frequency words** As you read aloud, point out high-frequency words students have learned so far. Have students read aloud the high-frequency words with you.	

* Use this menu to plan extra practice and center activities for use through the week. All the skills needed for an activity have been introduced by the first day of the range shown. See pages 80–81 for full descriptions.

Collaborative Learning and Independent Practice

 Phonological/Phonemic Awareness Activities

Phonemic Concentration:
Words with Short /u/ Sounds
Use on Days 1–5

Provide students with a set of the week's picture cards (page 89), two of each card, for a total of 24 cards. Instruct partners to arrange the cards face down to form a 4 x 6 grid to play a concentration game. The partners should alternate turning over two cards per turn. When a student uncovers a matching pair, he/she should use the word in an oral sentence and keep the pair of cards. The student who collects the most pairs wins the game.

Phonemic Classroom Clean-Up:
Words with Short /u/ Sounds, Inflectional Ending –s Sounds
Use on Days 3–5

Set up two bins, one with the *bug* picture card taped to it, and the other with the *hugs* picture card taped to it (page 89). Have partners pronounce each word, pointing out the middle /u/ sound in *bug* and the final /z/ sound in *hugs*. Point out that both words contain the /u/ sound. Then explain that if a word has BOTH sounds, the cards should go in the *hugs* bin. Scatter around the classroom the other ten picture cards. Instruct partners to find the cards and place words with the middle /u/ sound in the *bug* bin, and words with BOTH the middle /u/ sound and the final /z/ sound in the *hugs* bin.

Phonics Activities

Phonics Word Builder:
Words with Short /u/ Sounds
Use on Days 1–5

Label a spinner (BLM B) with the letters *a, e, i, o,* and *u,* and provide students with letter tiles (or cutouts) of each letter. Have students use the spinner and letter tiles to complete the activity on BLM 2 (page 83). Note that student answers may vary.

Craft Stick Chains:
Words with Short /u/ Sounds, Inflectional Ending –s Sounds
Use on Days 3–5

Use tongue depressors or craft sticks. Write a decodable word with a middle /u/ sound on one end of each stick and a word with an inflectional ending –s on the other end of each stick. Have partners take turns choosing a stick and placing it end-to-end with another stick, matching words with the middle /u/ or final –s sound.

Read/Draw/Label:
"Lots of Bugs Here!":
Words with Short /u/ Sounds, Inflectional Ending –s Sounds
Use on Days 3–5

Provide students with BLM 3 (page 84) and have them complete the activity.

Word Family Activities

Feed the Creatures: Word Families –ug, –up
Use on Days 1–5

Provide two small plastic bins. Label each with a word family, –ug or –up. Use a marker to make eyes or a face on each bin to turn the bins into creatures. Provide partners with the –ug and –up picture cards, and have them take turns "feeding" the creatures the appropriate cards:

• bug / dug / jug / rug / cup / pup

Word Family Spinners: Word Families –un, –ug, –up
Use on Days 3–5

Set up a word spinner (BLM B) for each of the week's word families. Write a word family on the long rectangular piece and initial letters around the circle. Provide three copies of the phonics house (BLM A) and have students label them –un, –ug, and –up. Ask students to form words using the spinners and to list each word they form in the appropriate word family house.

Word Family Towers: Word Family –un
Use on Days 3–5

Provide partners with interlocking blocks. On each block, place a piece of masking tape. Write –un words on half of the blocks, and other decodable words on the rest of the blocks. Have students find and stack the –un word blocks into a word family tower, pronouncing each word as they add it to the tower.

(Adapt this activity for the –ug or –up word families.)

High-Frequency Word Activities

High-Frequency Words Beanbag Toss
Use on Days 1–5

Gather Benchmark Advance high-frequency word cards for a beanbag toss. Use review words from previous weeks as well as some of the current week's words.

• and / are / come / for / go / have / here / jump / little / look / my / no / one / play / said / see / she / the / two / with / you

Have one student choose a word to read aloud, and another to toss the bag to cover the matching card.

High-Frequency Words Graph
Use on Days 3–5

Provide students with BLM 4 (page 85) and have them complete the activity.

Writing Activities

Reading/Writing: Respond to the Poem "Lots of Bugs Here!"
Use on Days 1–5

Provide copies of BLM 5 (page 86) and have students reread the poem and complete the activity.

Reading/Writing: Continue the Story "My Pup"
Use on Days 3–5

Provide copies of BLM 6 (page 87) and have students complete the activity.

BLM
1

Spelling Homework

Read each spelling word aloud with your child. Spell it aloud together. Then ask your child to write each spelling word and say it in a sentence.

bun _____

dug _____

up _____

come _____

cups _____

fun _____

hugs _____

of _____

Choose a different activity every day to practice this week's spelling words at home with your child.

Write it	Trace your words	Multi-colored words	Write it again	Letter tiles
Write the word, saying aloud each letter as you write it.	Use your finger to write each spelling word in sand, flour, or a similar material.	Write the spelling words with crayons or colored pencils, using a different color for each letter.	Write the word three times, and then circle the vowels.	Use letter tiles to spell the words and then write the words on a piece of paper.

Phonics Word Builder

Place a letter tile in each box to make a word.
Read the word aloud.
Be sure that you make real words.

b ☐ g

p ☐ g

b ☐ d

r ☐ g

h ☐ g

j ☐ g

p ☐ p

r ☐ b

Lots of Bugs Here!

Read the poem.
Circle all the words that have the short u sound.

See the little bug?

On the rug! On the rug!

See the big bugs?

In the tub! In the tub!

Lots of bugs here! Lots of bugs!

High-Frequency Words Graph

How many letters are in each word?
Write the words below the graph.
Color in the graph for each word.

come	here	to	of

1				
2				
3				
4				

_____

- -

_____

Little Cub

Read the poem.
Write a sentence about something else the little cub might do.

The little cub sits in the sun.

The little cub gets in the mud.

The little cub looks at a bug.

The little cub has lots of fun!

Come here for a hug, little cub!

_____

- -

_____

- -

_____

- -

_____

My Pup

Read the story.

Look at my pup!

My pup has fun!

My pup plays in the sun!

My pup plays with bugs!

My pup plays in the tub!

"Come here, pup!" I tell him.

I hug my pup.

Draw a picture to tell what happens next.

bug	jug
bun	pup
cup	rug
dug	runs
fun	sun
hugs	tugs

Advancing Phonics Every Day

Letters/sounds:
l-blends

	Day 1	Day 2	Day 3
Phonological/ Phonemic Awareness	**Syllable Blending** `Routine 4` **Model:** puddle, bucket **Practice:** cuddle, subway, buzzing **Extra practice:** number, maximum, sunshine	**Phoneme Addition** `Routine 12` Model: lock/block, lane/plane Practice: loss/gloss, lip/flip, low/glow Extra practice: lame/flame, lap/clap	**Phoneme Blending** `Routine 15` Model: block, glass Practice: flag, slip, clam Extra practice: clown, plane
Phonics	**Review previous week's sound/symbol focus** `Routine 17` **Model:** bus, tugs **Practice:** runs, fun, pup **Extra practice:** hugs, mug, sun, cup, rug	**Introduce sound/symbol correspondence: l-blends** `Routine 18` **Model:** blob, slob **Practice:** slot, glob, glad **Extra practice:** clip, slip, slit, plop, plan, Explain to students that each sound in a blend is pronounced separately. **Predecodable reader: "A Sled Club"** Use decodable reader ideas (p. 23).	**Blend words with l-blends** `Routine 18` **Model:** blob, slab **Practice:** plug, plan, flop, bless, fluff **Extra practice:** glass, flap
Word Families	Guide students to make a five-rung word ladder with the word family –ob at the top of the ladder and an –ob word on each rung of the ladder.	Use the following letter cards. Have students write words in the –ob family on their workmats. **Letter cards:** b, c, m, r, s, ob Students can record their answers on BLM A.	Display picture cards blocks, lock, clock, flock, and sock. Have students work in pairs, say the name of the picture, and write the word using BLM A word family house.
High-Frequency Words	**Introduce high-frequency words** `Routine 20` what, put, want	**Practice high-frequency words** what, put, want `Routine 21` **Predecodable reader: "A Sled Club"** Use decodable reader ideas (p. 23).	**Introduce high-frequency words** `Routine 20` this, saw
Writing	Have students use this week's high-frequency words and the words they made from the phonics activity to write a sentence about a boy named Bob.	Students work in pairs and use the words from their phonics activity to compose a simple sentence about a giant blob.	Have students use the new high-frequency words and the words they wrote for the word family activity to write a sentence.
Spelling	**Introduce spelling words** `Routines 20, 22` job, hot, lock, what	**Spell words in context** `Routines 21, 23` job, hot, lock, what	**Introduce spelling words** `Routines 20, 22` blot, clock, rock, this
Shared Reading	**"A Smart Hen"** **Review short u; inflectional ending -s** As you read aloud, review phonics elements short u and inflectional ending -s by pointing out words that contain these elements. Have students read the words aloud with you, emphasizing the phonics element(s).	**"A Smart Hen"** **Introduce high-frequency words: l-blends** As you read aloud, point out this week's high-frequency words and words with l-blends. Have students read these words aloud with you, emphasizing the phonics element.	**" A Smart Hen"** **Introduce word family words –ob, –ock** As you read aloud, point out words that contain the word family word patterns you have been learning, -ob and -ock. Have students read these words aloud with you, emphasizing the phonics element.

High-Frequency Words:	Spelling:	Word Families:
what, put, want, this, saw	Words with –ob, –ock	–ob, –ock

Day 4	Day 5	Collaborative Learning and Independent Practice*
Phoneme Deletion Routine 16 **Model:** block/lock **Practice:** play/lay, place/lace **Extra practice:** fat/at, lick/slick		• Phonemic Picnic: Words with l-Blends Days 1–5 • Phoneme Cubes: Words with l-Blends Days 3–5
Build words with l-blends Routine 19 **Model:** flip/clip/slip **Practice:** block/clock/flock flop/plop/slop **Extra Practice:** blot/clot/slot	**Predecodable reader: "A Sled Club"** Use decodable reader ideas (p. 23).	• Phonics Ice Cream Cones: Words with l-Blends Days 1–5 • Phonics Beanbag Toss: Words with l-Blends Days 3–5 • Read/Draw/Label: "A Little Clam": Words with –op Sounds and l-Blends Days 3–5
Distribute the following letter cards to students. Have them make as many words in the –ock word family as possible and write them on their workmats. **Letter cards:** d, l, m, r, s, o, c, k	**Review –ob and –ock words** Have students work in small groups and use the following letter cards and two BLM As to write words in word families –ock and –ob. Each student can then use one of the words in an oral sentence. **Letter cards:** d, j, l, r, s, o, c, k	• Word Family Books: –ob Days 1–5 • Word Family Sort: –ob, –ock Days 3–5
Practice high-frequency words Routine 21 what, put, want, this, saw	**Predecodable reader: "A Sled Club"** Use decodable reader ideas (p. 23).	• High-Frequency Words Concentration Days 1–5 • High-Frequency Words Yoga Days 3–5
Have students use the picture cards *blocks, clock, flock, glad, plug, sock* and the week's high-frequency words to write a silly sentence about a blob.	**Interactive writing** (see p. 22) **Story starter:** Glen and Bob got a job. **Word bank:** lock, block, clock, sob, sock, rock, flock	• Reading/Writing: Respond to the Story "The Black Cat" Days 1–5 • Reading/Writing: Respond to the Poem "Tom Has a Cat" Days 3–5
Spell words in context Routines 20, 22 blot, clock, rock, this	**Test words in dictation** Read out the spelling words for students to write. Then review their work.	• Spelling Homework: BLM 1 Days 1–5
"Chums" **Review this week's high-frequency words** As you read aloud, point out this week's high-frequency words. Have students say the words aloud with you.	**"Chums"** **Review l-blends; review –ob and –ock word families** As you read aloud, point out the words in the text that have l-blends and are a part of the –ob and –ock word families. Have students say these words aloud with you, emphasizing the phonics elements.	

* Use this menu to plan extra practice and center activities for use through the week. All the skills needed for an activity have been introduced by the first day of the range shown. See pages 92–93 for full descriptions.

© Benchmark Education Company, LLC

Grade 1 • Advancing Phonics Skills 91

Collaborative Learning and Independent Practice

 Phonological/Phonemic Awareness Activities

Phonemic Picnic:
Words with l-Blends
Use on Days 1–5

Fill a picnic basket (or lunch box) with toy foods. Each food should begin with a l-blend from this week (and, if desired, a phoneme from previous weeks) (for example: *black beans, blackberries, blueberries, clams, flan, plums*). Have partners sit on the floor as if ready for a picnic. They should take turns choosing a food, saying the name of the food, and passing it to their partner to "eat."

Phoneme Cubes:
Words with l-Blends
Use on Days 3–5

Gather multiple pairs of cubes (such as empty cube-shaped tissue boxes). Paste the week's picture cards (page 101) on the boxes. Students can take turns rolling the cubes, saying the two words that face up, identifying the beginning sound(s), and noting whether they are the same.

^A_C^B)) Phonics Activities

Phonics Ice Cream Cones:
Words with l-Blends
Use on Days 1–5

Provide students with BLM 2 (page 95) and have them complete the activity.

Phonics Beanbag Toss:
Words with l-Blends
Use on Days 3–5

Arrange the picture cards (page 101) for a beanbag toss. Provide the word cards, and have students take turns reading a word aloud and tossing the beanbag to the corresponding picture.

Read/Draw/Label:
"A Little Clam":
Words with –ock and l-Blends
Use on Days 3–5

Provide students with BLM 3 (page 96) and have them complete the activity.

Word Family Activities

Word Family Books: –ob
Use on Days 1–5

For each student, cut two index cards in half. Stack these four pieces of index cards, and then staple them to a single index card to form a "book" with four narrow pages and a final full-width page. Instruct students to write *ob* on the final index card so that those letters are always visible. Then have students form different word family words by writing a letter on each of the first four pages of their books, such as *bl, c, gl,* and *j.* (If necessary, support students by providing a bank of letters that will form real words: *b, bl, c, gl, j, m, r, s, sl.*) When finished, students can flip through the first four pages to form and read aloud different word family words (such as *blob, cob, glob, job*).

Word Family Sort: –ob, –ock
Use on Days 3–5

Provide students with BLM 4 (page 97) and have them complete the activity.

High-Frequency Word Activities

High-Frequency Words Concentration
Use on Days 1–5

Distribute to partners the following Benchmark Advance high-frequency word cards. Each set should contain two copies of each word, for a total of twenty-eight cards per pair of students.

- **are / come / for / here / jump / look / my / no / of / put / said / to / two / what**

Instruct partners to arrange the cards face down to form a 4 x 7 grid to play a concentration game. The partners should alternate turning over two cards per turn. When a student uncovers a matching pair, he/she uses the word in an oral sentence and keeps the pair of cards. The student who collects the most pairs wins the game.

High-Frequency Words Yoga
Use on Days 3–5

Form groups of three and four students. Provide each group of three with a three-letter HFW on an index card. Provide each group of four with a four-letter HFW on an index card. Instruct students to sound out each letter and read the word aloud. Then encourage students to pose in order to form the letters in the word with their bodies. Each student can then say his or her letter in order so that the group says the word.

Writing Activities

Reading/Writing: Respond to the Story "The Black Cat"
Use on Days 1–5

Provide copies of BLM 5 (page 98) and have students read and respond to the story by identifying phonics elements and writing a sentence using the sentence starter.

Reading/Writing: Respond to the Poem "Tom Has a Cat"
Use on Days 3–5

Provide copies of BLM 6 (page 99) and have students read and respond to the poem by identifying high-frequency words and writing a sentence using the sentence starter.

Spelling Homework

Read each spelling word aloud with your child. Spell it aloud together. Then ask your child to write each spelling word and say it in a sentence.

job _____   blot _____

hot _____   rock _____

lock _____   this _____

what _____   clock _____

Choose a different activity every day to practice this week's spelling words at home with your child.

Flashlight writing	Magnetic letters	Trace the word	Remember the word	Circle the word
Turn out the lights. Use a flashlight to spell each word on the wall.	Spell the words on a cookie sheet using magnetic letters and then write the words on a piece of paper.	Write the word with dotted lines, and then trace the dots with a different color.	Turn the paper over and write the word from memory.	Work with your child to write a sentence for each word on a sheet of paper and circle the spelling words.

Phonics Ice Cream Cones

Place the scoops of ice cream on the cones with the same sound.

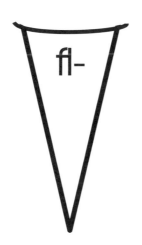

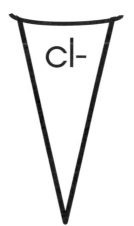

A Little Clam

Read the poem. Then circle the *-ock* words with one colored pencil. Underline the words with l-blends using a different colored pencil.

A little clam was in the mud.

The clam got on top of a rock.

The clam saw the dock.

The clam saw the fog.

The clam saw the cliffs.

The clam got off the rock

and hid in the mud. Plop!

Come back, little clam!

Word Family Sort

Cut out the words.

Place each word in the basket belonging to its word family.

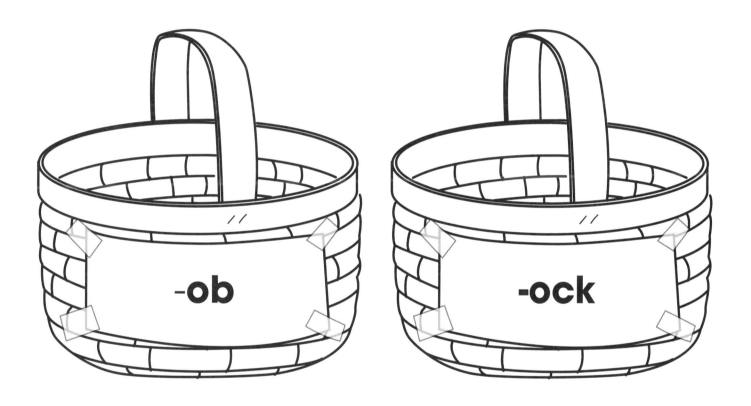

-ob

-ock

| rock | job | sock | block | slob |
| Bob | cob | clock | dock | rob |

The Black Cat

**Read the story. Circle all the words with *-op* with one colored pencil.
Underline all the words with l-blends with another colored pencil.
Then write a sentence about the cat.**

"Will you look for the black cat?" said Tom.

Did the cat jump in a sack?

Did the cat flop in a box?

Did the cat plop on the bed?

Mom sees the black cat.

The cat is on top of the hat.

Get off the hat, cat!

The cat

Name _____ Date_____

Tom Has a Cat

Read the poem. Circle the words "wants," "come," and "little."
Then write a sentence about where you like to nap.

Tom has a little cat.

The little cat is tan.

The cat wants to nap.

The cat wants to nap on the red cap.

Get off, cat!

Come nap on this flat mat.

I nap

Bob	**glad**
blocks	**lock**
clock	**plug**
cob	**sob**
pot	**sock**
flock	**flag**

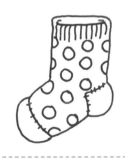

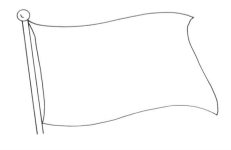

Advancing Phonics Every Day

Letters/sounds:
r-blends; possessives

	Day 1	Day 2	Day 3
Phonological/ Phonemic Awareness	**Word Awareness** `Routine 1` **Model:** Dad is cooking on the grill. **Practice:** The princess took the dragon's treasure. **Extra practice:** I am drawing the dragonfly in the grass.	**Sentence Awareness** `Routine 2` **Model:** I like grabbing grapes. **Practice:** Drake plays the drum. **Extra practice:** Fran took out the trash.	**Phoneme Segmentation** `Routine 11` **Model:** frog, crab **Practice:** drop, truck **Extra practice:** trap, grin
Phonics	**Review previous week's sound/symbol focus: l-blends** `Routine 18` **Model:** block, slip **Practice:** glad, plan, clock **Extra practice:** plug, slot, flat, flop **Introduce sound/symbol correspondence: r-blends** `Routine 18` **Model:** brim, drop **Practice:** drip, grip **Extra practice:** grin, drill, frog, trip, trick Remind students that each sound in a blend is pronounced separately.	**Blend words with r-blends** `Routine 18` **Model:** dress, track **Practice:** frill, grill, drop **Extra practice:** grin, grip, drip **Build words with r-blends** `Routine 19` **Model:** glass, grass **Other words:** grim, trim, crop, drop **Decodable reader: "Fran Grabs It!"** Use decodable reader ideas (p. 23).	**Introduce Possessives** Display the word card *Pam's*. Point out the apostrophe and the -s and tell students that when a noun ends with an apostrophe and an -s, it is called a possessive. When you possess something, you own it. Reinforce the idea by pointing to a student and saying the student's name and an article of clothing the student is wearing, such as *Jack's shirt*. Have students say their name and something they own using possessive form.
Word Families	Have students use the following letter cards to make as many words as they can in the word family –*im*. Students can write the words on their workmats. **Letter cards:** d, h, J, K, r, i, m	Guide students to draw a five-petal flower. Students will write –*im* in the center of the flower, and then use the following letter cards to write an –*im* word on each petal. **Letter cards:** d, h, J, K, r, T, i, m	Distribute the picture cards *drill* and *grill* to pairs of students. Have students write the name of the picture on their workmats.
High-Frequency Words	**Introduce high-frequency words** `Routine 20` now, do	**Introduce high-frequency words** `Routine 21` which, went	**Practice high-frequency words now, do** `Routine 20` **Decodable reader: "Fran Grabs It!"** Use decodable reader ideas (p. 23).
Writing	Have students use the words they made in the word family activity to write a sentence about Tim and Kim.	Have students use the high-frequency words that they practiced and choose from the words *drop, drip, trip*, and *grip* to write a sentence about a boy named Tim.	Have students use the words they wrote from the word family activity and the possessive form of a noun to write a sentence.
Spelling	**Introduce spelling words** `Routines 20, 22` him, grill, trim, now	**Spell words in context** `Routines 21, 23` him, grill, trim, now	**Introduce spelling words** `Routines 20, 22` Bill's, brick, trick, which
Shared Reading	**"The Amazing Butterfly"** **Review l-blends** As you read aloud, point out words in the text with l-blends. Have students say these words with you, emphasizing the phonics element.	**"The Amazing Butterfly"** **Introduce r-blends** As you read aloud, point out words that begin with r-blends. Have students read these words aloud with you, emphasizing the phonics element.	**"The Amazing Butterfly"** **Introduce r-blends, introduce possessives** As you read aloud, point out and review words that have r-blends. Have students read aloud with you words that show possession.

High-Frequency Words: now, do, which, went	Spelling: Words with –im, –ill, –ick	Word Families: –im, –ill, –ick

Day 4	Day 5	Collaborative Learning and Independent Practice*
Phoneme Blending Routine 12 **Model:** frogs, crib **Practice:** drag, trims, trap **Extra practice:** brick, grin, crack		• Phonemic Word Sort: Words with r–Blends Days 1–5 • Elkonin Boxes: Words with r–Blends, Possessives Days 3–5
Practice Possessive Words Review what students learned previously about possessive words. Recall that an apostrophe and an *s* at the end of a word show possession. Then display the picture cards below. Have student pairs write the name of the picture and add the apostrophe and *s* to show possessive form. **Picture cards:** hat, dad, bell, hen, jet, bug, pup, clock, sock, hill, brick	**Decodable reader: "Fran Grabs It!"** Use decodable reader ideas (p. 23).	• Phonics Classroom Clean-Up: Words with r–Blends Days 1–5 • Phonics Concentration: Words with r–Blends, Possessives Days 3–5 • Read/Draw/Label: "A Trick!": Words with r–Blends Days 3–5 R-Blends Picture
Have students use a five-rung ladder to write –*ick* word family words. Students write –*ick* at the top of the ladder and add an –*ick* word to each rung. **Letter cards:** k, l, p, N, R, s, t, i, c, k	**Review –im, –ill –ick words** Distribute letter cards and have students work in pairs. Have partners take turns building –*im*, –*ill*, and –*ick* words. As one student makes a word, the other student uses the word in an oral sentence.	• Word Family Tic-Tac-Toe: Word Families –im, –ill Days 1–5 • Word Family Picture Labels: Word Families –ill, –ick Days 3–5 • Word Family Scramble: Word Family –ick Days 3–5
Practice high-frequency words Routine 21 now, do, which, went	**Decodable reader: "Fran Grabs It!"** Use decodable reader ideas (p. 23).	• High-Frequency Words Board Game Days 1–5 • High-Frequency Words Go Fish Days 3–5
Have students use the words they wrote for the word family activity to write a simple sentence about a boy named Rick and his day.	**Interactive writing** (see p. 22) **Story starter:** What did Tim's pup Mick do now? **Word bank:** kick, lick, trick, hill, will, brick, drill, fill, him, trim	• Reading/Writing: Respond to the Poem "Fun with –ill" Days 1–5 • Reading/Writing: Respond to the Story "We See Brad" Days 3–5
Spell words in context Routines 21, 23 Bill's, brick, trick, which	**Test words in dictation** Read out the spelling words for students to write. Then review their work.	• Spelling Homework: BLM 1 Days 1–5
"Caterpillar" **Review high-frequency words: now, do, which, went; review possessives** As you read aloud, point out the week's high-frequency words and possessive nouns. Have students read these words aloud with you.	**"Caterpillar"** **Review –im, –ill, –ick** As you read aloud, point out words that are part of the word families –*im, –ill, –ick*. Have students read these words aloud with you, emphasizing the phonics element.	

* Use this menu to plan extra practice and center activities for use through the week. All the skills needed for an activity have been introduced by the first day of the range shown. See pages 104–105 for full descriptions.

Collaborative Learning and Independent Practice

🦻)) Phonological/Phonemic Awareness Activities

Phonemic Word Sort: Words with r–Blends
Use on Days 1–5

Distribute copies of this week's picture cards for words with r–blends (page 113). Have pairs of students work together to sort the cards by initial blend:

- **drill / drip**
- **grill / grin**
- **bricks / brim**

Elkonin Boxes: Words with r–Blends, Possessives
Use on Days 3–5

Provide the week's 12 picture cards (page 113). For each card, have students sound out the word, sliding a counter into a cell of an Elkonin box for each individual phoneme. Students can do this individually, or partners can take turns choosing from the picture cards.

ᴬᴮ)) Phonics Activities
C

Phonics Classroom Clean-Up: Words with r–Blends
Use on Days 1–5

Label seven bins with the initial r–blends, *br, cr, dr, fr, gr, pr*, and *tr*. Gather objects and toys from the classroom that begin with the r–blends (such as a *brush, bristle blocks, crayons, drawing paper*, and *green paint*). Instruct partners to "clean up" by putting each object in the appropriate bin.

Phonics Concentration: Words with r–Blends, Possessives
Use on Days 3–5

Provide students with a set of the week's picture and word cards (pages 112–113). Instruct partners to arrange the cards face down to form a 6 x 4 grid to play a concentration game. The partners should alternate turning over two cards per turn. When a student uncovers a matching pair (a picture and its corresponding word card), he/she should use the word in an oral sentence and keep the pair of cards. The student who collects the most pairs wins the game.

Read/Draw/Label: R-Blends Picture: Words with r–Blends
Use on Days 3–5

Provide students with BLM 3 (page 108) and have them complete the activity.

Word Family Activities

Word Family Tic-Tac-Toe: Word Families –im, –ill
Use on Days 1–5

Provide or have students draw a tic-tac-toe board. Have partners play tic-tac-toe using words belonging to the *–im* and *–ill* word families. One partner will use *–im* words instead of an X to mark his/her spots on the board. The other partner will use *–ill* words instead of an O.

Word Family Picture Labels: Word Families –ill, –ick
Use on Days 3–5

Provide students with BLM 2 (page 107) and word sliders (BLM C) for the *–ill* and *–ick* word families. Have students use the sliders to form word family words and complete the activity.

Word Family Scramble: Word Family –ick
Use on Days 3–5

Distribute BLM 4 (page 109) and have students complete the *–ick* word family activity.

High-Frequency Word Activities

High-Frequency Words Board Game:
Use on Days 1–5

Place copies of BLM D, a spinner (BLM B), and disks or coins for playing pieces in the center. Students use the spinner to advance on the board. When they land on a space with a high-frequency word, they read the word aloud and use it in an oral sentence. Students also follow directions on the squares that have them.

Label the squares with words and directions, making a path from the START square to the FINISH square (words and directions can be repeated, as necessary). Examples of words and directions include:

- **now, do, what, put, want, this, saw, come, here, to, of, are, said, two, look, my, for, no, jump, one, have, play, little, you, with, the, see, go, she, and**

- **"Move back two spaces"**

- **"Move forward five spaces"**

- **"Spin again"**

- **"Skip your next turn"**

High-Frequency Words Go Fish:
Use on Days 3–5

Pick twenty-five high-frequency words, including the four from this week, and write each word on two index cards to create fifty cards. Students might be instructed to draw fish on the other sides of the cards. Have groups of 2–4 students play "Go Fish" using this deck.

Writing Activities

Reading/Writing: Respond to the Poem "Fun with –ill"
Use on Days 1–5

Provide copies of BLM 5 (page 110) and have students read the passage and use the sentence starter to respond to the passage.

Reading/Writing: Respond to the Story "We See Brad"
Use on Days 3–5

Provide copies of BLM 6 (page 111) and have students read the story and use the sentence starter to write about the story.

Spelling Homework

Read each spelling word aloud with your child. Spell it aloud together. Then ask your child to write each spelling word and say it in a sentence.

him _____

Bill's _____

trim _____

brick _____

grill _____

trick _____

now _____

which _____

Choose a different activity every day to practice this week's spelling words at home with your child.

Trace your words	Remember the word	Flashlight writing	Multi-colored words	Circle the Word
Use your finger to write each spelling word in sand, flour, or a similar material.	Turn the paper over and write the word from memory.	Turn out the lights. Use a flashlight to spell each word on the wall.	Write the spelling words with crayons or colored pencils, using a different color for each letter.	Work with your child to write a sentence for each word on a sheet of paper and circle the spelling words.

Name _____ Date_____

Word Family Picture Labels

Say the name of the pictures aloud.
Write the word below each picture.

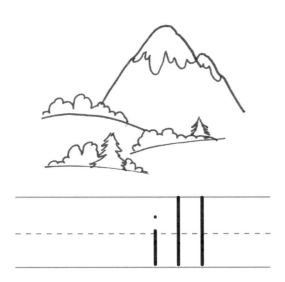

i l l

i c k

i c k

i l l

R-Blends Picture

Label things in the picture that are r-blends.
Then write a sentence to tell what is happening in this picture.

_____

- -

_____

- -

_____

- -

_____

Word Family Scramble

Cut out the tiles.
Arrange the tiles to spell the word.

t   ck   i   r

ck   i   s

k   ck   i

i   ck   l

Fun with -ill

Read the poem. Then write a sentence about something you will do that ends with -ill.

Tim and Nick went to play on a hill.

Kim and Mick went to set up a grill.

Jim and Rick went to get a drill.

Mom and Dad went to look at a mill.

Now what will you do with an -ill?

I will _____

_____

_____

We See Brad

Read the story.
Then write a sentence about a time you went on a trip.

We go on a trip to see Brad.

We see a lot of grass and hills.

But we do not see Brad yet.

We seee a frog and a crab.

Now we see Brad!

We can see Brad's hat.

Brad's hat is black with a tan brim.

Brad is glad to see us.

I went on a

trip

bricks	grin
drill	brim
drip	lick
frog	Pam's
grill	Rick
crib	track

Advancing Phonics Every Day

	Day 1	Day 2	Day 3
Phonological/ Phonemic Awareness	**Syllable Segmentation** `Routine 3` **Model:** sleeping, snowman **Practice:** sneaker, starfish, spider **Extra practice:** strawberry, spinach	**Syllable Blending** `Routine 4` **Model:** sticker, slipper **Practice:** student, starfish **Extra practice:** sweater, smoothie	**Phoneme Categorization** `Routine 13` **Model:** sleep/slip/soon **Practice:** stir/sip/stop, mall/small/smart **Extra practice:** snail/sail/snap
Phonics	**Review previous week's skill: r-blends** `Routine 18` **Model:** grin, drip **Practice:** drill, brick, trick, frog **Extra practice:** Fran, crop Remind students that each sound in a blend is pronounced. **Introduce s-blends** `Routine 18` **Model:** skip, spot **Practice:** skim, spin, slip **Extra practice:** smell, stick	**Blend with s-blends** `Routine 18` **Model:** slip, snug **Practice:** slob, snip, spell, skin **Extra practice:** slim, smock **Build with s-blends** `Routine 19` **Model:** skill, spill **Other words:** stack, slack, spin, swim **Decodable reader: "Stop! It's a Frog!"** Use decodable reader ideas (p. 23).	**Introduce contractions ('s)** `Routine 18` Tell students that a contraction is the shortened form of two words. Display the *he's* and *it's* picture cards. Note that *he's* is a contraction of *he is*; *it's* is a contraction of *it is*. The apostrophe replaces the left-out letter. **Model:** he's **Practice:** it's, she's
Word Families	Use the following letter cards. Have students work in pairs to form words in the *–ap* family and write them on their workmats. **Letter cards:** c, g, l, m, n, r, s, t, z , a, p	Guide students to make a five-rung word ladder for the word family *–am*. Have students write *–am* at the top of the ladder and then add a word to each rung of the ladder.	Distribute the following letter cards and have students use a phonics house (BLM A) to write words for the word family *–ag*. **Letter cards:** b, g, h, l, r, s, t, w, a
High-Frequency Words	**Introduce high-frequency words** `Routine 20` was, there	**Practice high-frequency words** was, there `Routine 21` **Decodable reader: "Stop! It's a Frog!"** Use decodable reader ideas (p. 23).	**Introduce high-frequency words** `Routine 20` then, out
Writing	Have students use the words they wrote for the word family activity to write a simple sentence about a boy named Stan.	Have students use the words they wrote for the word family activity to write a simple sentence about Sam's jam.	Have students use the *he's* and *it's* picture word cards, as well as words they wrote for the word family routine, to write a sentence about a dog.
Spelling	**Introduce spelling words** `Routines 20, 22` snap, slap, swam, there	**Spell words in context** `Routines 21, 23` snap, slap, swam, there	**Introduce spelling words** `Routines 20, 22` slam, drag, snag, out
Shared Reading	**"An Apple Grows"** **Review r-blends** As you read aloud, point out words with r-blends (*grows, trees*). Have students read these words aloud with you, emphasizing the phonics element.	**"An Apple Grows"** **Introduce words with s-blends** As you read aloud, point out words that have s-blends (*spot, starts*). Have students read the words aloud with you, emphasizing the phonics element.	**"An Apple Grows"** **Introduce contractions ('s); review word families –ap, –am, –ag** As you read aloud, point out the contractions ('s). Have students read the word and say the two words the contraction stands for. Also, point out words for word families *–ap, –am,* and *–ag.* Have students read them with you.

High-Frequency Words:	Spelling:	Word Families:
was, there, then, out	Words with –ap, –am, –ag	–ap, –am, –ag

Day 4	Day 5	Collaborative Learning and Independent Practice*
Phoneme Substitution Routine 14 **Model:** swing/sling **Practice:** spell/smell, slip/skip/snip **Extra practice:** snot/spot, scout/stout/snout/spout		• Phonemic Picnic: Words with s-Blends Days 1–5 • Phoneme Cubes: Contractions ('s), Words with s-Blends Days 3–5
Blend contractions ('s) Routine 18 **Model:** he's, it's **Practice:** she's, there's, what's **Extra practice:** here's **Build contractions ('s)** Routine 19 **Model:** It is a little dog. It's a little dog. **Other words:** He is sick. He's sick.	**Decodable reader: "Stop! It's a Frog!"** Use decodable reader ideas (p. 23).	• Letter Cup Substitution: Words with s-Blends Days 1–5 • Picture Word Cards: Words with s-Blends, Contractions ('s) Days 3–5 • Read/Circle/Underline: "The Slug": Words with s-Blends, Contractions ('s) Days 3–5
Display the *bag, tag, clam, jam, map,* and *stop* picture word cards. Have students read the words and then write a sentence using two of the words.	**Review –ap, –am, –ag words** Use the following picture word cards. Have pairs of students take turns looking at the picture, saying the word, and using the word in an oral sentence. **Picture word cards:** bag, clam, jam, map, tag, ham, Pam	• Word Family Crossword: –ap, –am Days 1–5 • Word Family Picture Labels: –ag, –ag Days 3–5 • Word Family Board Game: –ap, –ag Days 3–5
Practice high-frequency words Routine 21 was, there, then, out	**Decodable reader: "Stop! It's a Frog!"** Use decodable reader ideas (p. 23).	• High-Frequency Words Concentration Days 1–5 • High-Frequency Words Bug Catch Days 3–5
Have students use the high-frequency words to write a simple sentence about Sam, Pam, and Stan.	**Interactive writing** (see p. 22) **Story starter:** Cam and Tam can swim with Gram. **Word bank:** lap, trap, clam, swam, flag	• Reading/Writing: Continue the Story "Pam and Sam Swim" Days 1–5 • Reading/Writing: Respond to the Story "Stan's Snack" Days 3–5
Spell words in context Routines 21, 23 slam, drag, snag, out	**Test words in dictation** Read out the spelling words for students to write. Then review their work.	• Spelling Homework: BLM 1 Days 1–5
"Sunflower" **Review high-frequency words: was, there, then, out** As you read aloud, have students point out this week's high-frequency words. Have students say the words aloud with you.	**"Sunflower"** **Review s-blends** As you read aloud, point out words with s-blends (*standing*). Have students read the words aloud with you, emphasizing the phonics element.	

* Use this menu to plan extra practice and center activities for use through the week. All the skills needed for an activity have been introduced by the first day of the range shown. See pages 116–117 for full descriptions.

Collaborative Learning and Independent Practice

 **Phonological/Phonemic Awareness Activities**

Phonemic Picnic:
Words with s-Blends
Use on Days 1–5

Fill a picnic basket (or lunch box) with plastic food items. Each food item should begin with a phoneme from this week (and, if desired, from previous weeks) (for example, *spaghetti, steak, smoothie, sweet potato, stew, spinach*). Have partners sit on the floor as though they are going to have a picnic. Partners can take turns choosing a food item, saying the name of the food, and passing the item to their partner to "eat."

Phoneme Cubes:
Words with s-Blends, Contractions ('s)
Use on Days 3–5

Gather multiple pairs of cubes (such as empty cube-shaped tissue boxes). Paste this week's twelve picture cards (page 125) on each pair of boxes, six per box. Students can take turns rolling the cubes, saying the words for the two pictures that face up, identifying the final consonant sounds, and noting whether they are the same. Repeat and have students identify initial s-blends.

Phonics Activities

Letter Cup Substitution:
Words with s-Blends
Use on Days 1–5

Provide students with plastic cups that have an s-blend, letter(s), or vowel written on the outside of each. Place cups upside down in a row to spell a starting word. Have partners take turns fitting another cup over one of the original cups to make a new word. Examples include the following:

- **starting word: still / substitute with s-blends: sp, sk**
- **starting word: skim / substitute with s-blends: sw, sl**
- **starting word: slam / substitute with s-blends: sp, sw**
- **starting word: snip / substitute with s-blends: sl, sk**

Students should read each starting word and new words aloud and record the new words on a phonics house (BLM A) before continuing.

Picture Word Cards:
Words with s-Blends, Contractions ('s)
Use on Days 3–5

Distribute the following picture word cards:

- **it's, bag, jam, stop, Pam, ham, flag**
- **he's, clam, map, spill, tag**

Have partners take turns. Student 1 holds up a card with the picture facing student 2. Student 1 reads aloud the word on the card. Student 2 spells the word orally. If student 2 needs a clue, student 1 provides the first and last letters, and allows student 2 to provide the middle letter. (Point out to students that the words will not all start with an s-blend or be a contraction with 's.)

Read/Circle/Underline:
"The Slug":
Words with s-Blends, Contractions ('s)
Use on Days 3–5

Place copies of BLM 5 (page 122) in a center. Have student pairs take turns reading the poem. Then have them circle the words beginning with s-blends and draw a line under the contraction.

Word Family Activities

Word Family Crossword: –ap, –am
Use on Days 1–5

Provide students with BLM 2 (page 119) and have them complete the crossword activity.

Word Family Picture Labels: –ag, –ap
Use on Days 3–5

Distribute BLM 4 (page 121) and have students write the letters to complete the -ag and -ap words.

Word Family Board Game: –ag, –ap
Use on Days 3–5

Label the squares of BLM D with words and directions, making a path from START to FINISH. Words and directions might include:

- **bag, nag, sag, flag, tag, wag, cap, clap, flap, lap, map, nap, sap, snap, tap, pass, man, tan, tack, slam, mat, pat, flat**
- **"Move back two spaces"**
- **"Move forward five spaces"**
- **"Spin again"**
- **"Skip your next turn"**

Place the prepared BLM D, a spinner (BLM B), and disks or coins for playing pieces in the center. Students play by spinning the spinner to advance. If they land on a square with an –ap or –ag word, they use it in an oral sentence and spin again. If they don't land on an –ap or –ag word, the next player spins. Students should also follow the instructions on any squares that have them.

High-Frequency Word Activities

High-Frequency Words Concentration
Use on Days 1–5

Distribute to each pair of students a set of the following Benchmark Advance high-frequency word cards. (Each set should contain two copies of each word, for a total of twenty-eight cards per pair of students.)

- **come / do / here / now / put / said / saw / there / this / want / was / went / what / which**

High-Frequency Words Bug Catch
Use on Days 3–5

Write several high-frequency words, from this week and previous weeks, on index cards. Place the index cards face-up on a flat surface. Then provide each pair of students with a plastic fly swatter. Instruct students to take turns: one student should read a high-frequency word aloud, and then the other student should find and "swat" the index card showing that word.

Writing Activities

Reading/Writing: Continue the Story "Pam and Sam Swim"
Use on Days 1–5

Provide copies of BLM 3 (page 120) and have students write a sentence about the story.

Reading/Writing: Respond to the Story "Stan's Snack"
Use on Days 3–5

Provide copies of BLM 6 (page 123) and have students label each food.

Spelling Homework

Read each spelling word aloud with your child. Spell it aloud together. Then ask your child to write each spelling word and say it in a sentence.

snap _____   slam _____

slap _____   drag _____

swam _____   snag _____

there _____   out _____

Choose a different activity every day to practice this week's spelling words at home with your child.

Write it again	Letter tiles	Two-toned words	Magnetic letters	Circle the word
Have your child write the word three times on a sheet of paper and circle the vowels.	Use letter tiles to spell the words and then write the words on a sheet of paper.	Write spelling words with crayons or colored markers on a sheet of paper. Use one color for consonants and one for vowels.	Spell the words on a cookie sheet using magnetic letters and then write the words on a sheet of paper.	Work with your child to write a sentence for each word on a sheet of paper and circle the spelling words.

Word Family Crossword

**Complete the crossword puzzle. Use the pictures and the word bank.
Fill in the words for the pictures shown.**

Word Bank
cap
nap
clap
snap

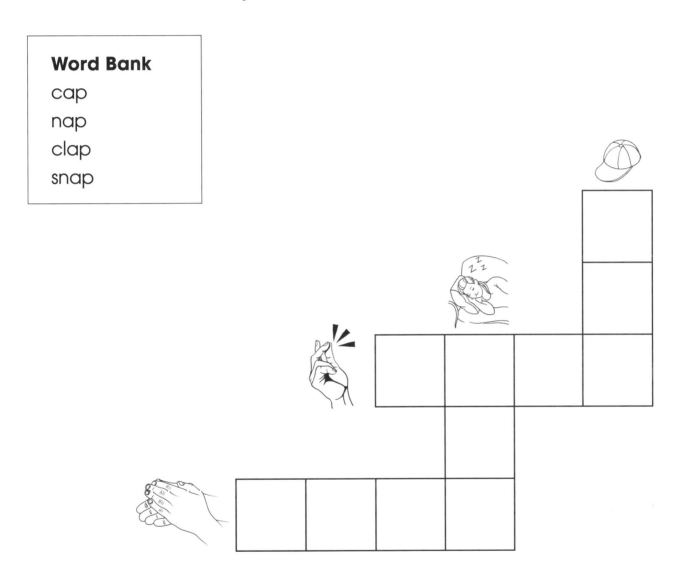

Pam and Sam Swim

Read the story. Then write a sentence about the story.

Pam and Sam go to swim.

Pam steps in. Sam jumps in. Plop!

Pam and Sam swim laps and play tag.

Then Pam and Sam stop and get out.

It's fun to swim!

_____

- -

_____

_____

- -

_____

_____

- -

_____

Word Family Picture Labels

Say the name of the picture aloud.
Write the beginning of the word below each picture.

ag

ap

ap

ag

The Slug

Read the poem. Circle all the words that have s-blends.
Then draw a line under the contraction ('s).

I am a slug.

My skin is slick.

I stick to stuff as I go.

I will slip in this slot here by two rocks.

Then I will slip out.

That's the skill of a slug!

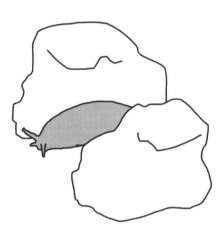

Stan's Snack

Read the story.

Stan wants a snack.

He gets a slab of ham.

He gets a bit of jam.

He gets a can of yams.

Yum! The snack hits the spot.

Then Stan has a nap.

Look at the pictures of the food. Label each picture.

 It's _____

 It's _____

 It's _____

bag	Pam
clam	ham
he's	flag
it's	spill
jam	stop
map	tag

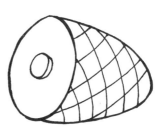

he+is=he's

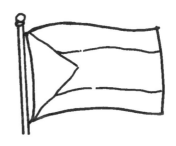

it+is=it's

Advancing Phonics Every Day

	Day 1	Day 2	Day 3
Phonological/ Phonemic Awareness	**Rhyme Recognition** `Routine 5` **Model:** land/hand, lump/stump **Practice:** cast/mast, limp/chimp, sunk/trunk **Extra practice:** hint/tint, best/rest	**Rhyme Production** `Routine 6` **Model:** spent/tent, test/west **Practice:** grand/band, jump/hump, blink/stink **Extra practice:** dust/must, camp/stamp	**Phoneme Addition** `Routine 15` **Model:** lend/blend, bank/blank **Practice:** lint/flint, ramp/tramp, rust/trust **Extra practice:** link/blink, and/sand
Phonics	**Review:** *s-blends* `Routine 18` **Model:** swim, slip **Practice:** snip, stop, spot **Extra Practice:** skip, smock `Routine 18` **Introduce final consonant blends: nd, nk, nt, mp, st** **Model:** bank, hunt, stamp, fast **Practice:** pink, went, bump, west **Extra practice:** fist, blink Explain that in words ending in *-nk*, the vowel sound sometimes changes.	**Blend words with final consonant blends: nd, nk, nt, mp, st** `Routine 18` **Model:** sand, link, mint, camp, west **Practice:** hand, rink, plant, bump, lost **Extra practice:** pond, drink **Build words with final consonant blends: nd, nk, nt, mp, st** `Routine 19` **Model:** pat, past, truck, lap **Other words:** trunk, lamp, ten, tent **Decodable reader: "The Best Nest"** Use decodable reader ideas (p. 23).	**Introduce: inflectional ending –ed** Display the *dented* word card. Use the word in a sentence, such as *I dropped the can, and it dented*. Explain that *–ed* at the end of an action word shows that the action happened in the past. The ending *–ed* can be added to many verbs to show that the action has already happened.
Word Families	Have students use the following letter cards to make words in the *–ent* word family. **Letter cards:** b, d, l, r, s, t, w, e, n	Guide students to make a five-rung ladder with *–ent* at the top. Have them write *–ent* words on each rung of the ladder.	Have students work in pairs to make *–est* words using the following letter cards. **Letter cards:** b, n, p, r, t, v, w, e, s
High-Frequency Words	**Introduce high-frequency words** `Routine 20` who, good	**Practice high-frequency words** who, good `Routine 21` **Decodable reader: "The Best Nest"** Use decodable reader ideas (p. 23).	**Introduce high-frequency words** `Routine 2` by, them
Writing	Have students write a sentence using some of the words they made in the word family activity and one of the high-frequency words.	Have students write a sentence using two of the *–ent* words from the word family activity.	Have students write a sentence about a nest using the word family words they made.
Spelling	**Introduce spelling words** `Routines 20, 22` bent, sent, hand, who	**Spell words in context** `Routines 21, 23` bent, sent, hand, who	**Introduce spelling words** `Routines 20, 22` best, pest, bumped, them
Shared Reading	**"A Tree for Sam"** **Review s-blends and contractions ('s)** As you read aloud, point out words that have s-blends (*small*) and contractions ('s) (*That's, It's*). Have students read these words aloud with you, emphasizing the phonics elements.	**"A Tree for Sam"** **Introduce final consonant blends nd, nk, nt, mp, st** As you read aloud, point out the words with the final consonant blends *nt* and *st* (*plant, just*). Have students read them with you, emphasizing the phonics element.	**"A Tree for Sam"** **Introduce inflectional ending –ed** As you read aloud, point out the words with the inflectional ending *–ed* (*wanted*). Have students read these words aloud with you.

High-Frequency Words:	Spelling:	Word Families:
who, good, by, them	Words with –ent, –est	–ent, –est

Day 4	Day 5	Collaborative Learning and Independent Practice*
Phoneme Deletion Routine 16 **Model:** sink/ink, pant/ant **Practice:** send/end, blast/last **Extra practice:** drink/rink, clamp/lamp		• Phonemic Classroom Clean-Up: Words with Final Consonant Blends: nd, nk, nt, mp, st Days 1–5 • Phonemic Word Sort: Words with Final /d/ Sound; Final Consonant Blends: nd, nk, nt, mp, st Days 3–5
Blend words with inflectional ending –ed Routine 18 **Model:** jumped, tested **Practice:** ended, hunted, yelled **Extra practice:** blended Explain that the -ed ending can be pronounced three ways: /d/ as in jumped, /t/ as in locked, and /ed/ as in tested. **Build words with inflectional ending –ed** Routine 19 **Model:** lock, locked, test, tested **Other words:** paint, panted, kick, kicked, bump, bumped	**Decodable reader: "The Best Nest"** Use decodable reader ideas (p. 23).	• Phonics Board Game: Words with Final Consonant Blends: nd, nk, nt, mp, st Days 1–5 • Word Rainbows: Words with Inflectional Ending -ed; Final Consonant Blends: nd, nk, nt, mp, st Days 3–5 • Read/Circle: "I Like to Camp!": Words with Final Consonant Blends: nd, nt Days 3–5
Have students make a five-petal flower with the letters –est in the middle of the flower. Students can write one –est word on each petal.	**Review –ent and –est words** Have students use a word family house (BLM A) for the word families –ent and –est. Students work in small groups to write –ent and –est words. Then each student uses one of the words in a sentence.	• Word Family Towers: –ent Days 1–5 • Word Family Spinners/Sliders: –ent, –est Days 3–5 • Word Family Ice Cream Cones: –ent, –est Days 3–5
Practice high-frequency words Routine 21 who, good, by, them	**Decodable reader: "The Best Nest"** Use decodable reader ideas (p. 23).	• High-Frequency Words Chatterboxes Days 1–5 • High-Frequency Words "Go Fish" Days 3–5
Have students choose two or three words from their five-petal flower and the week's high-frequency words to write a sentence.	**Interactive writing** (see p. 22) **Story starter:** Tink the cat just put a dent in the lamp. **Word bank:** bent, sent, spent, pest, rest	• Reading/Writing: Continue the Story "Junk in the Sand" Days 1–5 • Reading/Writing: Respond to the Story "A Fun Trip" Days 3–5
Spell words in context Routines 21, 23 best, pest, bumped, them	**Test words in dictation** Read aloud each of the week's spelling words for students to write. Then collect and review student work.	• Spelling Homework: BLM 1 Days 1–5
"Welcome, Ducklings!" **Review high-frequency words: who, good, by, them** As you read aloud, point out the week's high-frequency words (them, by). Have students read the words aloud with you.	**"Welcome, Ducklings!"** **Review final consonant blends: nd, nk, nt, mp, st** As you read aloud, point out words with the final consonant blends nd, nt, or st (just, plants). Have students read the words aloud with you, emphasizing the phonics element.	

* Use this menu to plan extra practice and center activities for use through the week. All the skills needed for an activity have been introduced by the first day of the range shown. See pages 128–129 for full descriptions.

Collaborative Learning and Independent Practice

 **Phonological/Phonemic Awareness Activities**

Phonemic Classroom Clean-Up:
Words with Final Consonant Blends nd, nk, nt, mp, st
Use on Days 1–5

Set up five bins, each with one of the following picture cards taped to it: *hand, bank, tent, lamp, nest* (page 137). Have partners say the word for each picture and identify its final blend sound. Scatter around the classroom the other picture cards of words with the target final blend sounds. Instruct partners to find the cards and place each one in the correct bin, for example, words with the /nd/ sound should go in the *hand* bin.

Phonemic Word Sort:
Words with Final /d/ Sound; Final Consonant Blends nd, nk, nt, mp, st
Use on Days 3–5

Distribute copies of the week's twelve picture cards (page 137). Have pairs of students work together to sort the cards by final blend sound:

- hand/pond
- bank/drink/sink
- tent
- lamp/stamp/stump
- nest/vest

ᴬᴮ꜀)) Phonics Activities

Phonics Board Game:
Words with Final Consonant Blends nd, nk, nt, mp, st
Use on Days 1–5

On a flat surface, place a game board (BLM D), a spinner (BLM B), and disks or coins to use as playing pieces. Label several squares on the board with a word or an instruction, making a path between the START square and the FINISH square (words and instructions can be repeated if necessary). Examples of words and instructions include the following:

- bank, pink, tank, band, hand, stand, pant, sent, tent
- stamp, clamp, stump, past, fast, fist, block, class, clock, pass, stick
- "Move back two spaces"
- "Move forward five spaces"
- "Spin again"
- "Skip your next turn"
- "Swap squares with the player across from you"

Students use the spinner to advance on the board. If they land on a square that has a word ending with the blends *nd, nk, nt, mp,* or *st,* they must use it in an oral sentence and spin again. If the word does not end with the blends *nd, nk, nt, mp,* or *st,* the next player spins. Students should follow the instructions on any squares that have them.

Word Rainbows: Words with Inflectional Ending -ed; Final Consonant Blends nd, nk, nt, mp, st
Use on Days 3–5

Provide students with the week's twelve picture cards (page 137). Instruct students to write each word, spelling each sound in the word with a different color. You might suggest that students choose rainbow colors and use them in that order.

Read/Circle: "I Camp!":
Words with Final Consonant Blends nd, nt
Use on Days 3–5

Place copies of BLM 5 (page 134) in a center. Have student pairs take turns reading the poem. Then have them circle the words ending in *nd* with one color and the words ending in *nt* with a different color.

Word Family Activities

Word Family Towers: –ent
Use on Days 1–5
Provide partners with interlocking blocks. On each block, place a piece of masking tape. Write -ent words on half of the blocks, and other decodable words on the rest of the blocks. Have students find and stack the -ent word blocks into a word family tower, pronouncing each word as they add it to the tower.

(This activity can be adapted for the -est word family.)

Word Family Spinners/Sliders: –ent, –est
Use on Days 3–5

Construct two word spinners (BLM B), one for each of the week's word families. Write the word family on the long rectangular piece and initial letters around the circle. Distribute copies of the phonics house (BLM A) and have students label the houses -ent and -est. Ask students to form words using the spinners and to list each word they form in the appropriate word family house. (This activity may also use word sliders [BLM C] instead of spinners.)

Word Family Ice Cream Cones: -ent, -est

Use on Days 3–5

Provide students with BLM 2 (page 131) and have them complete the activity.

High-Frequency Word Activities

High-Frequency Words Chatterbox
Use on Days 1–5

Fold BLM 4 (page 133) to form a "chatterbox." (See directions on page 390.) Instruct students to play with a partner. One student chooses a word on an outside flap, says the word, and spells it aloud while the other student opens and closes the chatterbox for each letter in the word. Then the other student should pick a word on an inside flap, say the word, and spell it aloud. Finally, the first student should open that flap and form an oral sentence using the word that is found there.

High-Frequency Words "Go Fish"
Use on Days 3–5

Pick twenty-five high-frequency words and write each word on two index cards to create fifty cards. Students can be encouraged to draw fish on the other sides of the cards. Have groups of two to four students play "Go Fish" using this deck.

Writing Activities

Reading/Writing: Continue the Story "Junk in the Sand"
Use on Days 1–5

Provide copies of BLM 3 (page 132) and have students describe what happens next.

Reading/Writing: Respond to the Story "A Fun Trip"
Use on Days 3–5

Provide copies of BLM 6 (page 135) and have students complete the activity.

Spelling Homework

Read each spelling word aloud with your child. Spell it aloud together. Then ask your child to write each spelling word and say it in a sentence.

bent _____

best _____

sent _____

pest _____

hand _____

bumped _____

who _____

them _____

Choose a different activity every day to practice this week's spelling words at home with your child.

Trace your words	Multi-colored words	Write it again	Remember the word	Circle the word
Use your finger to write each spelling word in sand, flour, or a similar material.	Write the spelling words with crayons or colored pencils, using a different color for each letter.	Have your child write the word three times on a sheet of paper and circle the vowels.	Turn the paper over and write the word from memory.	Work with your child to write a sentence for each word on a sheet of paper and circle the spelling words.

Word Family Ice Cream Cones

Place the scoops of ice cream on the correct word family cones.

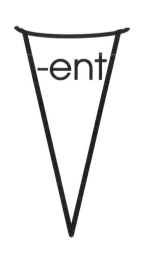

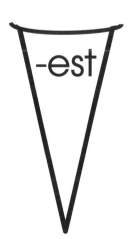

Junk in the Sand

Read the story.
Then write a sentence about what you might find in the sand.

I go to the pond a lot.

It's good to play in the damp sand,

but I see junk as well.

I pick up drink cans with rust.

I pick up stuff that is lost.

Then I see a pink cap!

That is not junk!

High-Frequency Words Chatterbox

Listen to the directions from your teacher.

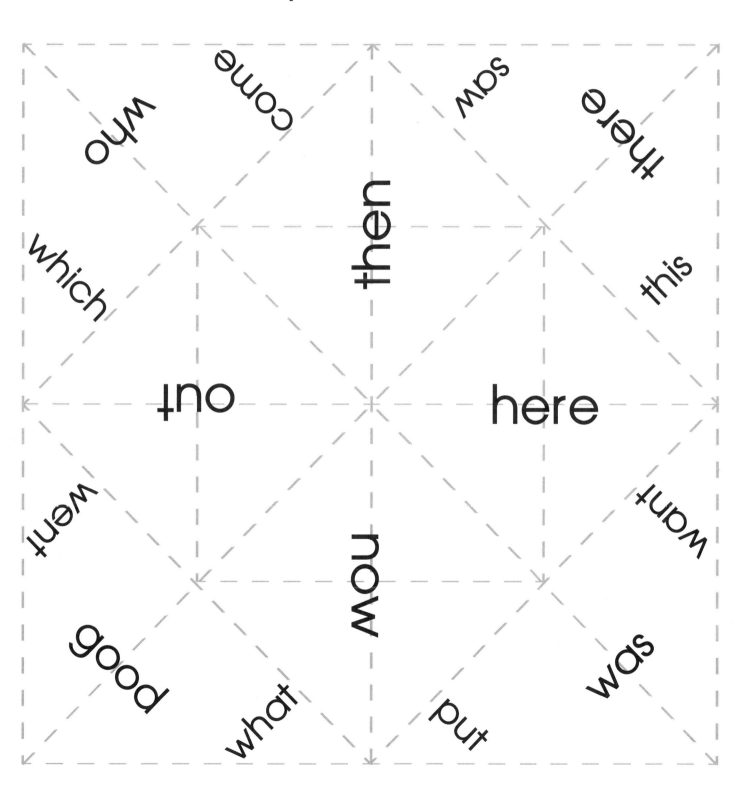

I Camp!

Read the poem.
Circle the words that end in -nd with one color.
Underline the words that end in -nt with a different color.

I camp at dusk.

I put my tent on the land.

I see an ant as I stand.

I see a print in the sand.

It is the print of a big hand.

It is fun to camp!

A Fun Trip

Read the story.
Write a sentence about a trip you have taken.

Kent and I went on a trip.

It was the best!

We camped in a tent.

We rafted and swam,

and then we rested on the sand.

We said to Mom and Dad,

"Our trip was good!"

I went

bank	nest
sink	pond
dented	stump
drink	stamp
hand	tent
lamp	vest

Advancing Phonics Every Day

Letters/sounds:
consonant digraphs th, sh, ng; inflectional ending -ing

	Day 1	Day 2	Day 3
Phonological/ Phonemic Awareness	**Word Awareness** *Routine 1* **Model:** Jill must rush to the house. **Practice:** Sherry takes a long bath. **Extra practice:** I think I will sing a song.	**Rhyme Recognition** *Routine 5* **Model:** moth/froth, ash/cash **Practice:** string/ding, math/path, wish/swish **Extra practice:** mash/flash, ping/ring	**Phoneme Recognition** *Routine 9* **Model:** bush/bash/brush, moth/math/mouth **Practice:** ring/ping/pong, mash/wash/wish, tooth/teeth/wreath **Extra practice:** cling/sling/clang, push/gosh/gush
Phonics	**Review final consonant blends: nd, nk, nt, mp, st** *Routine 18* **Model:** blend, tank **Practice:** last, jump, rent **Extra practice:** camp, plant **Introduce consonant digraphs th, sh, ng** *Routine 17* **Model:** thump, dish, hang **Practice:** math, ship, bang **Extra practice:** thick, path, cash Explain that the two letters make one sound. Explain that in words ending in *-ng*, the vowel sound sometimes changes.	**Blend words with consonant digraphs: th, sh, ng** *Routine 18* **Model:** think, wish, swing **Practice:** with, shed, sting **Extra practice:** thank, cloth, fish **Build words with consonant digraphs: th, sh, ng** *Routine 19* **Model:** bath, bash, bang **Other words:** with, wish, wing **Decodable reader: "A Fish Wish"** Use decodable reader ideas (p. 23).	**Learn inflectional ending –ing** Display the *winking* word card. Point out the *–ing* ending. Use the word in a sentence. *The cat is winking at m*e. Explain that when we add *–ing* to the end of a verb, we use another verb before it, such as *am*, *is*, *are*, *was* and *were*.
Word Families	Use the following letter cards and have partners make words in the *–ung* or *–ing* word family. Each student can use one of the words in an oral sentence. **Letter cards:** h, k, r, s, w , u, n, g, i	Use the *king, sing, wing, stung,* and *lung* picture cards. Have students work in pairs, say the word for each picture, and write the word in a word family house (BLM A) for *–ung* or *–ing*.	Use the following letter cards and have students work in pairs to make words in the *–ink* word family. **Letter cards:** l, m, p, r, s, w, i, n, k
High-Frequency Words	**Introduce high-frequency words** *Routine 20* were, our	**Practice high-frequency words** *Routine 21* were, our **Decodable reader: "A Fish Wish"** Use decodable reader ideas (p. 23).	**Introduce high-frequency words** *Routine 20* could, these
Writing	Have students write a sentence using one of the words from the word family activity and one of this week's high-frequency words.	Have students work in pairs. One partner writes a sentence using a word from their -ung word family house, and the other writes a sentence using a word from their -ing word family house.	Have students use the words from the word family activity to write a sentence about a cat named Wink.
Spelling	**Introduce spelling words** *Routines 20, 22* rush, sung, thing, our	**Spell words in context** *Routines 21, 23* rush, sung, thing, our	**Introduce spelling words** *Routines 20, 22* wing, drink, think, could
Shared Reading	**"Home Sweet Home"** **Review final consonant blends nd, nk, nt, mp, st** As you read aloud, point out words that end with *nk* (*slink, tank*). Have students say the words aloud with you.	**"Home Sweet Home"** **Introduce consonant digraphs th, sh, ng** As you read aloud, point out words that contain the consonant digraphs. Have students read these words aloud with you, emphasizing the phonics element.	**"Home Sweet Home"** **Introduce inflectional ending –ing** As you read aloud, point out words with the inflectional ending *–ing*. Have students read these words aloud with you, emphasizing the phonics element.

High-Frequency Words:	Spelling:	Word Families:
were, our, could, these	Words with –ung, –ing, –ink	–ung, –ing, –ink

Day 4	Day 5	Collaborative Learning and Independent Practice*
Phoneme Categorization Routine 13 **Model:** sung/sing/wink, bank/bush/brash **Practice:** wash/wig/wish, rash/rush/red, sing/sip/sling **Extra practice:** rash/rush/run, rung/rip/ring		• Elkonin Boxes: Words with /th/, /sh/, /ng/ Sounds Days 1–5 • Phonemic Concentration: Words with /ing/, /th/, /sh/, /ng/ Sounds Days 3–5
Practice words with inflectional ending –ing Display the *winking* word card. Review that verbs ending with –ing are used with the verbs *am, is, are, was,* and *were.* Work with students to add –ing to words, such as *play* and *sing.* Students can make up oral sentences using the words. Next, have student partners add –ing to the words *jump, drink, think,* and *rest.* They can use the –ing form of the word in an oral sentence.	**Decodable reader: "A Fish Wish"** Use decodable reader ideas (p. 23).	• Craft Stick Chains: Words with Consonant Digraphs th, sh, ng Days 1–5 • Picture Word Matching: Inflectional Ending –ing; Words with Consonant Digraphs th, sh, ng Days 3–5 • Read/Draw/Label: "In the Band!": Inflectional Ending –ing Days 3–5
Write *–ink* on the board. Have students write as many words as they can in this word family. Remind students that they can use r–, l–, and s-blends and the consonant digraphs *sh* and *th* to make words.	**Review -ung, -ing, -ink words** Have students work in groups of three. Each student chooses a different word family to write words for. After two minutes, students exchange papers, read the words aloud, and use one word in an oral sentence.	• Feed the Creatures: –ung, –ing Days 1–5 • Word Family Scramble: –ink Days 3–5 • Word Family Tic-Tac-Toe: –ing, –ink Days 3–5
Practice high-frequency words Routine 21 were, our, could, these	**Decodable reader: "A Fish Wish"** Use decodable reader ideas (p. 23).	• High-Frequency Words Parking Lot Days 1–5 • High-Frequency Words Beanbag Toss Days 3–5
Have students choose one or two of the words they wrote in the word family activity and one or more of this week's high-frequency words. Have them write a sentence using their chosen words.	**Interactive writing** (see p. 22) **Story starter:** Ming the cat and Tink the dog were singing. **Word bank:** sung, hung, ring, zing, wink, think, bring, thing, swung	• Reading/Writing: Respond to the Story "Singing Is Fun" Days 1–5 • Reading/Writing: Continue the Story "Stop the Plink, Ding, Ring!" Days 3–5
Spell words in context Routines 21, 23 wing, drink, think, could	**Test words in dictation** Read out the spelling words for students to write. Then review their work.	• Spelling Homework: BLM 1 Days 1–5
"Good Neighbors" **Review consonant digraphs sh, th, ng** As you read aloud, point out words with the consonant digraphs *sh* and *th* (*she, they, the*). Have students read these words aloud with you, emphasizing the phonics element.	**"Good Neighbors"** **Review high-frequency words** As you read aloud, point out the high-frequency word *good.* Have students read this word aloud with you and have volunteers use the word in an oral sentence.	

* Use this menu to plan extra practice and center activities for use through the week. All the skills needed for an activity have been introduced by the first day of the range shown. See pages 140–141 for full descriptions.

© Benchmark Education Company, LLC

Collaborative Learning and Independent Practice

Phonological/Phonemic Awareness Activities

Elkonin Boxes:
Words with /th/, /sh/, /ng/ Sounds
Use on Days 1–5

Provide ten of the week's picture cards (page 149) (do not include the *sink* or *winking* picture card). For each card, have students sound out the word for each picture, sliding a counter into a cell of an Elkonin box for each individual phoneme. Students can do this individually, or partners can take turns choosing from the picture cards.

Phonemic Concentration:
Words with /ing/, /th/, /sh/, /ng/ Sounds
Use on Days 3–5

Provide students with a double set of the week's picture cards (page 149), for a total of twenty-four cards. Instruct partners to arrange the cards face down in a 6 x 4 grid to play a concentration game. The partners should alternate turning over two cards at a time. When a student uncovers a matching pair, he/she should use the word in an oral sentence and keep the pair of cards. The student who collects the most pairs wins the game.

Phonics Activities

Craft Stick Chains:
Words with Consonant Digraphs th, sh, ng
Use on Days 1–5

Use tongue depressors or craft sticks. Write a decodable word with a /th/ (initial or final) sound on one end of several sticks and a word with a /sh/ sound (initial or final) on the other end of each stick. Do the same with other sticks and decodable words with the /ng/ sound (final) and more words with a /th/ or /sh/ sound. Have partners take turns choosing a stick and placing it end-to-end with another stick, matching words with the same sound.

Picture Word Matching:
Inflectional Ending –ing; Words with Consonant Digraphs th, sh, ng
Use on Days 3–5

Provide students with the week's twenty-four picture and word cards (pages 148–149). Have students match each picture to its word and then sort all the pairs in a variety of ways. For example:

- king, sing, winking, wing
- sink, winking
- thick, thin

Read/Circle:
"In the Band":
Inflectional Ending -ing
Use on Days 3–5

Place copies of BLM 5 (page 146) in a center. Have student pairs take turns reading the poem. Then have students complete the activity.

Word Family Activities

Feed the Creatures: –ung, –ing
Use on Days 1–5

Label each of two small plastic bins with -ung or -ing. Use a marker to make eyes or a face on each bin to turn it into a "creature." Provide partners with the following -ung and -ing picture cards, and have them take turns "feeding" each card to the appropriate creature:

- **stung, king, sing, wing**

Word Family Scramble: –ink
Use on Days 3–5

Distribute BLM 2 (page 143) and have students complete the -ink word family activity.

Word Family Tic-Tac-Toe: –ing, –ink
Use on Days 3–5

Provide or have students draw a tic-tac-toe board. Have partners play tic-tac-toe using words belonging to the -ing and -ink word families. One partner will use -ing words instead of an X to mark his/her spots on the board. The other partner will use -ink words instead of an O.

High-Frequency Word Activities

High-Frequency Words Parking Lot
Use on Days 1–5

Provide partners with a copy of BLM 4 (page 145) and several toy cars. Students take turns: One student reads a high-frequency word aloud, and the other student "parks" a toy car in that spot on the BLM and says a sentence using the word.

High-Frequency Words Beanbag Toss
Use on Days 3–5

Lay out several Benchmark Advance high-frequency word cards for a beanbag toss. Use review words from previous weeks as well as the current week's words.

- **come, could, here, of, our, put, saw, these, this, want, were, what**

Have one student choose a word to read aloud, and have another student toss a beanbag to cover the matching word card.

Writing Activities

Reading/Writing: Respond to the Story "Singing Is Fun"
Use on Days 1–5

Provide copies of BLM 3 (page 144) and have students draw a picture of the show.

Reading/Writing: Respond to the Story "Stop the Plink, Ding, Ring!"
Use on Days 3–5

Provide copies of BLM 6 (page 147) and have students continue the story.

Spelling Homework

Read each spelling word aloud with your child. Spell it aloud together. Then ask your child to write each spelling word and say it in a sentence.

rush _____   wing _____

sung _____   drink _____

thing _____   think _____

our _____   could _____

Choose a different activity every day to practice this week's spelling words at home with your child.

Flashlight writing	Trace your words	Two-toned words	Remember the word	Circle the Word
Turn out the lights. Use a flashlight to spell each word on the wall.	Use your finger to write each spelling word in sand, flour, or a similar material.	Write the spelling words with crayons or colored markers on a sheet of paper. Use one color for consonants and another for vowels.	Turn the paper over and write the word from memory.	Work with your child to write a sentence for each word on a sheet of paper and circle the spelling words.

BLM
2

Word Family Scramble

Cut out the tiles.
Arrange the tiles to spell the word.

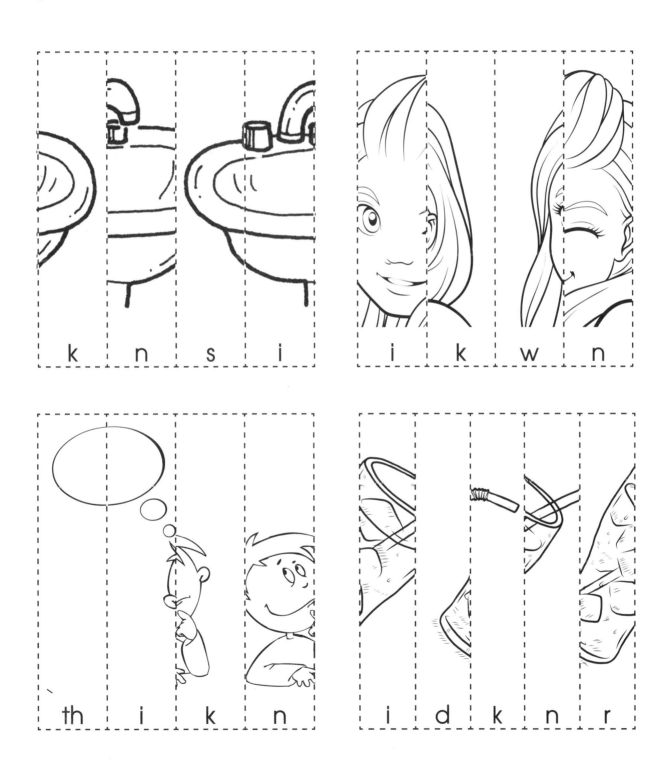

BLM
3

Singing Is Fun

Read the story. Draw a picture of the story.

I think that singing is fun.

"Could you sing a song with me?" I asked Ling.

We sang two songs.

Our songs were good!

Thad and Seth were there as Ling and I sang.

Thad and Seth gushed to us.

"You two sang so well!"

BLM
4

High-Frequency Words Parking Lot

Listen to the directions from your teacher.

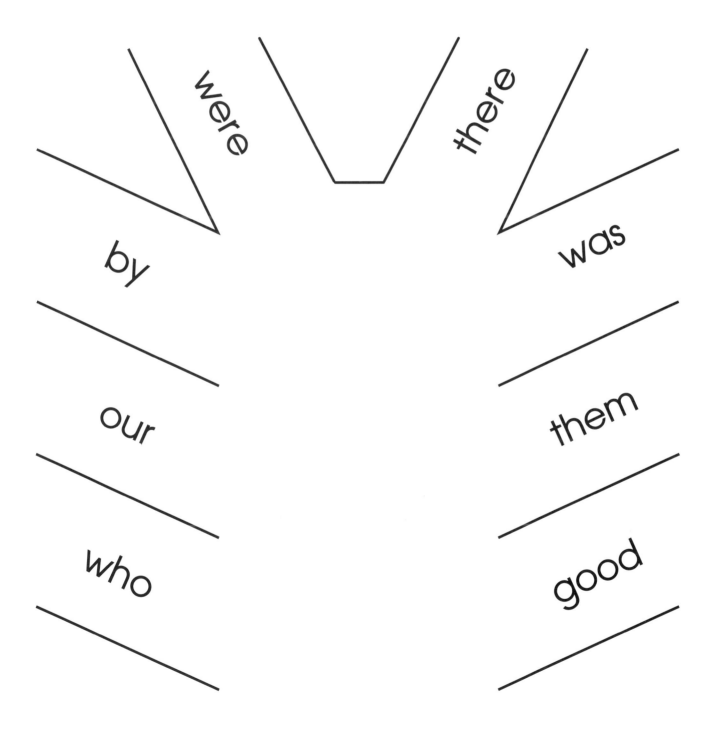

were

there

by

was

our

them

who

good

BLM

5

In the Band

**Read the story. Circle the words that end with -ing.
Then draw a picture of the story.**

The kids are in the band.

The kids are banging drums!

The kids are ringing bells!

The kids are clanging sticks!

The kids are playing songs!

The kids are in the band!

Stop the Plink, Ding, Ring!

**Read the story.
Then write a sentence to tell how the story ends.**

The tap went plink, plink, plink.

I could not think!

The bell went ring, ring, ring.

I could not sing!

The clock went ding, ding, dong.

I could not think of my song!

What could I do to make these things stop?

You could

king	stung
ring	lung
ship	thick
fish	thin
sing	wing
sink	winking

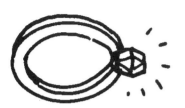

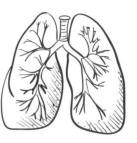

Advancing Phonics Every Day

Letters/sounds: consonant digraphs ch, –tch, wh; closed syllables

	Day 1	Day 2	Day 3
Phonological/ Phonemic Awareness	**Sentence Awareness** — Routine 2 **Model:** Where is Mitch? **Practice:** Patch is chatty. **Extra practice:** Chip whistles.	**Rhyme Production** — Routine 6 **Model:** hatch/catch **Practice:** patch/latch, truck/snuck **Extra practice:** pitch/ditch, much/such	**Phoneme Isolation** — Routine 10 **Model:** chain/check, watch/witch **Practice:** where/when, much/touch, ditch/catch **Extra practice:** chase/cheese, why/what
Phonics	**Review consonant digraphs th, sh, –ng** — Routine 17 **Model:** thing, dash **Practice:** thin, shot, hash, bang **Extra practice:** moth, shut, bring **Introduce consonant digraphs ch, –tch, wh** — Routine 17 **Model:** chip, match, whip **Practice:** much, itch, when **Extra practice:** which, check, catch	**Blend words with consonant digraphs ch, –tch, wh** — Routine 18 **Model:** chill, pitch, whip **Practice:** ditch, batch, when, which **Extra practice:** chop, match, patch **Build words with consonant digraphs ch, –tch, wh** — Routine 19 **Model:** hat, chat, risk, whisk **Other words:** chunk, hunk, pat, patch **Decodable reader: "Lunch for Patch"** Use decodable reader ideas (p. 23).	**Learn closed syllables** Display the *chess, duck,* and *lamp* picture cards. Guide students to see that each word has a short vowel sound. Tell students that to make this sound the vowel must be "closed in" by a consonant. This makes the word a closed syllable. Explain that these words just have one syllable, but other words can have more, such as *magnet* and *rabbit*.
Word Families	Students use the following letter cards to write words for the word family –unk on word family houses (BLM A). **Letter cards:** b, d, h, j, s, u, n, k	Have partners create two five-rung ladders, one with –unk at the top and the other with –ump at the top. Each partner can fill in one of the ladders, writing an –unk word or an –ump word on each rung.	Have students work in pairs to complete a BLM A word family house for –ump words. They can use the following letter cards to generate words. **Letter cards:** b, d, l, p, t, y, j, u
High-Frequency Words	**Introduce high-frequency words** — Routine 20 once, upon	**Practice high-frequency words** once, upon — Routine 21 **Decodable reader: "Lunch for Patch"** Use decodable reader ideas (p. 23).	**Introduce high-frequency words** — Routine 20 hurt, that
Writing	Have students continue the word family activity and write more words for –unk and –ump using l–, r–, and s-blends.	Have students swap word family ladders and add two more rungs with –unk or –ump words.	Have students write a sentence using one or two of the word family words they created and one of this week's high-frequency words.
Spelling	**Introduce spelling words** — Routines 20, 22 such, chunk, bump, once	**Spell words in context** — Routines 21, 23 such, chunk, bump, once	**Introduce spelling words** — Routines 20, 22 thump, latch, whiff, that
Shared Reading	**"A Big Fish?"** **Review consonant digraphs th, sh, –ng** As you read aloud, point out words that contain the consonant digraphs *th, sh, ng* (*fish, their, think, looking*). Have students read the words, emphasizing the phonics element.	**"A Big Fish?"** **Introduce consonant digraphs ch, –tch, wh** As you read aloud, point out words containing the consonant digraphs *ch* and *-tch* (*Chip, catch*). Have students read these words with you, emphasizing the phonics elements.	**"A Big Fish?"** **Introduce closed-syllable words** Point out words with closed syllables (e.g., *big, fish, Jen, Chip, catch, gets, rod, runs*). Have students read these words aloud with you, clap the syllables and call out the short vowel sounds.

High-Frequency Words:	Spelling:	Word Families:
once, upon, hurt, that	Words with –unk, –ump	–unk, –ump

Day 4	Day 5	Collaborative Learning and Independent Practice*
Phoneme Substitution Routine 14 **Model:** bump/dump, cinch/pinch **Practice:** pitch/stitch, why/try, match/catch **Extra practice:** batch/hatch		• Phonemic Word Sort: Words with Consonant Digraphs ch, -tch Days 1–5 • Phonemic Classroom Clean-Up: Words with Closed Syllables Days 3–5
Practice closed syllables Display the *chess, duck,* and *lamp* picture and word cards. Review that words have parts called syllables, and that short vowel sounds followed by consonants create closed syllables. Write the following words on the board: *chip, rich, bump, snap, frog.* Have students work in pairs to read each word, write them on their workmats to show syllables, and identify the short vowel–consonant pattern in each syllable.	**Decodable reader: "Lunch for Patch"** Use decodable reader ideas (p. 23).	• Letter Cup Substitution: Words with Consonant Digraphs ch, -tch, wh Days 1–5 • Phonics Board Game: Words with Closed Syllables Days 3–5 • Read/Circle: "Little Skunk": Words with Final Blends -ump, -unk Days 3–5
Have students choose one of the two word families, *–unk* or *–ump,* and write it on their workmat. Call out a letter and if students can, they write a word in their word family that begins with that letter.	**Review –unk, –ump words** Have students work in pairs and use the following letter cards. One student picks a letter card and says a word in one of this week's word families. The other student uses the word in an oral sentence. **Letter cards:** b, d, h, j, l, p, u, n, k, m	• Word Family Spinners/Sliders: -unk, -ump Days 1–5 • Word Family Cube: -uck Days 3–5 • Word Family Sort: -unk, -ump Days 3–5
Practice high-frequency words Routine 21 once, upon, hurt, that	**Decodable reader: "Lunch for Patch"** Use decodable reader ideas (p. 23).	• High-Frequency Words "Go Fish" Days 1–5 • High-Frequency Words Bug Catch Days 3–5
Have students write a sentence with one or more of the words that they wrote on their workmats.	**Interactive writing** (see p. 22) **Story starter:** Skunk and Duck have fun. **Word bank:** jump, luck, bump, pump	• Reading/Writing: Respond to the Story "What Is It?" Days 1–5 • Reading/Writing: Continue the Story "Catch the Ball!" Days 3–5
Spell words in context Routines 21, 23 thump, latch, whiff, that	**Test words in dictation** Read out the spelling words for students to write. Then review their work.	• Spelling Homework: BLM 1 Days 1–5
"My Mom, the Vet"" **Review closed-syllable words** As you read aloud, point out words with closed syllables (e.g., *mom, vet, help, get, sick, dogs, cats, pets*). Have students read these words aloud with you and identify the short vowel–consonant combinations.	**"My Mom, the Vet"** **Review consonant digraphs ch, –tch, wh** As you read aloud, point out the word *when,* featuring the consonant digraph *wh.* Have students read the word with you, emphasizing the phonics element.	

* Use this menu to plan extra practice and center activities for use through the week. All the skills needed for an activity have been introduced by the first day of the range shown. See pages 152–153 for full descriptions.

Collaborative Learning and Independent Practice

Phonological/Phonemic Awareness Activities

Phonemic Word Sort:
Words with Consonant Digraphs ch, –tch
Use on Days 1–5

Distribute copies of six of the week's picture cards (page 161). Have pairs of students work together to sort the cards by the position of the digraph:

- chest/chess
- catch/patch/match/itch

Phonemic Classroom Clean-Up:
Words with Closed Syllables
Use on Days 3–5

Set up four bins, and label with the vowels *a, e, i, u*. Scatter around the classroom the picture cards. Instruct partners to find the cards and pronounce each word, paying close attention to the vowel sound. Instruct partners to place the cards in the bin with the correct vowel sound.

Phonics Activities

Letter Cup Substitution:
Words with Consonant Digraphs ch, –tch, wh
Use on Days 1–5

Provide students with plastic cups that have a letter, digraph, or vowel team written on the outside of each. Place cups upside down in a row to spell a starting word. Have partners take turns adding cups (including placing another cup over one of the original cups) to make a new word. Students should read each word aloud and record it on a phonics house (BLM A) before continuing. Examples include the following:

- starting word: dip / substitute initial letter/digraph: wh, ch, sh
- starting word: pad / substitute final letter(s)/digraph: tch, th, ss

Phonics Board Game:
Words with Closed Syllables
Use on Days 3–5

Label the squares of BLM D with words and directions, making a path from START to FINISH. (Repeat words and directions as necessary.) Words and directions might include:

- chest, when, patch, pitch, ditch, whip, chip, chop, chat, chin, whiff, batch, catch
- "Move back two spaces"
- "Move forward five spaces"
- "Spin again"
- "Skip your next turn"

Place the prepared BLM D, a spinner (BLM B), and disks or coins for playing pieces in the center. Students play by spinning the spinner to advance. If they land on a square that has a word with a digraph at the end, they must pronounce it, use it in an oral sentence, and spin again. If the word has a digraph at the beginning, students pronounce the word, and the next player spins.

Read/Circle: "Little Skunk":
Words with Final Blends -unk, -ump
Use on Days 3–5

Place copies of BLM 5 (page 158) in a center. Have student pairs take turns reading the poem. Then have students complete the circling activity.

 # Word Family Activities

Word Family Spinners/Sliders: –unk, –ump
Use on Days 1–5

Construct two word spinners (BLM B), one for each of the week's first two word families. Write the word family on the long rectangular piece and write initial letters around the circle. Provide each student with two copies of the phonics house (BLM A). Have students label the houses -unk and -ump. Ask students to form words using the spinners and to list each word they form in the appropriate word family house. (This activity may also use word sliders [BLM C] instead of spinners.)

Word Family Picture Labels: –unk, –ump
Use on Days 3–5

Distribute BLM 2 (page 155) and have students say the name of the word and write the missing letters.

Word Family Sort: –unk, –ump
Use on Days 3–5

Provide students with BLM 4 (page 157) and have them complete the activity.

 # High-Frequency Word Activities

High-Frequency Words "Go Fish"
Use on Days 1–5

Pick twenty-five high-frequency words (excluding *hurt* and *that*), and write each word on two index cards to create fifty cards. Students can be instructed to draw fish on the other sides of the cards. Have groups of two to four students play "Go Fish" using this deck.

High-Frequency Words Bug Catch
Use on Days 3–5

Write several high-frequency words, from this week and previous weeks, on index cards. Place the index cards face up on a flat surface. Then provide each pair of students with a plastic fly swatter. Instruct students to take turns: one student should read a high-frequency word aloud, and then the other student should find and "swat" the index card showing that word.

Writing Activities

Reading/Writing: Respond the Story "What Is It?"
Use on Days 1–5

Provide copies of BLM 3 (page 156) and have students write about what is in the box.

Reading/Writing: Continue the Story "Catch the Ball!"
Use on Days 3–5

Provide copies of BLM 6 (page 159) and have students write an ending for the story.

Spelling Homework

**Read each spelling word aloud with your child. Spell it aloud together.
Then ask your child to write each spelling word and say it in a sentence.**

such _____

thump _____

chunk _____

latch _____

bump _____

whiff _____

once _____

that _____

**Choose a different activity every day to practice
this week's spelling words at home with your child.**

Flashlight writing	Two-toned words	Remember the word	Multi-colored words	Circle the word
Turn out the lights. Use a flashlight to spell each word on the wall.	Write the spelling words with crayons or colored markers on a sheet of paper. Use one color for consonants and another for vowels.	Turn the paper over and write the word from memory.	Write the spelling words with crayons or colored pencils, using a different color for each letter.	Work with your child to write a sentence for each word on a sheet of paper and circle the spelling words.

Word Family Picture Labels

Say the name of the picture aloud.
Write the beginning of the word below each picture.

_____ ump

_____ ump

_____ unk

_____ unk

What Is It?

Read the story. Write a sentence to tell what is in the box.

Dad handed Mitch a big box.

"What is it, Dad?" said Mitch.

"It is a gift," said Dad.

Mitch looked at the box.

"You will like what is in the box," said Dad.

Mitch thumped the box.

"Can I check in the box?" said Mitch.

"Yes, you can check!" said Dad.

There is

Word Family Sort

Cut out the words.

Place each word in the basket for its word family.

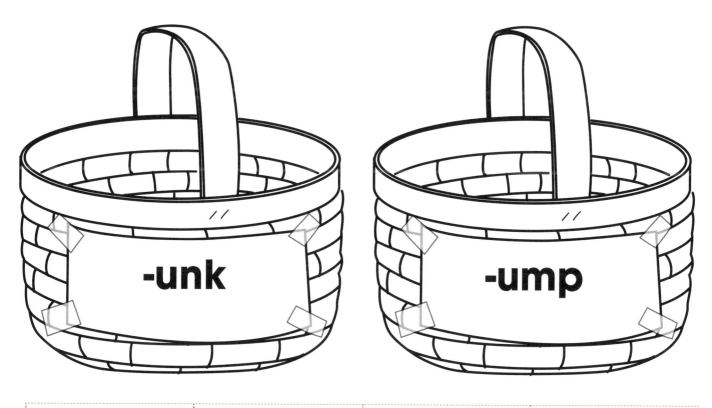

bunk	chunk	pump	dump
junk	lump	clump	skunk
stump	trunk		

Little Skunk

Read the poem. Circle the words with *-ump*.
Underline the words ending in *-unk*.
Then draw a picture of the story.

Once there was a little skunk.

He hid in a stump.

He munched on grass and bugs.

Then a cat jumped on the stump.

The skunk did not want to get hurt.

He let out a bad smell. It stunk!

The cat was shocked! She left.

The skunk could rest.

Catch the Ball!

Read the story. Then write a sentence to tell how the story ends.

Mitch and Chuck played catch.

Chuck pitched to Mitch.

Then they switched.

Mitch pitched to Chuck.

They were a good match!

Then Mitch missed a catch.

He fell in a patch of grass.

He clutched his hand. It hurt!

Chuck said, "That was bad luck."

chest	lamp
chess	stump
catch	truck
duck	trunk
match	whisk
patch	stitch

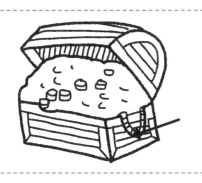

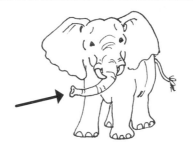

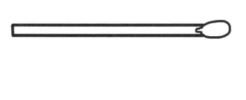

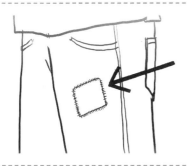

Advancing Phonics Every Day

Letters/sounds:
Three-letter blends (spl, spr, squ, str); plurals (-es)

	Day 1	Day 2	Day 3
Phonological/ Phonemic Awareness	**Syllable Segmentation** `Routine 3` **Model:** squishes, straighten **Practice:** springy, splashing, stretches, sprouting **Extra practice:** squeakier, splendid	**Phoneme Segmentation** `Routine 11` **Model:** sprung, splash **Practice:** spring, string, squid **Extra practice:** splat, stretch	**Phoneme Addition** `Routine 15` **Model:** print, sprint **Practice:** truck, struck, platter, splatter **Extra practice:** trip, strip
Phonics	**Review consonant digraphs ch, –tch, wh** `Routine 17` **Model:** chat, catch, whip **Practice:** crunch, when, stitch, chill **Extra practice:** fetch, which `Routine 18` **Introduce: three-letter blends (spl, spr, squ, str)** **Model:** splash, spring **Practice:** squish, strap, split **Extra practice:** strip, sprint Remind students that each sound in a blend is pronounced separately.	**Blend words with three-letter blends spl, spr, squ, str** `Routine 18` **Model:** splat, spring **Practice:** squint, struck, splash **Extra practice:** string, sprint **Build words with three-letter blends spl, spr, squ, str** `Routine 19` **Model:** slit, split, trap, strap **Other words:** print, sprint, train, strain **Decodable reader: "Squid Twins"**	**Learn plurals (–es)** Display the *dishes* and *lashes* word cards. Point out the –es endings. Use each word in a sentence, such as *Dad and I picked up the dishes.* Explain that to form the plural of nouns ending in *s, ss, x, sh, ch*, and *tch*, we add –es to the end of the word. **Learn compound words** Remind students that they learned about syllables, or word parts. Compound words have two or more syllables. They are made of two smaller words put together.
Word Families	Use the following letter cards. Have students write words in the –ash family on their workmats. **Letter cards:** b, c, d, l, m, r, a, s, h	Have students use a five-rung ladder to write –ash word family words. Students write –ash at the top of the ladder and add an –ash word to each rung.	Guide students to draw a five-petal flower. Students will write –ack in the center of the flower, and then use the following letter cards to write an –ack word on each petal. **Letter cards:** b, p, r, s, t, a, c, k
High-Frequency Words	**Introduce high-frequency words** `Routine 20` because, from	**Practice high-frequency words** because, from `Routine 21` **Decodable reader: "Squid Twins"** Use decodable reader ideas (p. 23).	**Introduce high-frequency words** `Routine 20` their, when
Writing	Have students use the words they wrote in the word family activity and one of the high-frequency words to write a sentence.	Have students add two more rungs to the ladder they made in the word family activity. Have students add two more –ash words. Remind them that they can use words with s–, l–, and r-blends.	Have students use the word family words they wrote on their five-petal flower to write a sentence about a boy named Jack.
Spelling	**Introduce spelling words** `Routines 20, 22` cash, crash, splash, because	**Spell words in context** `Routines 21, 23` cash, crash, splash, because	**Introduce spelling words** `Routines 20, 22` strap, shack, track, their
Shared Reading	**"The Kickball Game"** **Review consonant digraphs ch, –tch, wh** As you read aloud, point out consonant digraphs *ch* and *wh* (*Ouch, When, lunchtime*). Have students say these words with you, emphasizing the phonics elements.	**"The Kickball Game"** **Introduce three-letter blends spl, spr, squ, str** As you read aloud, point out the word *strong*. Have students read this word aloud with you and use it in an oral sentence.	**"The Kickball Game"** **Introduce high-frequency words** As you read aloud, point out one of this week's high-frequency words (*When*). Have students read this word aloud with you.

High-Frequency Words:	Spelling:	Word Families:
because, from, their, when	Words with –ash, –ack	–ash, –ack

Day 4	Day 5	Collaborative Learning and Independent Practice*
Phoneme Addition Routine 15 **Model:** ash/splash, etch/stretch **Practice:** ring/string, lint/splint, out/sprout **Extra practice:** rung/sprung, it/split		• Phonemic Picnic: Words with Three-Letter Blends spl, spr, squ, str Days 1–5 • Phonemic Concentration: Plurals (-es); Words with Three-Letter Blends spl, spr, squ, str Days 3–5
Practice plurals (–es) Display the *dishes* and *lashes* word cards again. Review that –es is added to the end of some nouns to mean more than one. Have students work in pairs and form the plural of the words *box, fox, glass, lunch, wish*. One student can form the plural and the other can use the plural word in an oral sentence. **Practice compound words** Review that compound words are made from two smaller words put together. Have students work in pairs to make compound words from these words: pig, pen, dish, rag, sun, set, bed, bug, bath, tub.	**Decodable reader: "Squid Twins"** Use decodable reader ideas (p. 23).	• Phonics Word Builder: Words with Three-Letter Blends spl, spr, squ, str Days 1–5 • Phonics Classroom Clean-Up: Plurals (-es); Words with Three-Letter Blends spl, spr, squ, str Days 3–5 • Read/Circle: "The Dog's Bath": Words with Three-Letter Blends spl, squ Days 3–5
Write *–ack* on the board. Give students three minutes to make as many –ack words as they can on their workmats.	**Review –ash, –ack words** Distribute BLM A and write either –ash or –ack at the top of the house. As you say the following letters, have students write a word in that word family. **Letter cards:** b, d, h, l, m, p, r, s, t, a, h, c, k	• Word Family Towers: -ash Days 1–5 • Word Family Board Game: -ash, -ack Days 3–5
Practice high-frequency words Routine 21 because, from, their, when	**Decodable reader: "Squid Twins"** Use decodable reader ideas (p. 23).	• High-Frequency Words Chatterboxes Days 1–5 • High-Frequency Words Beanbag Toss Days 3–5
Students will use words from the word family activity and this week's high-frequency words to write a sentence.	**Interactive writing** (see p. 22) **Story starter:** Zack and Nash dash to the back. **Word bank:** pack, snack, stack, flash, mash, trash	• Reading/Writing: Continue the Story "Nash Sprints" Days 1–5 • Reading/Writing: Continue the Story "Jack and Ash" Days 3–5
Spell words in context Routines 21, 23 strap, shack, track, their	**Test words in dictation** Read out the spelling words for students to write. Then review their work.	• Spelling Homework: BLM 1 Days 1–5
"I Had a Little Hen" **Review plurals (–es)** As you read aloud, point out the word with the plural ending –es (*dishes*). Have students read the word with you and clap the syllables.	**"I Had a Little Hen"** **Review –ash words** As you read aloud, point out the word belonging to the –ash word family. Have students read the word aloud with you, emphasizing the phonics element.	

* Use this menu to plan extra practice and center activities for use through the week. All the skills needed for an activity have been introduced by the first day of the range shown. See pages 164–165 for full descriptions.

Collaborative Learning and Independent Practice

🦻)) Phonological/Phonemic Awareness Activities

Phonemic Picnic:
Words with Three-Letter Blends spl, spr, squ, str
Use on Days 1–5

Fill a picnic basket (or lunch box) with plastic food items. Each item should begin with a blend from this week (and, if desired, phonemes from previous weeks) (examples: *split peas, sprouts, squash, string cheese*). Have partners sit on the floor as though they are about to have a picnic. They should take turns choosing a food, saying the name of the food, and passing it to their partner to "eat."

Phonemic Concentration:
Plurals (–es); Words with Three-Letter Blends spl, spr, squ, str
Use on Days 3–5

Provide students with a set of this week's picture cards (page 173), consisting of two of each card, for a total of twenty-four cards. Instruct partners to arrange the cards face down in a 6 x 4 grid to play a concentration game. The partners should alternate turning over two cards at a time. When a student uncovers a matching pair, he/she should use the word in an oral sentence and keep the pair of cards. The student who collects the most pairs wins the game.

ᴬᵦ𝖼)) Phonics Activities

Phonics Word Builder:
Words with Three-Letter Blends spl, spr, squ, str
Use on Days 1–5

Label a spinner (BLM B) with the letters *a, e, i, o,* and *u,* and provide students with letter tiles (or cutouts) of each letter. Have students use the spinner and letter tiles to complete the activity on BLM 2 (page 167). Note that student answers may vary.

Phonics Classroom Clean-Up:
Plurals (–es);
Words with Three-Letter Blends spl, spr, squ, str
Use on Days 3–5

Label a bin with the letters *–es.* Remind students that some plural nouns end in the /es/ sound. Label another bin with the three-letter blends *spl, spr, squ,* and *str.* Gather objects and toys from the classroom that, when made plural, end in the /es/ sound or that contain three-letter blend sounds (such as *spring toys, brushes, string, watches, scrap paper*). Instruct partners to "clean up" by putting each object in the appropriate bin.

Read/Circle: "The Dog's Bath":
Words with Three-Letter Blends spl, squ
Use on Days 3–5

Place copies of BLM 5 (page 170) in the center. Have student pairs take turns reading the poem. Then have students complete the circling activity.

Word Family Activities

High-Frequency Word Activities

Writing Activities

Word Family Towers: –ash
Use on Days 1–5

Provide partners with interlocking blocks. On each block, place a piece of masking tape. Write -ash words on half of the blocks, and other decodable words on the other half. Have students find and stack the -ash word blocks into a word family tower, pronouncing each word as they add it to the tower.

Word Family Board Game: Compound Words

Use on Days 3–5

On a flat surface, place a game board (BLM D), a spinner (BLM B), and disks or coins to use as playing pieces. Label several squares on the board with a word or an instruction, making a path between the START square and the FINISH square (words and instructions can be repeated if necessary). Examples of words and instructions include the following:

- **splash, stash, smack, stack, track, cramp, scrap, stamp, strap, strip, tramp, handstand, sandbox, bunkbed, shellfish, backpack, jackpot, kickoff, lipstick**
- **"Move back two spaces"**
- **"Move forward five spaces"**
- **"Spin again"**
- **"Skip your next turn"**

Students use the spinner to advance on the board. If they land on a square that has a compound word, they use it in an oral sentence and spin again. If the word is not from a compound word, the next player spins. Students should follow the instructions on any squares that have them.

High-Frequency Words Chatterbox
Use on Days 1–5

Fold BLM 4 (page 169) to form a "chatterbox." (See directions on page 390.) Instruct students to play with a partner. One student chooses a word on an outside flap, says the word, and spells it aloud while the other student opens and closes the chatterbox for each letter in the word. Then the other student should pick a word on an inside flap, says the word, and spells it aloud. Finally, the first student should open that flap and form an oral sentence using the word that is found there.

High-Frequency Words Beanbag Toss
Use on Days 3–5

Gather Benchmark Advance high-frequency word cards for a beanbag toss. Use review words from previous weeks as well as the current week's words.

- **because / come / from / their / once / upon / hurt / that / were / could / our / these**

Have a student read one of the words aloud, and have another student toss a beanbag onto the matching card.

Reading/Writing: Continue the Story "Nash Sprints"
Use on Days 1–5

Provide copies of BLM 3 (page 168) and have students write an ending for the story.

Reading/Writing: Continue the Story "Jack and Ash"
Use on Days 3–5

Provide copies of BLM 6 (page 171) and have students write about the snack.

Spelling Homework

**Read each spelling word aloud with your child. Spell it aloud together.
Then ask your child to write each spelling word and say it in a sentence.**

cash _____   strap _____

crash _____   shack _____

splash _____   track _____

because _____   their _____

Choose a different activity every day to practice
this week's spelling words at home with your child.

Flashlight writing	**Trace your words**	**Magnetic letters**	**Letter tiles**	**Remember the word**
Turn out the lights. Use a flashlight to spell each word on the wall.	Use your finger to write each spelling word in sand, flour, or a similar material.	Spell the words on a cookie sheet using magnetic letters and then write the words on a sheet of paper.	Use letter tiles to spell the words and then write the words on a sheet of paper.	Turn the paper over and write the word from memory.

Phonics Word Builder

Place a letter tile in each box to make a word.
Read the word aloud.
Be sure that you make real words.

spl☐sh   squ☐nt

spr☐nt   str☐p

spr☐ng   spl☐t

str☐ng   str☐tch

Nash Sprints

Read the story. Then write a sentence to tell how the story ends.

Nash was out sprinting.

He dashed here and there.

Then he fell!

Nash fell because he did not look as he sprinted.

He crashed on the track and scratched his leg.

Then he stretched and split his pants!

What could Nash do?

High-Frequency Words Chatterbox

Listen to the directions from your teacher to use this page.

once

our

their

from

because

that

when

these

were

who

upon

by

could

them

hurt

good

The Dog's Bath

Read the poem. Circle the words that start with *scr* in blue crayon. Underline the word that starts with *spl* in red crayon and the word that starts with *spr* in green.

"Can you give the dog a bath?" Mom asked.

"Yes, I will get him wet."

"You must scrub his back and legs," she said.

"Yes, I can, you bet!"

"He will scratch and splash a lot."

"I will mop up the mess!"

"He could jump out and sprint off!"

"Mom, I will do my best!"

Jack and Ash

Read the story. Then write a sentence about Jack and Ash.

Jack wants to see the sunset.

He brings Ash with him.

Ash has a backpack with snacks.

Jack and Ash go uphill to sit on a bench.

Just then, a snack slips out of the backpack.

A stinkbug snatches it!

"Scram!" Ash yells.

Jack tells Ash, "It's the bug's snack!

Let's catch the sunset!"

_____

- -

_____

_____

- -

_____

black	spring
splash	squid
dishes	tack
lashes	trash
split	cash
pack	strap

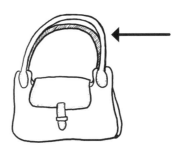

Advancing Phonics Every Day

Letters/sounds:
Long a (final –e)

	Day 1	Day 2	Day 3
Phonological/ Phonemic Awareness	**Syllable Blending** — Routine 4 **Model:** became, awake **Practice:** nickname, celebrate, parade, lemonade **Extra practice:** rattlesnake, calculate	**Onset and Rime Blending** — Routine 8 **Model:** shake, name **Practice:** take, save, shame, base **Extra practice:** pane, Dave	**Phoneme Blending** — Routine 12 **Model:** game, lake **Practice:** tame, shake, made, chase **Extra practice:** same, faze
Phonics	**Introduce sound/symbol correspondence: long a (final e)** — Routine 17 **Model:** ape, late **Practice:** cave, maze, trade, plane **Extra practice:** gave, blaze Explain that letter a can make two sounds, short a and long a. When a is followed by a consonant and the letter e, the vowel sound is strong.	**Blend words with long a (final e)** — Routine 18 **Model:** gate, cane **Practice:** made, shade, plate, skate **Extra practice:** graze, crane **Decodable reader: "Shade Lake"** Use decodable reader ideas (p. 23).	**Blend words with long a (final e)** — Routine 18 **Model:** late, lane **Practice:** fade, wade, state **Extra practice:** craze, plane Remind students that the final e makes the vowel sound long. The final e is silent.
Word Families	Use the following letter cards. Have students form as many –ame words as they can and write the words on their workmats. **Letter cards:** c, f, g, n, s, t, a, m, e	Distribute BLM 2 (page 179) and have students complete the –ame word family activity.	Have student pairs make a word wheel with –ake in the center and five write-on lines leading from the wheel. Students will write words in the –ake word family on the lines.
High-Frequency Words	**Introduce high-frequency words** — Routine 20 why, many	**Practice high-frequency words** — Routine 21 why, many **Decodable reader: "Shade Lake"** Use decodable reader ideas (p. 23).	**Introduce high-frequency words** — Routine 20 right, start
Writing	Have students write a sentence using one or two of the words they made in the word family activity.	Students can write a sentence using one of the words they made in the word family activity.	Have student pairs continue the word wheel from the word family activity, adding two or three more write-on lines and words. Encourage students to use blends and consonant digraphs.
Spelling	**Introduce spelling words** — Routines 20, 22 blame, came, tame, why	**Spell words in context** — Routines 21, 23 blame, came, tame, why	**Introduce spelling words** — Routines 20, 22 wake, brake, shake, start
Shared Reading	**"Carrier Pigeons"** **Review three-letter blends spl, spr, squ, str** As you read aloud, point out the word beginning with the three-letter blend str (strap). Have students read this word with you, emphasizing the phonics element.	**"Carrier Pigeons"** **Introduce long a (final e)** As you read aloud, point out words with a long a (final e) (take, takes). Have students read these words with you, emphasizing the phonics element.	**"Carrier Pigeons"** **Introduce word family –ake** As you read aloud, point out words in the –ake word family (take, takes). Have students read these words with you.

High-Frequency Words:	Spelling:	Word Families:
why, many, right, start	Words with –ame, –ake	–ame, –ake

Day 4	Day 5	Collaborative Learning and Independent Practice*
Phoneme Deletion `Routine 16` **Model:** cape/ape, plane/lane **Practice:** late/ate, crave/rave **Extra practice:** flake/lake, plate/late		• Elkonin Boxes: Words with Long a (Final e) Days 1–5 • Phonemic Concentration: Words with Long a (Final e) Days 3–5
Build words with long a (final e) `Routine 19` **Model:** fade, lane **Practice:** tape, base, wave, vase **Extra practice:** gaze, shave	**Decodable reader: "Shade Lake"** Use decodable reader ideas (p. 23).	• Phonics Picture Word Cards: Words with Long a (Final e) Days 1–5 • Word Rainbows: Words with Long a (Final e) Days 3–5 • Read/Underline/Write: "The Same Name": Words with Long a (Final e) Days 3–5
Have student pairs use a word family house (BLM A). They can write –ake at the top of the house and use the following letter cards to make –ake words. Have students write the words on the lines in the house. **Letter cards:** b, c, f, l, m, r, t, w, a, k, e	**Review –ame, –ake words** Display the *cake, flake, frame,* and *rake* picture cards. Have students take turns saying the word for one of the pictures and then using the word in an oral sentence.	• Word Family Scramble: -ame Days 1–5 • Word Family Ice Cream Cones: -ame, -ake Days 3–5 • Word Family Tic-Tac-Toe: -ame, -ake Days 3–5
Practice high-frequency words `Routine 21` why, many, right, start	**Decodable reader: "Shade Lake"** Use decodable reader ideas (p. 23).	• High-Frequency Words Board Game Days 1–5 • High-Frequency Words Yoga Days 3–5
Have students choose from the words that they made in the word family activity and this week's high-frequency words to write a sentence.	**Interactive writing** (see p. 22) **Story starter:** Jake likes to bake cakes. **Word bank:** came, name, fame, take, shake, flake, make	• Reading/Writing: Respond to the Story "Nate and Kate Skate" Days 1–5 • Reading/Writing: Continue the Story "The Bake Sale" Days 3–5
Spell words in context `Routines 21, 23` wake, brake, shake, start	**Test words in dictation** Read aloud each of the week's spelling words for students to write. Then collect and review student work.	• Spelling Homework: BLM 1 Days 1–5
"Atom's Day Off" **Review word families –ash, –ack** As you read aloud, point out the words in the –ash and –ack word families (*track*). Have students read these words aloud with you, emphasizing the phonics element.	**"Atom's Day Off"** **Review inflectional ending –ed** As you read aloud, point out the verbs ending in –ed (*beeped*). Have students read these words aloud with you.	

* Use this menu to plan extra practice and center activities for use through the week. All the skills needed for an activity have been introduced by the first day of the range shown. See pages 176–177 for full descriptions.

Collaborative Learning and Independent Practice

🔊 Phonological/Phonemic Awareness Activities

Elkonin Boxes:
Words with Long a (Final e)
Use on Days 1–5

Provide the week's twelve picture cards (page 185). For each card, have students sound out the word, sliding a counter into a cell of an Elkonin box for each individual phoneme. Students can do this individually, or partners can take turns choosing from the picture cards.

Phonemic Concentration:
Words with Long a (Final e)
Use on Days 3–5

Provide students with a set of this week's picture cards (page 185), comprising of two of each card, for a total of twenty-four cards. Instruct partners to arrange the cards face down in a 6 x 4 grid and play a concentration game. The partners should alternate turning over two cards at a time. When a student uncovers a matching pair, he/she should use the word in an oral sentence and keep the pair of cards. The student who collects the most pairs wins the game.

ᴬᴮC🔊 Phonics Activities

Phonics Picture Word Cards:
Words with Long a (Final e)
Use on Days 1–5

Distribute the following picture word cards:

- **bake, flame, flake, rake, cake, Kate**
- **frame, snake, base, cave, Jake, shake**

Have partners take turns. Student 1 holds a card with the picture. Student 1 reads aloud the word. Student 2 spells the word orally. If student 2 needs a clue, student 1 provides the first and last consonants, and allows student 2 to indicate the middle and final vowels.

Spelling Rules:
Words with Long a (Final e)
Use on Days 3–5

Provide students with the week's twelve picture cards (page 185). Instruct students to write each word. Have students underline the final -e because it does not make its own sound. Then have students draw an arrow from the final -e to the vowel to show that the -e makes the vowel sound long.

Read/Underline/Write:
"The Same Name":
Words with Long a (Final e)
Use on Days 3–5

Place copies of BLM 5 (page 182) in the center. Have student pairs take turns reading the poem. Then have students complete the underlining and writing activities.

Word Family Activities

Word Family Scramble: -ame
Use on Days 1–5

Distribute BLM 2 (page 179) and have students complete the -ame word family activity.

Word Family Ice Cream Cones: -ame, -ake
Use on Days 3–5

Provide students with BLM 4 (page 181) and have them complete the activity.

Word Family Tic-Tac-Toe: -ame, -ake
Use on Days 3–5

Provide or have students draw a tic-tac-toe board. Have partners play tic-tac-toe using words belonging to the -ame and -ake word families. One partner will use -ame words instead of an X to mark his/her spots on the board. The other partner will use -ake words instead of an O.

High-Frequency Word Activities

High-Frequency Words Board Game
Use on Days 1–5

On a flat surface, place a game board (BLM D), a spinner (BLM B), and disks or coins to use as playing pieces. Label several squares on the board with a word or an instruction, making a path between the START square and the FINISH square (words and instructions can be repeated if necessary). Examples of words and instructions include the following:

- **why, many, because, from, when, once, upon, now, do, went, hurt, that, were, our, could, who, good, by, them, was, then, out**
- **"Move back two spaces"**
- **"Move forward five spaces"**
- **"Spin again"**
- **"Skip your next turn"**
- **"Switch squares with the player to your left"**

Students use the spinner to advance on the board. If they land on a square that has a high-frequency word, they use it in an oral sentence. Students should follow the instructions on any squares that have them.

High-Frequency Words Yoga
Use on Days 3–5

Form groups of five students. Provide each group with a five-letter high-frequency word on an index card (*right, start, their, these, there, which*). Instruct students to sound out each letter and read the word aloud. Then encourage students to pose so that their bodies form the letters in the word. Each student can then say his or her letter in order.

Writing Activities

Reading/Writing: Respond to the Story "Nate and Kate Skate"
Use on Days 1–5

Provide copies of BLM 3 (page 180) and have students write a sentence about what they like to do outside.

Reading/Writing: Respond to the Story "The Bake Sale"
Use on Days 3–5

Provide copies of BLM 6 (page 183) and have students draw and write about what happens next.

Spelling Homework

**Read each spelling word aloud with your child. Spell it aloud together.
Then ask your child to write each spelling word and say it in a sentence.**

blame _____

wake _____

came _____

brake _____

tame _____

shake _____

why _____

start _____

Choose a different activity every day to practice
this week's spelling words at home with your child.

Write it	Write it again	Letter tiles	Magnetic letters	Remember the word
Work with your child to write the word, saying aloud each letter as you write it.	Have your child write the word three times on a sheet of paper and circle the vowels.	Use letter tiles to spell the words and then write the words on a sheet of paper.	Spell the words on a cookie sheet using magnetic letters and then write the words on a sheet of paper.	Turn the paper over and write the word from memory.

Word Family Scramble

Cut out the tiles.
Arrange the tiles to spell the word.

m e a g

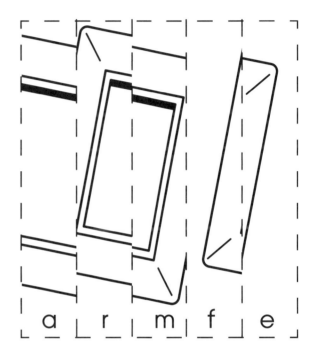

a r m f e

m e a s

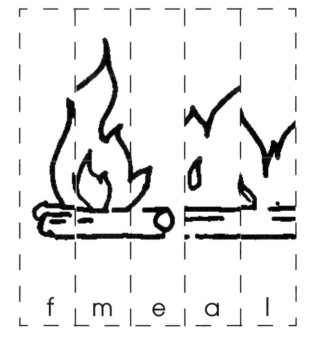

f m e a l

Nate and Kate Skate

Read the story.
Then write a sentence about something you like to do.

Nate likes to skate.

Many times, Kate comes to skate with Nate.

Kate and Nate have the same skates.

"Why do you like to skate?" asks Kate.

"I like to go fast!" says Nate.

"I like to skate fast, too!" says Kate.

_____

_____

_____

_____

_____

_____

Word Family Ice Cream Cones

Place the scoops of ice cream on the correct word family cones.

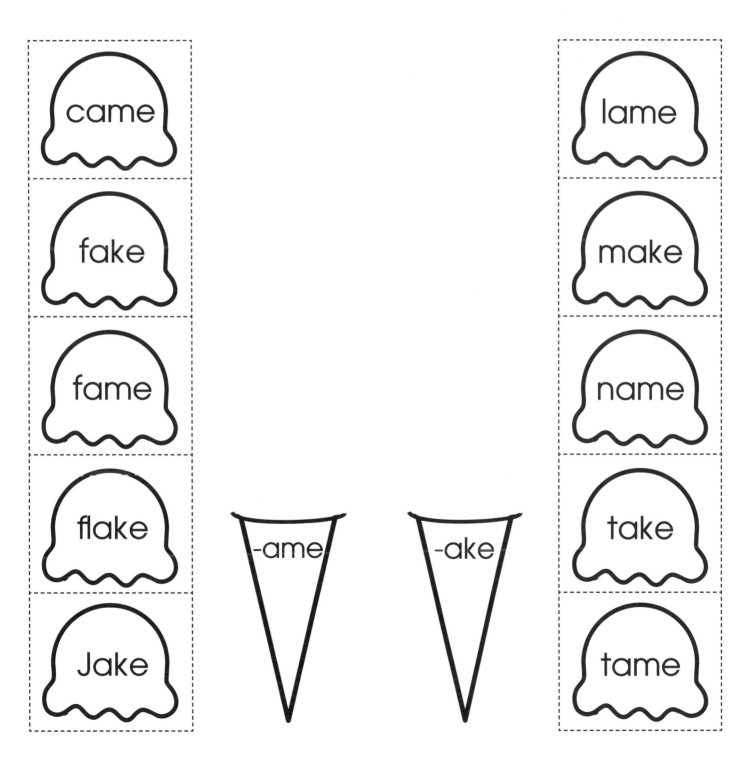

The Same Name

Read the poem. Draw a line under words that have the long a sound. Then write your own name.

My name is James.

My dad's name is James.

Our names are the same!

My mom's name is Lane.

Our names are not the same.

My dog's name is Socks.

I do not want to trade for that name.

My name is _____

_____

_____

_____

The Bake Sale

**Read the story. Draw a picture to show what happens in the story.
Write to tell about your picture.**

Jane and Jake will bake.

What will Jane and Jake bake?

Jane and Jake will bake two cakes.

One cake will be little and one cake will be big,

but the cakes will look the same.

bake	Kate
shake	cave
cake	base
flake	rake
flame	Jake
frame	snake

Advancing Phonics Every Day

Letters/sounds:
Long o (final e)

	Day 1	Day 2	Day 3
Phonological/ Phonemic Awareness	**Syllable Segmentation** Routine 3 **Model:** joker, overalls **Practice:** alone, frozen **Extra practice:** Oklahoma, tadpole	**Phoneme Recognition** Routine 9 **Model:** rose/robe/rope, close/cone/cove **Practice:** spoke/slope/stove, drove/dose/dome **Extra practice:** home/hose/hope, pole/poke/pose	**Onset and Rime Segmentation** Routine 7 **Model:** globe, code **Practice:** robe, vote **Extra practice:** phone, rose
Phonics	**Review previous week's sound/symbol focus: Long a (final e)** Routine 17 **Model:** flame, bake **Practice:** graze, shave, chase **Extra practice:** crane, brave **Introduce sound/symbol correspondence: Long o (final e)** **Model:** joke, those **Practice:** pole, home, vote **Extra practice:** smoke, globe	**Blend words with long o (final e)** Routine 18 **Model:** rode, woke **Practice:** bone, hole, froze **Extra practice:** zone, note Remind students that in words that end in long e, the vowel sound is long as the e is silent. **Decodable reader: "Cole and Rose"** Use decodable reader ideas (p. 23).	**Blend words with long o (final e)** Routine 18 **Model:** stove, broke **Practice:** spoke, cone, slope **Extra practice:** drove, stone
Word Families	Use the following letter cards. Have students form as many –ope words as they can and write the words on their workmats. **Letter cards:** h, m, n, p, r	Have student pairs make a five-rung word ladder with –ope at the top. On each rung, students write a word in the –ope word family.	Use the following letter cards. Have students form as many –ape words as they can and write the words on the workmats. **Letter cards:** c, g, t, sh, gr, dr
High-Frequency Words	**Introduce high-frequency words** Routine 20 find, how	**Practice high-frequency words** Routine 21 find, how **Decodable Reader: "Cole and Rose"** Use decodable reader ideas (pg. 23).	**Introduce high-frequency words** Routine 20 over, under
Writing	Have students write a sentence using one or two of the words they made in the word family activity.	Students can write a sentence using one of the words they made in the word family activity and one of the week's high-frequency words.	Have students write a sentence using words they made in the word family activity and high-frequency words.
Spelling	**Introduce spelling words** Routines 20, 22 hope, rope, slope, how	**Spell words in context** Routines 21, 23 hope, rope, slope, how	**Introduce spelling words** Routines 20, 22 drape, grape, tape, over
Shared Reading	**"A Handy Machine"** **Review long a (final e)** As you read aloud, point out words with long a (final e) (*make, same*). Have students read these words with you, emphasizing the phonics element.	**"A Handy Machine"** **Introduce long o (final e)** As you read aloud, point out the word with the long o (final e) (*code*). Have students read this word with you, emphasizing the phonics element.	**"A Handy Machine"** **Review high-frequency words** As you read aloud, point out the high-frequency words *how* and *their*. Have students read these words with you.

High-Frequency Words:	Spelling:	Word Families:
find, how, over, under	Words with –ope, –ape	–ope, –ape

Day 4	Day 5	Collaborative Learning and Independent Practice*
Phoneme Isolation Routine 10 **Model:** doze, wove **Practice:** nose, broke, throne **Extra practice:** stroke, close		• Phonemic Word Sort: Words with Long o and Long a (Final e) Days 1–5 • Phoneme Cubes: Words with Long o (Final e) Days 3–5
Build words with long o (final *e*) Routine 19 **Model:** code, cone, lone **Practice:** role, robe, lobe, globe **Extra practice:** smoke, spoke, poke, pole	**Decodable reader: "Cole and Rose"** Use decodable reader ideas (p. 23).	• Phonics Beanbag Toss: Words with Long o (Final e) Days 1–5 • Phonics Crossword: Words with Long o (Final e) Days 3–5 • Read/Circle/Draw: "Joke on My Dog": Words with Long o (Final e) Days 3–5
Write –*ape* on the board. Give students three minutes to write as many –*ape* words as they can on their workmats. Have student choose one of their words and use it in an oral sentence.	**Review –ope, –ape words** Display the *cape, grapes, rope, scrape, shapes,* and *slope* picture cards. Have students take turns saying the word for each picture and then using the word in an oral sentence.	• Word Family Picture Labels: -ope Days 1–5 • Feed the Creatures: -ope, -ape Days 3–5 • Word Family Spinners/Sliders: -ope, -ape Days 3–5
Practice high-frequency words Routine 21 find, how, over, under	**Decodable reader: "Cole and Rose"** Use decodable reader ideas (p. 23).	• High-Frequency Words Concentration Days 1–5 • High-Frequency Words "Go Fish" Days 3–5
Have students use one or two of the words they made in the word family activity to write a sentence.	**Interactive writing** (see p. 22) **Story starter:** Can Rose jump rope? **Word bank:** hope, nope, scrape, joke, home, over, under	• Reading/Writing: Continue the Story "Jake's Pancakes" Days 1–5 • Reading/Writing: Respond to the Story "The Big Trip" Days 3–5
Spell words in context Routines 21, 23 drape, grape, tape, over	**Test words in dictation** Read out the spelling words for students to write. Then review their work.	• Spelling Homework: BLM 1 Days 1–5
"Two Places at Once" **Review long o (final e)** As you read aloud, point out the long o (final e) word *phone*. Have students read this word with you, emphasizing the phonics element.	**"Two Places at Once"** **Review high-frequency words** As you read aloud, point out this week's high-frequency words (*find, over*). Have students read these words aloud with you.	

* Use this menu to plan extra practice and center activities for use through the week. All the skills needed for an activity have been introduced by the first day of the range shown. See pages 188–189 for full descriptions.

Collaborative Learning and Independent Practice

 ## Phonological/Phonemic Awareness Activities

Phonemic Word Sort:
Words with Long o (Final e) and Long a (Final e)
Use on Days 1–5

Distribute copies of the following ten picture cards (page 197). Have pairs of students work together to sort the cards by final sound:

- **bone / cone / grape / shapes**
- **rope / slope**
- **ape / tape / scrape / cape**

Phoneme Cubes:
Words with Long o (Final e)
Use on Days 3–5

Gather multiple pairs of cubes (such as empty, cube-shaped tissue boxes). Paste the week's twelve picture cards (page 197) on the boxes, six per box. Students can take turns rolling the cubes, saying the two words that face up, identifying the middle vowel sounds, and noting whether the two sounds are the same.

Phonics Activities

Phonics Beanbag Toss:
Words with Long o (Final e)
Use on Days 1–5

Arrange the twelve picture cards (page 197) for a beanbag toss. Provide the word cards (page 196), and have students take turns reading a word aloud and tossing the beanbag onto the corresponding picture.

Phonics Crossword:
Words with Long o (Final e)
Use on Days 3–5

Provide students with BLM 2 (page 191) and have them complete the crossword activity.

Read/Circle/Draw:
"Joke on My Dog":
Words with Long o (Final e)
Use on Days 3–5

Place copies of BLM 5 (page 194) in a center. Have student pairs take turns reading the story. Then have students complete the circling and drawing activities.

Word Family Activities

High-Frequency Word Activities

Writing Activities

Word Family Picture Labels: -ope
Use on Days 1–5

Provide students with BLM 4 (page 193) and a word slider (BLM C) for the -ope word family. Have students use the slider to form word family words and complete the activity.

Feed the Creatures: -ope, -ape
Use on Days 3–5

Provide two small plastic bins. Label each bin with either -ope or -ape. Use a marker to make eyes or a face on each bin to turn it into a creature. Provide partners with the following -ope and -ape picture cards, and have them take turns "feeding" the creatures the appropriate cards:

*   rope / slope / cape / grapes / scrape / shapes

Word Family Spinners/Sliders: -ope, -ape
Use on Days 3–5

Construct two word spinners (BLM B), one for each of the week's word families. Write the word family on the long rectangular piece and initial letters around the circle. Provide copies of the phonics house (BLM A), and have students label the houses -ope or -ape. Ask students to form words using the spinners and to list each word they form in the appropriate word family house. (This activity may also use word sliders [BLM C] instead of spinners.)

High-Frequency Words Concentration
Use on Days 1–5

Distribute a set of *Benchmark Advance* high-frequency word cards to partners. Each set should contain two copies of each of the following words, for a total of twenty-eight cards per pair of students.

*   are / come / find / here / how / jump / one / play / said / the / there / two / what / who

Instruct partners to arrange the cards face down in a 4 x 7 grid and play a concentration game. The partners should alternate turning over two cards at a time. When a student uncovers a matching pair, he/she uses the word in an oral sentence and keeps the pair of cards. The student who collects the most pairs wins the game.

High-Frequency Words "Go Fish"
Use on Days 3–5

Pick twenty-five high-frequency words, and write each word on two index cards to create fifty cards. Students might be instructed to draw fish on the other sides of the cards. Have groups of two to four students play "Go Fish" using this deck.

Reading/Writing: Continue the Story "Jake's Pancakes"
Use on Days 1–5

Provide copies of BLM 3 (page 192) and have students draw and write about what happens next.

Reading/Writing: Respond to the Story "The Big Trip"
Use on Days 3–5

Provide copies of BLM 6 (page 195) and have students write about what Rose did in Rome.

Spelling Homework

Read each spelling word aloud with your child. Spell it aloud together. Then ask your child to write each spelling word and say it in a sentence.

hope _____

drape _____

rope _____

grape _____

slope _____

tape _____

how _____

over _____

Choose a different activity every day to practice this week's spelling words at home with your child.

Flashlight Writing	Write it	Two-Toned Words	Write It Again	Remember the Word
Turn out the lights. Use a flashlight to spell each word on the wall.	Work with your child to write the word, saying aloud each letter as you write it.	Write the spelling words with crayons or colored markers on a sheet of paper. Use one color for consonants and another for vowels.	Have your child write the word three times on a sheet of paper and circle the vowels.	Turn the paper over and write the word from memory.

Phonics Crossword

**Complete the crossword puzzle.
Fill in the words for the pictures shown.**

Word Bank
cape
scrape
shapes
slope

Jake's Pancakes

Read the story.
Draw a picture and then write a sentence to tell what happens next.

Jake woke up late.

He put on a robe.

He made pancakes on the stove.

Then Jake smelled smoke.

No! The pancakes got too hot!

Jake had to trade the pancakes

for a plate of grapes.

Word Family Picture Labels

Say the name of the picture aloud.
Write the beginning of the word below each picture.

ope

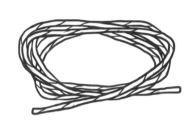

ope

ope

ope

Joke on My Dog

Read the story. Circle all of the words with the long o sound.

I played a joke on my dog, Cole.

I put his little bone under a stone.

Cole could not find his little bone.

Cole sniffed and sniffed our home with his nose.

I did not want to make Cole sad.

I gave Cole the bone and said,

"I will not trick you, Cole."

Draw a picture to show what happens at the end of the story.

The Big Trip

Read the story. Write a sentence to tell something else Rose did in Rome.

Rose wanted to take a trip to Rome.

To go there, Rose would cross the globe!

Rose packed a case with things to take.

Then she got on a plane.

The plane landed in Rome.

There, Rose sniffed a rose in a vase.

She ate a plate of grapes.

Rose was glad to be in Rome.

bone	pole
cape	rope
cone	ape
grapes	scrape
home	shapes
tape	slope

Advancing Phonics Every Day

Letters/sounds:
Soft c, g; Contractions with not

	Day 1	Day 2	Day 3
Phonological/ Phonemic Awareness	**Phoneme Recognition** *Routine 9* **Model:** rice, ace, page, cage **Practice:** pace, stage **Extra practice:** gem, cent	**Onset and Rime Blending** *Routine 8* **Model:** face, gem **Practice:** place, mice **Extra practice:** pace, rage	**Phoneme Segmentation** *Routine 11* **Model:** face, grace **Practice:** trace, twice **Extra practice:** cell, wage
Phonics	**Review previous week's sound/symbol focus** *Routine 17* **Model:** mole, rope **Practice:** code, hose **Extra practice:** choke, stole, clone, close, note **Introduce sound/symbol correspondence: soft c, g** *Routine 17* **Model:** cent, age **Practice:** face, gem **Extra practice:** cell, cage	**Blend words with soft c, g** *Routine 18* **Model:** pace, page **Practice:** gel, cent **Extra practice:** space, cage, race **Build words with soft c, g** *Routine 19* **Model:** stage, sage, rage, race **Other words:** place, lace, ace **Predecodable reader: "Grace and Ace"** Use decodable reader ideas (p. 23).	**Learn contractions with not** Display word cards *isn't* and *wasn't*. Note the apostrophe and remind students that a contraction is a short way to put two words together. Some words can make a contraction with the word *not*. Write *is not* and *was not* on the board. Demonstrate how the words were combined to make contractions. Remind students that the apostrophe replaces the left-out letter.
Word Families	Have student pairs make a five-rung ladder with *–ace* at the top. Have them use the following letter cards to write words on each rung of the ladder. **Letter cards:** f, l, p, r, sp	Have student pairs make a five-petal flower with *–ace* in the center. Have them add an *–ace* word to each of the petals.	Use the following letter cards and have students write words in the *–age* word family on their workmats. **Letter cards:** c, p, r, st, w
High-Frequency Words	**Introduce high-frequency words** try, give *Routine 20*	**Practice high-frequency words** try, give *Routine 21* **Predecodable reader: "Grace and Ace"** Use decodable reader ideas (p. 23)	**Introduce high-frequency words** far, too *Routine 20*
Writing	Have students write a sentence using the words that they made in the Word Families activity.	Have students write and illustrate a sentence using the Word Families words about a place they have been.	Have students use the words from the Word Families routines and high-frequency words to write a sentence about being onstage.
Spelling	**Introduce spelling words** *Routines 20, 22* give, race, place, space	**Spell words in context** *Routines 21, 23* give, race, place, space	**Introduce spelling words** *Routines 20, 22* far, cage, page, stage
Shared Reading	**"Unplug"** **Review long o (final e)** As you read aloud, point to long o (final e) words. Have students read these words with you, emphasizing the phonics element.	**"Unplug"** **Introduce soft c, g** As you read aloud, point out words with soft c and g. Have students read these words with you, emphasizing the phonics element.	**"Unplug"** **Introduce contractions with not** As you read aloud, point out contractions with *not*. Have students read these words with you, and tell the two words that formed the contraction.

High-Frequency Words:	Spelling:	Word Families:
try, give, far, too	Words with –ace, –age	–ace, –age

Day 4	Day 5	Collaborative Learning and Independent Practice*
Phoneme Blending `Routine 12` **Model:** page, cent **Practice:** gem, cell **Extra practice:** stage, lace		• Phonemic Word Sort: Words with Soft c, Soft g Days 1–5 • Elkonin Boxes: Contractions with not Days 3–5
Practice contractions with not Review contractions with the word cards *isn't* and *wasn't*. Have students tell the two words that make up each contraction. Write on the board *had not, has not, did not, have not, are not*, and *could not*. Have students tell how to make contractions with the verb phrases. For extra practice write *will not* and *do not* on the board. Discuss how the contractions for these words change spelling or pronunciation.	**Predecodable reader: "Grace and Ace"** Use decodable reader ideas (p. 23).	• Craft Stick Chains: Words with Soft c, Soft g Days 1–5 • Picture Word Matching: Words with Soft c, Soft g; Contractions with not Days 3–5 • Read/Draw/Label: "On the Table": Words with Soft c, Soft g Days 3–5
Write *–age* on the board. Give students three minutes to write as many *–age* words as they can on their workmats.	**Review –ace, –age words** Display picture cards *face, lace, race, space*, and *stage*. Have students take turns saying the picture name and then using the word in an oral sentence.	• Word Family Towers: -ace Days 1–5 • Word Family Crossword: -ace, -age Days 3–5 • Word Family Tic-Tac-Toe: -ace, -age Days 3–5
Practice high-frequency words try, give, far, too `Routine 21`	**Predecodable reader: "Grace and Ace"** Use decodable reader ideas (p. 23).	• High-Frequency Words Parking Lot Days 1–5 • High-Frequency Words Bug Catch Days 3–5
Have students use the words that they made in the Word Families activity to write and illustrate a sentence.	**Interactive writing** (see p. 22) **Story starter:** Grace takes a trip to space! **Word bank:** face, pace, race, place, age, stage, page	• Reading/Writing: Respond to the Story "Ten Cents" Days 1–5 • Reading/Writing: Continue the Story "Grace Sings" Days 3–5
Spell words in context `Routines 21, 23` far, cage, page, stage	**Test words in dictation** Read aloud each of the week's spelling words for students to write. Then collect and review student work.	• Spelling Homework: BLM 1 Days 1–5
"I Wonder" **Review –ace and –age word families** As you read aloud, point out the words from the *–ace* and *–age* word families. Have students read these words aloud with you.	**"I Wonder"** **Review soft c, g and contractions with not** As you read aloud, point out words in the *–ace* and *–age* word families. Have students read them aloud with you.	

* Use this menu to plan extra practice and center activities for use through the week. All the skills needed for an activity have been introduced by the first day of the range shown. See pages 200–201 for full descriptions.

Collaborative Learning and Independent Practice

Phonological/Phonemic Awareness Activities

Phonemic Word Sort:
Words with Soft c, Soft g
Use on Days 1–5

Distribute copies of ten of the week's picture cards (page 209). Do not include the cards with contractions. Have pairs of students work together to sort the cards by the soft c or soft g sound:

- cent / face / lace / race / space / brace
- gem / stage / cage / page

Phoneme Cubes:
Contractions with not
Use on Days 3–5

Gather multiple pairs of cubes (such as empty cube-shaped tissue boxes.) Write contractions with "not" on the boxes, six per box. Students can take turns rolling the cubes, saying the contraction that is facing up, and identifying the two words that it is made from.

Phonics Activities

Craft Stick Chains:
Words with Soft c, Soft g
Use on Days 1–5

Use tongue depressors or craft sticks. Write a decodable word with a soft c /s/ sound (*ace, race, trace*) on one end of each stick and a word with a soft g /j/ sound (*cage, page, stage*) on the other end of each stick. Have partners take turns choosing a stick and placing it end-to-end with another stick, matching words with the same sound.

Picture Word Matching:
Words with Soft c, Soft g; Contractions with not
Use on Days 3–5

Provide students with the week's twenty-four picture and word cards (pages 208–209). Have students match each picture to its word and then sort all the pairs by soft c, soft g, or contraction (*cent/face/lace/race/space/brace, gem/cage/stage, isn't/wasn't*).

Read/Draw/Label:
"On the Table":
Words with Soft c, Soft g
Use on Days 3–5

Place copies of BLM 5 (page 206) in the center. Have student pairs work together to complete the activity.

 Word Family Activities

Word Family Towers: -ace
Use on Days 1–5

Provide partners with interlocking blocks. On each block, place a piece of masking tape. Write –ace words on half of the blocks, and other decodable words on the rest of the blocks. Have students find and stack the –ace word blocks into a word family tower, pronouncing each word as they add it to the tower.

(This activity can be adapted for the –age word family.)

Word Family Crossword: -ace, -age
Use on Days 3–5

Provide students with BLM 2 (page 203) and have them complete the crossword activity.

Word Family Tic-Tac-Toe: -ace, -age
Use on Days 3–5

Provide or have students draw a tic-tac-toe board. Have partners play tic-tac-toe using words belonging to the –ace and –age word families. One partner will use –ace words instead of an X to mark his/her spots on the board. The other partner will use –age words instead of an O.

 High-Frequency Word Activities

High-Frequency Words Parking Lot
Use on Days 1–5

Provide partners with BLM 4 (page 205) and toy cars, and have them complete the activity. Students should take turns: One student should read a high-frequency word aloud, and the other student should "park" a toy car in that spot and say a sentence using the word.

High-Frequency Words Bug Catch
Use on Days 3–5

Write a series of high-frequency words, from this week and previous weeks, on index cards, and place the index cards on the floor or on a table. Then provide a pair of students with plastic fly swatters. Instruct students to take turns: One student should read a high-frequency word aloud, and then the other student should "swat" it.

Writing Activities

Reading/Writing: Respond to the Story "Ten Cents"
Use on Days 1–5

Provide copies of BLM 3 (page 204) and have students write a sentence about something they can buy for ten cents.

Reading/Writing: Continue the Story "Grace Sings"
Use on Days 3–5

Provide copies of BLM 6 (page 207) and have students draw a picture of what happens next.

BLM
1

Spelling Homework

**Read each spelling word aloud with your child. Spell it aloud together.
Then ask your child to write each spelling word and use it in a sentence.**

race _____

cage _____

place _____

page _____

space _____

stage _____

give _____

far _____

Choose a different activity every day to practice this week's spelling words at home with your child.

Flashlight writing	Write it	Trace the word	Letter tiles	Circle the Word
Turn out the lights. Use a flashlight to spell each word on the wall.	Write the word, saying aloud each letter as you write it.	Write the word with dotted lines on a sheet of paper, and then trace the dots with a different color.	Use letter tiles to spell the words and then write the words on a piece of paper.	Write one sentence for each word and circle the spelling words.

Word Family Crossword

Complete the crossword puzzle. Fill in the words for the pictures shown.

Word Bank
place
page
cage
lace

BLM
3

Ten Cents

Read the story.
Then write a sentence about something you can get for ten cents.

Jace is at a shop.

She wants to get something for ten cents.

Jace can't get lace for ten cents.

She can't get a gem for ten cents.

She can't get a bracelet for ten cents.

But Jace can get a pencil for ten cents!

Good find, Jace!

I can get

High-Frequency Words Parking Lot

Listen to the directions from your teacher.

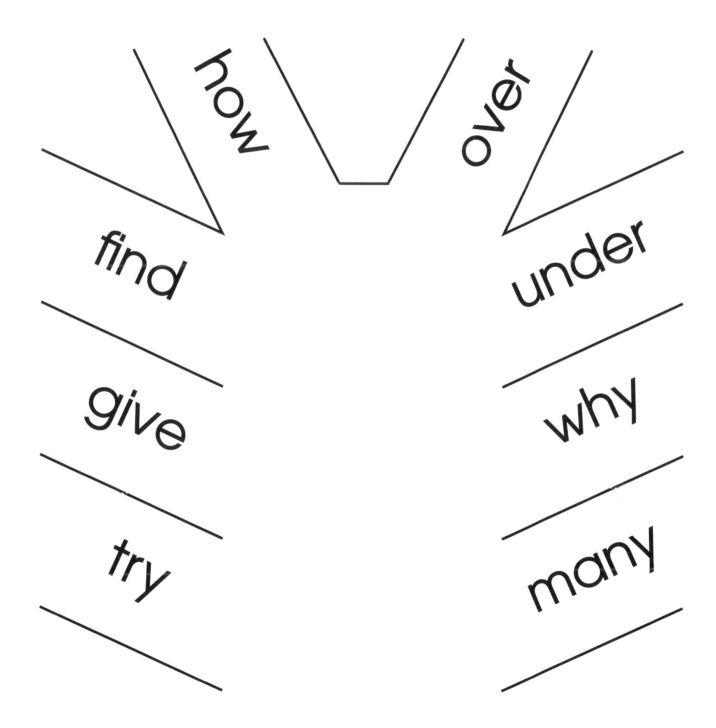

On the Table

Label the things you see in this picture of a table.

Hint: All of the words have the soft c or soft g sound.

_____   _____   _____

- - - - - - - - - - - -   - - - - - - - - - - - -   - - - - - - - - - - - -

_____   _____   _____

Grace Sings

Read the story.

Grace likes to sing onstage.

Her dress is made of lace.

Her necklace is filled with gems.

Grace sings like an ace.

You can tell Grace likes to sing.

Just look at her face!

Draw a picture to tell what happens next.

page	lace
cage	brace
cent	race
face	space
gem	stage
isn't	wasn't

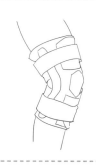

is + not = isn't

was + not = wasn't

Advancing Phonics Every Day

Letters/sounds: long i (final e), vowel-C-e syllables

	Day 1	Day 2	Day 3
Phonological/ Phonemic Awareness	**Word Awareness** — Routine 1 **Model:** I ride on the slide. **Practice:** Let's hide inside from the rain. **Extra practice:** The white bike is outside.	**Phoneme Recognition** — Routine 9 **Model:** ride, bike, nice **Practice:** drive, smile, bride **Extra practice:** like, white, rice	**Phoneme Categorization** — Routine 13 **Model:** wife/side/sink, ride/rip/rice **Practice:** knit/nine/nice, tide/line/pin, bike/dip/bite **Extra practice:** wide/dine/pin, pill/side/pile
Phonics	**Review previous week's sound/symbol focus** — Routine 17 **Model:** page, place **Practice:** trace, grace, cage **Extra practice:** race, rage, cent **Introduce long i (final e)** — Routine 17 **Model:** ripe, smile **Practice:** side, stride, life **Extra practice:** slide, wife	**Blend long i (final e) words** — Routine 18 **Model:** stripe, slide **Practice:** dime, pile, bite, glide, time **Build words with long i (final e)** — Routine 19 **Model:** kite, bite, bike **Other words:** spine, pine, pile, mile **Decodable reader: "Why Kittens Hide"** Use decodable reader ideas (p. 23)	**Review words with vowel-C-e syllables** — Routine 18 **Model:** pride, lifetime **Practice:** bike, ripe, inside, hive **Extra practice:** slide, sunshine
Word Families	Guide students to draw a simple five-band rainbow with a cloud at one end. Have them write *-ine* in the cloud and an *-ine* word in each color band. Repeat for the *-ife* word family.	Distribute letter cards to student pairs, and instruct them to form words in the *-ine* word family. Have them write their words on their workmats. **Letter cards:** d, e, f, i, l, m, n, p	Guide students to draw a square that is divided into four squares. Have them write an *-ide* word in each square.
High-Frequency Words	**Introduce high-frequency words** — Routine 20 after, call	**Practice high-frequency words** — Routine 21 after, call **Decodable reader: "Why Kittens Hide"** Use decodable reader ideas (p. 23)	**Introduce high-frequency words** — Routine 20 large, her
Writing	Have student pairs work together to write a sentence using one of the *-ine* or *-ife* words they wrote on their rainbows.	Have student pairs work together to write a sentence using one of the *-ine* words they made in the word families activity. Repeat using an *-ife* word.	Have student pairs work together to write a sentence using one of the *-ide* words they wrote in their squares.
Spelling	**Introduce spelling words** — Routines 20, 22 after, fine, dine, wife	**Spell words in context** — Routines 21, 23 after, fine, dine, wife	**Introduce spelling words** — Routines 20, 22 call, glide, bride, wide
Shared Reading	**"Not So Scary** **Review soft c, g** As you read aloud, review phonics elements soft c, g in the words *nice, dance*. Have students read them aloud, emphasizing the phonics element.	**"Not So Scary** **Introduce long i (final e)** As you read aloud, point out the long i (final e) in the words *likes, nice, like, outside*. Have volunteers to read a word aloud and use it in an oral sentence.	**"Not So Scary** **Review high-frequency words: too, large, find** Point out the high-frequency words *too, large, find*. Have students say each word aloud with you as you read.

High-Frequency Words:	Spelling:	Word Families:
after, call, large, her	Words with -ine, -ife, -ide	-ine, -ife, -ide

Day 4	Day 5	Collaborative Learning and Independent Practice*
Phoneme Substitution Routine 14 **Model:** ride/hide, life/wife **Practice:** fine/dine, side/wide, line/pine **Extra practice:** mine/nine, slide/glide		• Phonemic Picnic: Words with Long i Sounds Days 1–5 • Phoneme Cubes: Words with Long i (Final e); Vowel-C-e Syllables Days 3–5
Build words with vowel-C-e syllables Routine 19 **Model:** tribe, bribe, bride **Practice:** chive, hive, hide, ride **Extra practice:** fine, file, mile, smile	**Decodable reader: "Why Kittens Hide"** Use decodable reader ideas (p. 23).	• Spelling Rules: Words with Long i (Final e) Days 1–5 • Phonics Board Game: Words with Vowel-C-e Syllables Days 3–5 • Read/Draw/Label: "The Mice": Words with Long i (Final e) Days 3–5
Distribute the following letter cards to student pairs, and instruct them to form words in the -ide word family. Have them write the words on their workmats. **Letter cards:** d, e, h, i, r, s, t, w, pr, gl	**Review -ine, -ife, -ide words** Distribute picture cards (page 221) and letter cards to student pairs. Have students spell each word using the letter cards and write it on their workmats. **Picture cards:** nine, vine, line, wife, ride, slide **Letter cards:** d, e, f, i, l, n, n, r, s, v, w	• Word Family Ice Cream Cones: -ine, -ife Days 1–5 • Word Family Cube: -ide Days 3–5 • Feed the Creatures: -ine, -ife, -ide Days 3–5
Practice high-frequency words Routine 21 after, call, large, her	**Decodable reader: "Why Kittens Hide"** Use decodable reader ideas (p. 23).	• High-Frequency Words Beanbag Toss Days 1–5 • High-Frequency Words Concentration Days 3–5
Have student pairs work together to form another word using the letter cards from the word families activity, and write a sentence using the word.	**Interactive writing** (see p. 22) **Story starter:** Nine kids went to the park. **Word bank:** line, ride, mine, outside, beside, glide, slide	• Reading/Writing: Continue the Poem "Here We Go!" Days 1–5 • Reading/Writing: Respond to the Poem "Nine Swine" Days 3–5
Spell words in context Routines 21, 23 call, glide, bride, wide	**Test words in dictation** Read the spelling words for students to write. Then review their work.	• Spelling Homework: BLM 1 Days 1–5
"The Strongest Things **Review long i (final e)** As you read aloud, review phonics element long i (final e): *like, times.* Have students read each word aloud with you, and invite volunteers to use one of the words in an original sentence.	**The Strongest Things** **Review long i (final e)** As you read aloud, review phonics element long i (final e): *size, quite.* Have students read each word aloud with you, and emphasize the phonics element.	

* Use this menu to plan extra practice and center activities for use through the week. All the skills needed for an activity have been introduced by the first day of the range shown. See pages 212–213 for full descriptions.

Collaborative Learning and Independent Practice

 Phonological/Phonemic Awareness Activities

Phonemic Picnic:
Words with Long i Sounds
Use on Days 1–5

Fill a picnic basket (or lunch box) with toy foods. Each food should contain the long i sound (and, if desired, phonemes from previous weeks) (for example: *rice, ice cream, French fries, limes, pie, pineapple*). Have partners sit on the floor as if ready for a picnic. They should take turns choosing a food, say the name of the food, and passing it to their partner to "eat."

Phoneme Cubes:
Words with Long i (Final e);
Vowel-C-e Syllables
Use on Days 3–5

Gather multiple pairs of cubes (such as empty cube-shaped tissue boxes). Paste the week's twelve picture cards (page 221) on the boxes, six per box. Students can take turns rolling the cubes, saying the two words that face up, identifying the final (or only) vowel sounds, and noting whether they are the same.

Phonics Activities

Spelling Rules:
Words with Long i (Final e)
Use on Days 1–5

Provide students with the week's twelve picture cards (page 221). Instruct students to write each word. Have students underline the final e because it does not make its own sound. Then have students draw an arrow from the final e to the vowel to show that the e makes the vowel sound long.

Phonics Board Game:
Words with Vowel-C-e Syllables
Use on Days 3–5

Place copies of BLM D, a spinner (BLM B), and disks or coins for playing pieces in the center. Students use the spinner to advance on the board. If they land on a space that has a word with a vowel-C-e syllable, or the word is a vowel-C-i word, they use it an oral sentence and spin again. If the word does not have a vowel-C-e syllable or is not a vowel-C-e word, the next player spins. Students also follow directions on the squares that have them.

Label the squares with words and directions, making a path from the START square to the FINISH square (words and directions can be repeated, as necessary). Examples of words and directions include:

- **reptile, inside, tadpole, invite, mistake, bike, like, Mike, bite, kite, dine, fine, line, mine, nine, pine, shine, vine, life, wife, ride, side**
- **rabbit, stack, clock, fetch, flash, wishes**
- **"Move back two spaces"**
- **"Move forward five spaces"**
- **"Spin again"**
- **"Skip your next turn"**
- **"Switch squares with the player across from you"**

Read/Draw/Label:
"The Mice":
Words with Long i (Final e)
Use on Days 3–5

Place copies of BLM 5 (page 218) in the center. Have student pairs take turns reading the story. Then have students complete the drawing activity to show what happens next.

 **Word Family Activities**

Word Family Ice Cream Cones: -ine, -ife
Use on Days 1–5

Provide students with BLM 2 (page 215) and have them complete the activity.

Word Family Labels: -ide, -ide, -ine
Use on Days 3–5

Distribute BLM 4 (page 217) and have students complete the words by writing the missing letter or letters on the line.

Feed the Creatures: -ine, -ife, -ide
Use on Days 3–5

Provide three small plastic bins. Label each with a word family, –ine, –ife, or –ide. Use a marker to make eyes or a face on each bin to turn the bins into creatures. Provide partners with the following –ine, –ife, and –ide picture cards, and have them take turns "feeding" the creatures the appropriate cards:

- line / nine / vine / wife / ride / slide

High-Frequency Word Activities

High-Frequency Words Beanbag Toss
Use on Days 1–5

Gather Benchmark Advance high-frequency word cards for a beanbag toss. Use review words from previous weeks as well as the current week's words.

- after / are / because / call / far / find / from / give / how / hurt / many / over

Have one student choose a word to read aloud, and another to toss the bag to cover the matching card.

High-Frequency Words Concentration
Use on Days 3–5

Distribute to partners the following Benchmark Advance high-frequency word cards. Each set should contain two copies of each word, for a total of 28 cards per pair of students. Have students take turns finding the matching high-frequency words.

- after / and / call / come / do / good / here / jump / look / now / of / put / right / start

Writing Activities

Reading/Writing: Continue the Poem "Here We Go!"
Use on Days 1–5

Provide copies of BLM 3 (page 216) and have students complete the activity.

Reading/Writing: Respond to the Story "Nine Swine"
Use on Days 3–5

Provide copies of BLM 6 (page 219) and have students write about the nine swine.

Name _____ Date _____

BLM 1

Spelling Homework

Read each spelling word aloud with your child. Spell it aloud together. Then ask your child to write each spelling word and say it in a sentence.

after _____   call _____

fine _____   glide _____

dine _____   bride _____

wife _____   wide _____

Choose a different activity every day to practice this week's spelling words at home with your child.

Trace the word	Multi-Colored Words	Flashlight writing	Magnetic letters	Circle the word
Use your finger to write each spelling word in sand, flour, or a similar material.	Write the spelling words with crayons or colored pencils, using a different color for each letter.	Turn out the lights. Use a flashlight to spell each word on the wall.	Spell the words on a cookie sheet using magnetic letters and then write the words on a sheet of paper.	Work with your child to write a sentence for each word on a sheet of paper and circle the spelling words.

Word Family Ice Cream Cones

Place the scoops of ice cream on the correct word family cones.

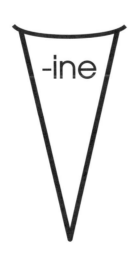

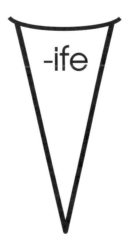

Here We Go!

Read the poem. Circle all the words that have both a long i sound and end with the letter e. Then write a sentence about what will happen next in the poem.

I sit at the top of the slide.

I like it just fine.

It's my time to ride!

But there are kids in line

Who want to go after me,

So I push off the side

And there I go! Nice!

_____

_____

_____

_____

_____

_____

Word Family Labels

Say the name of the picture aloud. Complete the word below each picture.

_____ ine

_____ ide

_____ ice

_____ ice

The Mice

Read the story. Draw a picture to show what happens next.

I see a line of five white mice.

I call to the mice,

But the mice hide from me.

I give them a little rice.

Will they like the rice?

Will they think it is nice?

Nine Swine

Read the story.
Then write a sentence about the nine swine.

Nine large swine stand under the pines.

The nine swine dine on rice.

After that, they nap in the sunshine.

The swine think their life is so nice!

Can't you see them smile?

The nine swine

_____

_____

_____

_____

bike	mice
bite	ride
rice	vine
bride	slide
line	ice
nine	pine

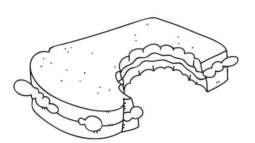

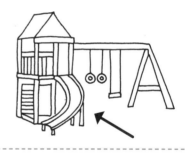

9

Advancing Phonics Every Day

Letters/sounds:
Long e (final e), long u (final e), Inflectional endings (-ed, -ing, dropping the final e)

	Day 1	Day 2	Day 3
Phonological/ Phonemic Awareness	**Syllable Segmentation** — Routine 3 **Model:** delete, perfume **Practice:** concrete, excuse **Extra practice:** confuse, amuse	**Syllable Blending** — Routine 4 **Model:** compete, costume **Practice:** delete, volume **Extra practice:** complete, refuse	**Phoneme Segmentation** — Routine 11 **Model:** fuse, eve **Practice:** cube, these **Extra practice:** mule, tubee
Phonics	**Review previous week's sound/symbol focus: long i (final e)** — Routine 17 **Model:** mine, bite **Practice:** drive, nine, pine, tribe **Introduce sound/symbol correspondence: long e (final e)** — Routine 17 **Model:** huge, these **Practice:** fume, use, mule **Extra practice:** theme, cube Long u can make two slightly different sounds, as in *tube* and *cube*.	**Blend words with long e (final e), long u (final e)** — Routine 18 **Model:** flute, Pete **Practice:** fume, Steve **Extra practice:** use, mule **Build words with long e (final e), long u (final e)** — Routine 19 **Model:** eve, Steve **Other words:** tune, tube, cube **Decodable reader: "Pete Mule's Hat"** Use decodable reader ideas (p. 23).	**Build words with inflectional endings (-ed, -ing, dropping the final e)** — Routine 19 **Model:** fume, fumed, fuming **Practice:** tune, tuned, tuning **Extra practice:** compete, competed, competing Explain to students that when *-ed* or *-ing* is added to a word ending in *e*, the *e* is dropped to make the new word. Model with *race, racing*.
Word Families	Guide students to draw a simple three-step ladder. Have them write an *-une* word in each rung. Explain that long u can make two slightly different sounds, as in *tube* and *cube*.	Distribute letter cards to student pairs, and instruct them to form words in the *-ale* word family. Have them write their words on their workmats. Repeat for the *-ane* word family. **Letter cards:** a, e, l, p, t, s, c, m, n	Guide students to draw a simple word web with a center circle and five satellite circles. Have them write *-ale* in the center and an *-ale* word in each satellite circle. Repeat for the *-ane* word family.
High-Frequency Words	**Introduce high-frequency words** — Routine 20 house, long	**Practice high-frequency words** — Routine 21 house, long **Decodable reader: "Pete Mule's Hat"** Use decodable reader ideas (p. 23).	**Introduce high-frequency words** — Routine 20 off, small
Writing	Have student pairs work together to write a sentence using one of the *-une* words they wrote in their ladders.	Have student pairs work together to write a sentence using one of the *-ale* words they made in the word families activity. Repeat the activity using one of the *-ane* words.	Have student pairs work together to write a sentence using one of the *-ale* or *-ane* words they wrote on their word webs.
Spelling	**Introduce spelling words** — Routines 20, 22 house, whale, plane, eve	**Spell words in context** — Routines 21, 23 house, whale, plane, eve	**Introduce spelling words** — Routines 20, 22 long, tune, cube, dune
Shared Reading	**"Pete Saves the Day"** **Review long i (final e)** As you read aloud, review phonics elements long i (final e): *bike* Have students read the word aloud with you, and emphasize the phonics element.	**"Pete Saves the Day"** **Introduce long e (final e)** As you read aloud, point out the long e (final e) words *Pete, these*. Have students read the words aloud with you, and invite them to use one in an original sentence.	**"Pete Saves the Day"** **Review high-frequency words: small, long** Point out the high-frequency words *small* and *long*. Have students use one of the words in an original sentence.

High-Frequency Words:	Spelling:	Word Families:
house, long, off, small	Words with -ale, -ane, -une	-ale, -ane, -une

Day 4	Day 5	Collaborative Learning and Independent Practice*
Phoneme Categorization Routine 13 **Model:** these/theme/thick, tube/tin/tune **Practice:** fume/feet/fuse, cute/cube/catch **Extra practice:** complete/delete/drier, perfume/volume/vanish		• Phonemic Word Sort: Words with Long Vowel Sounds Days 1–5 • Phonemic Concentration: Words with Long Vowel Sounds; Inflectional Endings (-ed, -ing, Dropping Final e) Days 3–5
Blend words with inflectional endings (-ed, -ing, dropping the final e) Routine 18 **Model:** hiked, hoping **Practice:** raked, diving, joked, using **Extra practice:** striving, spiced **Build words with inflectional endings (-ed, -ing, dropping the final e)** Routine 19 **Model:** bake, baked, baking **Practice:** use, used, using **Extra practice:** complete, completed, completing	**Decodable reader: "Pete Mule's Hat"** Use decodable reader ideas (p. 23).	• Phonics Ice Cream Cones: Words with Long e (Final e) and Long u (Final e) Days 1–5 • Picture Word Cards: Words with Inflectional Endings (-ed, -ing, Dropping Final e) Days 3–5 • Read/Draw/Label: "The Tube Race": Words with Long e (Final e) and Long u (Final e) Days 3–5
Distribute the following letter cards to student pairs, and instruct them to form words in the –une word family. Have them write the words on their workmats. **Letter cards:** t, d, J, pr, u, n, e	**Review -ale, -ane, -une words** Distribute picture cards (page 233) to student pairs. Have students sort the words by word family. **Picture cards:** crane, June, whale, tune, plane, sale	• Word Family Sort: -ale, -ane Days 1–5 • Word Family Towers: -une Days 3–5 • Word Family Spinners/Sliders: -ale, -ane, -une Days 3–5
Practice high-frequency words Routine 21 house, long, off, small	**Decodable reader: "Pete Mule's Hat"** Use decodable reader ideas (p. 23).	• High-Frequency Words Board Game Days 1–5 • High-Frequency Words "Go Fish" Days 3–5
Have student pairs work together to write a sentence using one of the -une words they made in the word families activity.	**Interactive writing** (see p. 22) **Story starter:** Pete the mule is cute. **Word bank:** be, he, these, huge, use	• Reading/Writing: Respond to the Poem "The Rude Mule" Days 1–5 • Reading/Writing: Respond to the Poem "Cute Flute" Days 3–5
Spell words in context Routines 21, 23 long, tune, cube, dune	**Test words in dictation** Read out the spelling words for students to write. Then review their work.	• Spelling Homework: BLM 1 Days 1–5
"Dog and His Bone" **Review long o (final e)** As you read aloud, review phonics element long o (final e): bone Have students read the word aloud with you, and invite volunteers to use the word in an original sentence.	**"Dog and His Bone"** **Review possessives** As you read aloud, point out the possessive dog's. Have student volunteers use dog's in an original sentence.	

* Use this menu to plan extra practice and center activities for use through the week. All the skills needed for an activity have been introduced by the first day of the range shown. See pages 224–225 for full descriptions.

Collaborative Learning and Independent Practice

 **Phonological/Phonemic Awareness Activities**

ABC)) Phonics Activities

Phonemic Word Sort:
Words with Long Vowel Sounds
Use on Days 1–5

Distribute copies of the week's picture cards (page 233). Have pairs of students work together to sort the cards by long vowel sound:

- crane / plane / sale / whale / raked / raking
- June / mule / tune / flute / cubed
- Pete

Phonemic Concentration:
Words with Long Vowel Sounds; Inflectional Endings (-ed, -ing, Dropping Final e)
Use on Days 3–5

Provide students with a set of the week's picture cards (page 233), two of each card, for a total of twenty-four cards. Instruct partners to arrange the cards face down to form a 6 x 4 grid to play a concentration game. The partners should alternate turning over two cards per turn. When a student uncovers a matching pair, he/she should use the word in an oral sentence and keep the pair of cards. The student who collects the most pairs wins the game.

Phonics Ice Cream Cones:
Words with Long e (Final e) and Long u (Final e)
Use on Days 1–5

Provide students with BLM 2 (page 227) and have them complete the activity.

Picture Word Cards:
Words with Inflectional
Endings (-ed, -ing, Dropping Final e)
Use on Days 3–5

Distribute the following Benchmark Advance picture word cards:

- raked, raking
- skated, skating

Have partners take turns. Student 1 holds a card with the picture-only side, facing student 2. Student 1 reads aloud the word on the card. Student 2 spells the word orally. If student 2 needs a clue, student 1 provides the letters of the -ed or -ing ending, and allows student 2 to indicate the remaining letters.

Read/Draw/Label:
"The Tube Race":
Words with Long e (Final e) and Long u (Final e)
Use on Days 3–5

Place copies of BLM 5 (page 230) in the center. Have student pairs take turns reading the story. Then have students complete the writing activity.

Word Family Activities

Word Family Sort: -ale, -ane
Use on Days 1–5

Provide students with BLM 4 (page 229) and have them complete the activity.

Word Family Towers: -une
Use on Days 3–5

Provide partners with interlocking blocks. On each block, place a piece of masking tape. Write –une words on half of the blocks, and other decodable words on the rest of the blocks. Have students find and stack the –une word blocks into a word family tower, pronouncing each word as they add it to the tower.

(This activity can be adapted for the –ale or -ane word family.)

Word Family Spinners/Sliders: -ale, -ane, -une
Use on Days 3–5

Construct three word spinners (BLM B), one for each of the week's word families. Write the word family on the long rectangular piece and initial letters around the circle. Provide copies of the phonics house (BLM A) and have students label the houses -ale, -ane, and -une. Ask students to form words using the spinners and to list each word they form in the appropriate word family house. (This activity may also use word sliders [BLM C] instead of spinners.)

High-Frequency Word Activities

High-Frequency Words Board Game
Use on Days 1–5

Place copies of BLM D, a spinner (BLM B), and disks or coins for playing pieces in the center. Students use the spinner to advance on the board. When they land on a space with a high-frequency word, they read the word aloud and use it in an oral sentence. Students also follow directions on the squares that have them.

Label the squares with words and directions, making a path from the START square to the FINISH square (words and directions can be repeated, as necessary). Examples of words and directions include:

- **house, long, large, her, try, give, too, why, their, when, once, could, by, then, out, which, saw, this, look, said**
- **"Move back two spaces"**
- **"Move forward five spaces"**
- **"Spin again"**
- **"Skip your next turn"**
- **"Switch squares with the player to your left"**

High-Frequency Words "Go Fish"
Use on Days 3–5

Pick twenty-five high-frequency words, and write each word on two index cards to create fifty cards. Students might be instructed to draw fish on the other sides of the cards. Have groups of 2–4 students play "Go Fish" using this deck.

Writing Activities

Reading/Writing: Respond to the Poem "The Rude Mule"
Use on Days 1–5

Provide copies of BLM 3 (page 228) and have students read the poem and write about an animal they think is cute.

Reading/Writing: Respond to the Poem "Cute Flute"
Use on Days 3–5

Provide copies of BLM 6 (page 231). Have students read the poem and write about something they think is cute.

Spelling Homework

Read each spelling word aloud with your child. Spell it aloud together. Then ask your child to write each spelling word and use it in a sentence.

house _____

long _____

whale _____

tune _____

plane _____

cube _____

eve _____

dune _____

Choose a different activity every day to practice this week's spelling words at home with your child.

Trace the word	Multi-colored words	Two-toned words	Remember the word	Circle the word
Write the word with dotted lines on a sheet of paper, and then trace the dots with a different color.	Write the spelling words with crayons or colored pencils, using a different color for each letter.	Write the spelling words with crayons or colored markers on a sheet of paper. Use one color for consonants and another for vowels.	Turn the paper over and write the word from memory.	Work with your child to write a sentence for each word on a sheet of paper and circle the spelling words.

Phonics Ice Cream Cones

Place the scoops of ice cream on the cones with the same sound.

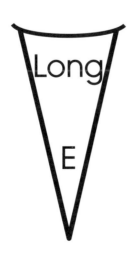

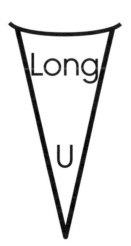

The Rude Mule

Read the poem. Then write a sentence about an animal you think is cute.

I see a mule named Pete.

He is cute as can be.

I call him, but

He will not come to me.

That is rude!

But I still want to stay

To see Pete eat a bale of hay.

I think that

Word Family Sort

Cut out the words.
Place each word under the plane belonging to its word family.

crane	kale	male	vane	tale
bale	lane	pane	pale	mane

Grade 1 • Advancing Phonics Skills 229

The Tube Race

**Read the story. Circle the words with the long u sound.
Then write a sentence about what happens next.**

It is a hot day in June.

Pete is racing Gene in the water.

Pete and Gene are floating in huge tubes.

Pete likes to compete with Gene.

The kids have fun riding their tubes in the water.

Who will win the tube race?

I think

Name _____ Date_____

Cute Flute

Read the poem.
Then write a sentence about something you think is cute.

Deke is playing some tunes.

He is using his flute.

I am taping these tunes

Because the tunes are cute.

Here you go, Deke, here's a tape!

Deke has started to eat his grapes.

I think

crane	raked
flute	raking
June	cubed
mule	sale
Pete	tune
plane	whale

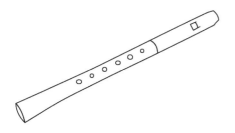

Advancing Phonics Every Day

Letter/sounds:
Long a vowel teams (ai, ay); Inflectional endings (-ed, -ing, double final consonant)

	Day 1	Day 2	Day 3
Phonological/ Phonemic Awareness	**Syllable Segmentation** — Routine 3 **Model:** explain, haystack **Practice:** raindrop, daytime, pigtail **Extra practice:** painless, runway, playing	**Onset and Rime Blending** — Routine 8 **Model:** train, clay **Practice:** snail, gray **Extra practice:** drain, pail, stray	**Phoneme Blending** — Routine 12 **Model:** braided, laying **Practice:** mailbox, Sunday, painted **Extra practice:** raining, paying, subway
Phonics	**Review previous week's sound/symbol focus: Long u and e (final e)** — Routine 17 **Model:** Pete, cute **Practice:** these, huge **Introduce sound/symbol correspondence: ai, ay** — Routine 17 **Model:** rain, day **Practice:** braid, clay **Extra practice:** main, paint, stay, stray Explain that the *ai* spelling is usually seen in the middle of a word, while the *-ay* spelling is usually at the end of a word.	**Blend words with ai, ay** — Routine 18 **Model:** mail, way **Practice:** paint, spray, play **Extra practice:** braids, train **Build words with ai, ay** — Routine 19 **Model:** hay, pay, play **Other words:** mail, nail, snail **Decodable reader: "A Snail in May"** Use decodable reader ideas (p. 23).	**Learn inflectional endings: -ed, -ing** Display and read aloud the words *shopped* and *shopping*. Point out the different endings. Use each word in a sentence, such as *The man is shopping now* and *I shopped for food yesterday.* Explain how the verb endings affect meaning. Point out that for verbs that end in a vowel and a consonant, like *shop*, we double the consonant before adding an *-ed* or *-ing* ending.
Word Families	Guide students to draw a simple five-petal flower, and write *-ail* in the middle and an *-ail* word on each petal. Repeat for the *-ain* word family.	Distribute picture cards (page 245) and letter cards to student pairs. Have students spell each word using the letter cards and write each word on their workmats. **Picture cards:** chain, nail, stain, rain, brain, train **Letter cards:** a, b, c, h, i, l, n, r, s, t	Guide students to draw a simple five-step ladder, and write *-ay* at the top and an *-ay* word on each rung.
High-Frequency Words	**Introduce high-frequency words** — Routine 20 brown, work	**Practice high-frequency words** brown, work — Routine 21 **Decodable reader: "A Snail in May"** Use decodable reader ideas (p. 23).	**Introduce high-frequency words** — Routine 20 brown, work, year, live
Writing	Have student pairs work together to write a sentence using one of the *-ail* or *-ain* words they wrote on their flowers.	Have student pairs work together to form another word using the letter cards from the word families activity, and write a sentence using the word.	Have student pairs work together to write a sentence using one of the *-ay* words they wrote on their ladders.
Spelling	**Introduce spelling words** — Routine 22 brown, brain, train, pail	**Spell words in context** — Routine 23 brown, brain, train, pail	**Introduce spelling words** — Routine 22 year, sail, spray, play
Shared Reading	**"Why Bear Has a Short Tail"** **Review long i (final e) and long u (final e)** **As you read aloud, review phonics elements:** long i (final e): *ice*; long u (final e): *use.* Have students read the words aloud with you, and emphasize the phonics element.	**"Why Bear Has a Short Tail"** **Introduce long a vowel teams (ai, ay)** As you read aloud, point out the *ai* vowel team in *tail* and *waited*, and the *ay* vowel team in *day.* Have students read the words aloud with you, and invite volunteers to use one of the words in an original sentence.	**"Why Bear Has a Short Tail"** **Review inflectional ending: -ed (no spelling change)** Point out the *-ed* ending in *asked* and *wanted.* Remind students that there is no spelling change because the words do not end in a vowel + consonant pattern. Have students read the words aloud with you, clapping the syllables.

High-Frequency Words: brown, work, year, live	Spelling: Words with -ail, -ain, -ay	Word Families: -ail, -ain, -ay

WEEK 18

Day 4	Day 5	Collaborative Learning and Independent Practice*
Phoneme Substitution `Routine 14` **Model:** mail/pail, clay/stay **Practice:** brain/stain, hay/play, nail/sail **Extra practice:** raining/training, day/stray		• Musical Chairs with Picture Cards: Words with Long a Vowel Teams Days 1–5 • Board Game: Words with Long a Vowel Teams Days 3–5
Practice inflectional endings: -ed, -ing Review the previous day's instruction on inflectional endings, including the spelling rule for words that end in a vowel and a consonant. Then work with students to add -ed and -ing endings to the word run, writing the word forms on the board as you do so. Invite volunteers to come up with oral sentences using each word. Next, have partners write -ed and -ing forms of the words *spin* and *step* and create oral sentences for each.	**Decodable reader: "A Snail in May"** Use decodable reader ideas (p. 23).	• Brush-n-Blend: Inflectional Endings Days 1–5 • Phonics-Go-Round: Inflectional Endings Days 3–5 • Read/Draw/Label a Story: "May and the Train": Long a Vowel Teams Days 3–5
Distribute the following letter cards to student pairs, and instruct them to form words in the -ay word family. Have them write the words on their workmats. **Letter cards:** a, d, m, r, s, t, w, y	**Review -ail, -ain, ay words** Distribute letter cards a, d, f, h, i, l, m, r, t, w, y. Have partners take turns building -ail, -ain, and -ay words, forming an oral sentence using the word.	• Word Family Scramble: Long a Vowel Teams Days 1–5 • Word Family Picture Labels: Long a Vowel Teams Days 3–5 • Word Family Spinner: Long a (-ay) Days 3–5
Practice high-frequency words `Routine 21` brown, work, year, live	**Decodable reader: "A Snail in May"** Use decodable reader ideas (p. 23).	• High-Frequency Words Bug Catch Days 1–5 • High-Frequency Words Carnival Game Days 3–5
Have student pairs work together to form another word using the letter cards from the word families activity, and write a sentence using the word.	**Interactive Writing** (see p. 22) **Story starter:** Sam and June went to the beach. **Word bank:** clay, pail, play, rain, snail, spray	• Reading/Writing: Respond to the Story "Hay for May" Days 1–5 • Reading/Writing: Continue the Story "At the Lake" Days 3–5
Spell words in context `Routine 23` year, sail, spray, play	**Test words in dictation** Read aloud each of the week's eight spelling words. Then collect and review students' work.	• Spelling Homework: BLM 1 Days 1–5
"What Do Animals Eat?" **Review /e/, /u/, /r/** As you read aloud, review phonics elements: initial /e/: *elephants*; medial /u/: *hunt*; initial /r/: *rabbits*. Have students read each word aloud with you, clapping the syllables.	**"What Do Animals Eat?"** **Review /u/, /b/, /h/** As you read aloud, review phonics elements: initial /h/: *Here, hunt*; initial /b/: *both*. Have students read each word aloud with you, emphasizing the phonics elements.	

* Use this menu to plan extra practice and center activities for use through the week. All the skills needed for an activity have been introduced by the first day of the range shown. See pages 236–237 for full descriptions.

Collaborative Learning and Independent Practice

Phonological/Phonemic Awareness Activities

Musical Chairs:
Words with Long a Vowel Teams
Use on Days 1–5

Set up a circle of chairs. Place a picture card of an object with a long a vowel team on all the chairs except for one. On this remaining chair, place a picture card of an object without a long a vowel team. Say the long a vowel sound over and over as students walk in a circle. When you stop, instruct students to sit and name the object on their chair's picture card. The student who gets a picture card of an object without a long a vowel sound is out.

Some picture cards with long a vowel words to use include:

- **crayon, hay, May, tray**

- **rain, train, chain, nail**

Board Game:
Words with Long a Vowel Teams
Use on Days 3–5

Provide small groups of students with game pieces and a board from a board game. Instruct students to take turns rolling a number cube. Players must say a certain number of words with the long a vowel depending on the number he or she rolled. Then the student can move ahead the same number of spaces. (For example, if a student rolls a two, the student might say "brain" and "May" and then move two spaces.)

ᴬᴮC)) Phonics Activities

Brush-n-Blend:
Inflectional Endings
Use on Days 1–5

On squares of heavy paper, use a white crayon to write decodable words containing the inflectional endings -ed or -ing. Provide these papers to students along with a paint brush and watered-down paint. Instruct students to paint the paper from left to right. As students "discover" each letter, they should practice sounding out the word.

Phonics-Go-Round:
Inflectional Endings
Use on Days 3–5

Organize groups of students. Assign each group an inflectional ending (-ed or -ing). Instruct students to take turns going around the circle identifying words that contain these inflectional endings.

Read/Draw/Label a Story:
"May and the Train": Long a Vowel Teams
Use on Days 3–5

Place copies of BLM 5 (page 242) in a center. Have student pairs take turns reading the story. Then have them complete the drawing activity.

Word Family Activities

Word Family Scramble:
Long a Vowel Teams
Use on Days 1–5

Distribute BLM 2 (page 239) and have students complete the long a vowel team word family activity.

Word Family Picture Labels:
Long a Vowel Teams
Use on Days 3–5

Distribute BLM 4 (page 241) and have students complete the long a vowel team word family activity.

Word Family Spinner:
Long a (-ay)
Use on Days 3–5

Prepare copies of BLM B (word family spinner) for use with the -ay word family. Write the letters d, h, m, p, and s on the dial and place the spinner in a center. Have partners alternate turning the dial to make words. One partner makes a word and says it aloud. The other partner then uses the word in an oral sentence.

High-Frequency Word Activities

High-Frequency Words Bug Catch
Use on Days 1–5

Gather Benchmark Advance high-frequency word cards for a game of Bug Catch.

Use review words from previous weeks as well as the current week's words.

- **brown / work / year / live / house / long / off / small**

Place the word cards face-up on the floor or table. Provide pairs of students with fly swatters. Tell students to take turns. One student says a high-frequency word aloud, and the other student needs to swat it.

High-Frequency Words Carnival Game
Use on Days 3–5

Write the current week's high-frequency words on four paper or plastic cups, one word per cup. Draw a star on two more cups.

- **brown / work / year / live**

Then stack the cups in a tower (three cups in the first row, two cups balanced on that row, and one cup on top). Students should take turns throwing a bean bag to try to knock down as many cups as possible in one try. Students should read the high-frequency words on the cups they knock down.

Writing Activities

Reading/Writing:
Respond to the Story "Hay in May"
Use on Days 1–5

Provide copies of BLM 3 (page 240) and have students use the sentence starter to write about the story.

Reading/Writing:
Continue the Story "At the Lake"
Use on Days 3–5

Provide copies of BLM 6 (page 243) and have students complete the writing activity.

Spelling Homework

Read each spelling word aloud with your child. Spell it aloud together. Then ask your child to write each spelling word and say it in a sentence.

brain _____

sail _____

train _____

spray _____

pail _____

play _____

brown _____

year _____

Choose a different activity every day to practice this week's spelling words at home with your child.

Flashlight writing	Letter tiles	Write it again	Remember the word	Circle the word
Turn out the lights. Use a flashlight to spell each word on the wall.	Use letter tiles to spell the words and then write the words on a sheet of paper.	Have your child write the word three times on a sheet of paper and circle the vowels.	Turn the paper over and write the word from memory.	Work with your child to write a sentence for each word on a sheet of paper and circle the spelling words.

Word Family Scramble

Cut on the dotted lines. Make a picture with each strip.
Read the word you see on the strip.

ai | t | n | r

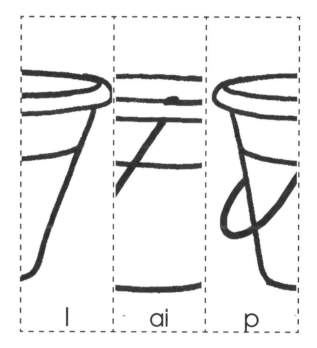

l | ai | p

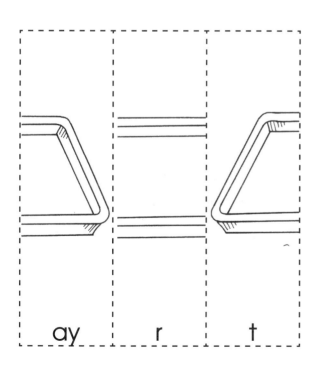

ay | r | t

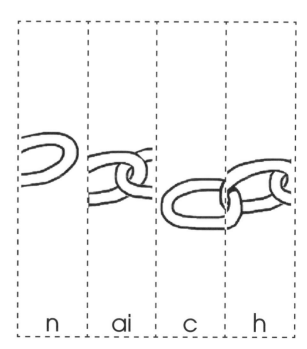

n | ai | c | h

Hay in May

Read the story.
Then write a sentence about something you do in May.

We raise hens.

In May, we cut the hay.

If we wait, the hay will get too brown.

After we cut the hay, we put it into bales.

The hens use the hay to lay their eggs.

Then we give the hens a pail of grain.

In May, I _____

_____

_____

_____

_____

Word Family Picture Labels

Say the name of the picture aloud.
Write the beginning of the word below each picture.

ail

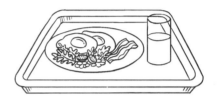

ay

ail

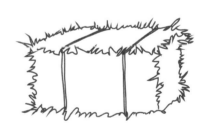

ay

May and the Train

Read the story.
Draw a picture to tell what happens next.

May waits for a train in the rain.

She is on her way to work.

She bites her nails.

Will the train be late?

Will she stay here all day?

May can see the train!

She will not be late.

At the Lake

Read the story. Then write a sentence about something else you can do at the lake.

I am at the lake.

The sun shines on my face.

I sail my little ship.

I fill my pail with water.

I see snails make trails in the sand.

I could stay at the lake the whole day.

crayon	paint
hay	May
tray	stain
brain	braid
rain	train
chain	nail

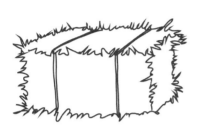

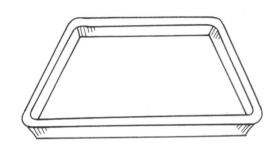

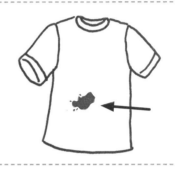

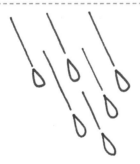

Advancing Phonics Every Day

Letters/sounds:
Long o vowel teams and single letters (o, oa, ow, oe)

	Day 1	Day 2	Day 3
Phonological/ Phonemic Awareness	**Syllable Segmentation** `Routine 3` **Model:** program, oboe **Practice:** goldfish, oatmeal, elbow **Extra practice:** download, banjo	**Syllable Blending** `Routine 4` **Model:** window, cargo **Practice:** yellow, open, shadow **Extra practice:** program, follow	**Phoneme Blending** `Routine 12` **Model:** boat, mow **Practice:** goat, bowl, toe **Extra practice:** snow, float
Phonics	**Review previous week's sound/symbol focus** `Routine 17` **Model:** lay, train **Practice:** spray, braid, paint, nail **Extra practice:** rain, plain, play, trail **Introduce sound/symbol correspondence: oa, ow, oe** `Routine 17` **Model:** oak, mow **Practice:** soak, crow, toe **Extra practice:** snow, road	**Blend words with oa, ow, oe** `Routine 18` **Model:** groan, bowl **Practice:** window, roast **Extra practice:** elbow, coach **Build words with oa, ow, oe** `Routine 19` **Model:** coat, coast, roast **Other words:** low, flow, glow **Decodable reader: "Go Slow, Go Fast"** Use decodable reader ideas (p. 23).	**Blend words with o, oa, ow, oe** `Routine 18` **Model:** foam, pillow **Practice:** load, grow, show, fold **Extra practice:** cold, roast Explain that the *oa* spelling is usually seen in the middle of words, while the *ow* and *oe* spellings are usually at the end of words.
Word Families	Guide students to draw a simple house outline with triangle roof and square house. Divide the house into four equal squares. Have them write -*ow* in the roof and an -*ow* word in each square. Repeat for the -*oat* family.	Distribute letter cards to student pairs, and instruct them to form words in the -*ow* word family. Have them write their words on their workmats. Repeat for the -*oat* word family. **Letter cards:** a, b, c, f, g, l, o, t, w	Guide students to fold their papers into six equal boxes, and write an -*old* word in each box.
High-Frequency Words	**Introduce high-frequency words** found, your `Routine 20`	**Practice high-frequency words** found, your `Routine 21` **Decodable reader: "Go Slow, Go Fast"** Use decodable reader ideas (p. 23).	**Introduce high-frequency words** know, always `Routine 20`
Writing	Have student pairs work together to form another word using the letter cards from the Word Families activity and write a sentence using the word.	Have student pairs work together to write a sentence using one of the –*ow* words they made in the Word Families activity. Repeat the activity using one of the -*oat* words.	Have student pairs work together to write a sentence using one of the words they wrote in the Word Families activity.
Spelling	**Introduce spelling words** `Routines 20, 22` found, row, glow, float	**Spell words in context** `Routines 21, 23` found, row, glow, float	**Introduce spelling words** `Routines 20, 22` your, hold, cold, gold
Shared Reading	**"Horses to the Rescue"** **Review long a vowel teams (ay, ain)** As you read aloud, review phonics elements, long a vowel teams (*ay, ain*). Have students read the word aloud with you, and emphasize the phonics element.	**"Horses to the Rescue"** **Review long o vowel teams and single letters (oa, o)** As you read aloud, review phonics element long o vowel teams and single letters (*oa, o*) (*groaned, road, going*). Have volunteers read each word aloud with you, and use the word in an original sentence.	**"Horses to the Rescue"** **Review inflectional endings -ed, -ing** Point out the words with inflectional endings -*ed, -ing* (*tossed, pulled*). Have students use one of the words in an original sentence.

High-Frequency Words:	Spelling:	Word Families:
found, your, know, always	Words with -ow, -oat, -old	-ow, -oat, -old

Day 4	Day 5	Collaborative Learning and Independent Practice*
Phoneme Addition Routine 15 Model: oat, coat Practice: row, grow, low, glow Extra practice: old, fold		• Elkonin Boxes: Words with Long o Sounds Days 1–5 • Phonemic Picnic: Words with Long o Sounds Days 3–5
Blend words with o, oa, ow, oe Routine 18 Model: soap, flow Practice: blow, loan, flown Extra practice: cocoa, row **Build words with o, oa, ow, oe** Routine 19 Model: bow, blow, blown Practice: row, grow, grown Extra practice: bowl, bowled, bowling	**Decodable reader: "Go Slow, Go Fast"** Use decodable reader ideas (p. 23).	• Phonics Beanbag Toss: Words with Long o Vowel Teams and Single Letters (ow, oa) Days 1–5 • Letter Cup Substitution: Words with Long o Vowel Teams and Single Letters (o, oa, ow, oe) Days 3–5 • Read/Draw/Label: "The Cold Road": Words with Long o Sounds Days 3–5
Distribute the following letter cards to student pairs, and instruct them to form words in the -old word family. Have them write the words on their workmats. Letter cards: b, c, d, l, m, o, s, t	Review -ow, -oat, -old words. Distribute picture and letter cards (pages 256–257) to student pairs. Have students spell words and write them on their workmats. Picture cards: boat, bow, cold, goat, grow, shadow Letter cards: a, b, c, d, g, h, l, o, r, s, t, w	• Word Family Board Game: -ow, -oat Days 1–5 • Feed the Creatures: -ow, -oat, -old Days 3–5
Practice high-frequency words Routine 21 found, your, know, always	**Decodable reader: "Go Slow, Go Fast"** Use decodable reader ideas (p. 23).	• High-Frequency Words Chatterbox Days 1–5 • High-Frequency Words Graph Days 3–5
Have student pairs work together to write a sentence using one of the -old words they made in the Word Families activity.	**Interactive writing** (see p. 22) Story starter: He floated in the boat. Word bank: row, old, cold, coast, shallow, toe	• Reading/Writing: Continue the Story "The Toad's Joke" Days 1–5 • Reading/Writing: Respond to the Poem "Old Joe" Days 3–5
Spell words in context Routines 21, 23 your, hold, cold, gold	**Test words in dictation** Read out the spelling words for students to write. Then review their work.	• Spelling Homework: BLM 1 Days 1–5
"The First Cars" **Introduce long o vowel teams (oa, ow)** As you read aloud, point out the long o vowel teams (oa, ow) words (road, slow). Have students read the words aloud with you, and invite volunteers to use one of the words in an original sentence.	**"The First Cars"** **Review inflectional ending –ed** As you read aloud, point out the words with inflectional ending –ed. Have student volunteers use one of the words in an original sentence.	

* Use this menu to plan extra practice and center activities for use through the week. All the skills needed for an activity have been introduced by the first day of the range shown. See pages 248–249 for full descriptions.

Collaborative Learning and Independent Practice

Phonological/Phonemic Awareness Activities

Elkonin Boxes:
Words with Long o Sounds
Use on Days 1–5

Provide the week's twelve picture cards (page 257). For each card, have students sound out the word, sliding a counter into a cell of an Elkonin box for each individual phoneme. Students can do this individually, or partners can take turns choosing from the picture cards.

Phonemic Picnic:
Words with Long o Sounds
Use on Days 3–5

Fill a picnic basket (or lunch box) with toy foods. Each food should contain the long o sound (and, if desired, phonemes from previous weeks) (for example: *coconut, macaroni, mango, oatmeal, okra, pepperoni, roast beef, toast, tofu, tomato*). Have partners sit on the floor as if ready for a picnic. They should take turns choosing a food, saying the name of the food, and passing it to their partner to "eat."

Phonics Activities

Phonics Beanbag Toss:
Words with Long o Vowel Teams and Single Letters (ow, oa)
Use on Days 1–5

Arrange the eight picture cards for words with long o spelled *ow* and *oa* (page 257) for a beanbag toss. Provide the word cards, and have students take turns reading a word aloud and tossing the beanbag to the corresponding picture.

Letter Cup Substitution:
Words with Long o Vowel Teams and Single Letters (o, oa, ow, oe)
Use on Days 3–5

Provide plastic cups with a letter, digraph, or vowel team written on the outside of each. Place upside-down cups in a row to spell a word. Have partners take turns fitting other cups over one of the original cups, making a new word. Students should read each word aloud and record it on a phonics house (BLM A) before continuing. Examples:

- **starting word: bow / substitute initial letter: fl, gl, gr, l, m, sh, t**
- **starting word: boat / substitute initial letter: c, fl, g, m**
- **starting word: doe / substitute initial letter: h, J, t**

Read/Draw/Label:
"The Cold Road" Long o Sounds
Use on Days 3–5

Place copies of BLM 5 (page 254) in the center. Have student pairs take turns reading the poem. Then have students complete the drawing and labeling activity.

Word Family Activities

 # High-Frequency Word Activities

 # Writing Activities

Word Family Board Game: -ow, -oat
Use on Days 1–5

Label the squares of BLM D with words and directions, making a path from START to FINISH. (Repeat words and directions as necessary.) Words and directions might include:

- **bow, blow, flow, grow, low, boat, coat, float, goat, moat, cone, bone, nose, rose, hot, log, spot, joke, poke, woke**
- **"Move back two spaces"**
- **"Move forward five spaces"**
- **"Spin again"**
- **"Skip your next turn"**
- **"Switch squares with another player"**

Place the prepared BLM D, a spinner (BLM B), and disks or coins for playing pieces in the center. Students play by spinning the spinner to advance. If they land on a space that has an *–ow* or *–oat* word family word, they use it in an oral sentence and spin again. If the word is not from an *–ow* or *–oat* word family, the next player spins. Students also follow directions on the squares that have them.

Feed the Creatures: -ow, -oat, -old
Use on Days 3–5

Provide two small plastic bins. Label each with a word family, *–ow, –oat,* or *–old.* Use a marker to make eyes or a face on each bin to turn the bins into creatures. Provide partners with the following *–ow, –oat,* and *–old* picture cards, and have them take turns "feeding" the creatures the appropriate cards:

- **bow / grow / shadow / boat / goat / road / cold / coat**

High-Frequency Words Chatterbox
Use on Days 1–5

Fold BLM 2 (page 251) to form a "chatterbox." (See directions on page 390.) Instruct students to play with a partner. One student chooses a word on an outside flap, says the word, and spells it aloud while the other student opens and closes the chatterbox for each letter in the word. Then the other student should pick a word on an inside flap, says the word, and spells it aloud. Finally, the first student should open that flap and form an oral sentence using the word that is found there.

High-Frequency Words Graph
Use on Days 3–5

Provide students with BLM 4 (page 253) and have them complete the activity.

Reading/Writing: Continue the Story "The Toad's Joke"
Use on Days 1–5

Provide copies of BLM 3 (page 252) and have students write about what happens next in the story.

Reading/Writing: Respond to the Poem "Old Joe"
Use on Days 3–5

Provide copies of BLM 6 (page 255) and have students write about something they like very much.

Spelling Homework

Read each spelling word aloud with your child. Spell it aloud together. Then ask your child to write each spelling word and say it in a sentence.

found _____   your _____

row _____   hold _____

glow _____   cold _____

float _____   gold _____

Choose a different activity every day to practice this week's spelling words at home with your child.

Flashlight writing	Trace the word	Multi-colored words	Remember the word	Circle the word
Turn out the lights. Use a flashlight to spell each word on the wall.	Write the word with dotted lines on a sheet of paper, and then trace the dots with a different color.	Write the spelling words with crayons or colored pencils, using a different color for each letter.	Turn the paper over and write the word from memory.	Work with your child to write a sentence for each word on a sheet of paper and circle the spelling words.

High-Frequency Words Chatterbox

Listen to the directions from your teacher.

her

house

brown

try

year

your

long

found

small

live

large

off

far

call

after

give

The Toad's Joke

Read the story. Write a sentence about what the goat does next.

The goat was on the road.

The road led to a moat.

A moat is like a lake.

The goat didn't see the moat.

The goat fell in the moat!

A toad saw the goat go in the moat.

The toad asked: "Do you want soap?"

"No!" said the goat.

Then, the goat

BLM
4

High-Frequency Words Graph

**How many letters are in each word? Write the words below the graph.
Color in the graph for each word.**

found	your	know	always

6				
5				
4				
3				
2				
1				

The Cold Road

Read the poem. Then draw a picture to show a part of the poem. Label anything in your picture that has a long o sound.

The day of the snow

I put on my coat,

And went for a stroll on the road.

By the end of the road,

My toes were so cold

That I came home to sit by the stove.

Old Joe

Read the poem.
Then write a sentence about something you like very much.

Old Joe was a little crow

With one goal in life:

To get gold rings, or yellow strings,

Or just old things that shined.

He dove into a pond of golden fish!

But they had no gold, you know.

I just hope Old Joe did not try to go

And get that shining gold sun.

boat	mow
bow	grow
cold	no
coat	road
go	shadow
goat	toe

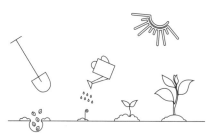

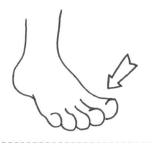

Advancing Phonics Every Day

Letters/sounds: Long e vowel teams and single letters (e, ee, ea, ie), prefixes un-, re-

	Day 1	Day 2	Day 3
Phonological/ Phonemic Awareness	**Rhyme Recognition** — Routine 5 **Model:** me/we, tree/see, eat/meat **Practice:** beach/teach, shield/field, tea/sea, three/free **Extra practice:** achieve/believe, team/dream	**Rhyme Production** — Routine 6 **Model:** seat/treat, niece/piece **Practice:** feet/meet, bee/fee, pea/tea, **Extra practice:** peach/beach, keeper/deeper	**Phoneme Categorization** — Routine 13 **Model:** seat/set/heat, me/we/wet **Practice:** Tim/tee/fee, meal/seal/mile, teach/tongue/beach **Extra practice:** wield/wild/yield, him/team/seam
Phonics	**Review previous week's sound/symbol focus** — Routine 17 **Model:** roast, mow **Practice:** go, flow, told, toad **Extra practice:** below, oat, fold **Introduce sound/symbol correspondence: e, ee, ea, ie** — Routine 17 **Model:** fee, brief **Practice:** weep, steam, field, be **Extra practice:** keep, beach	**Blend words with e, ee, ea, ie** — Routine 18 **Model:** chief, dream **Practice:** treat, three, brief **Extra practice:** season, green **Build words with e, ee, ea, ie** — Routine 19 **Model:** beam, seam, steam **Other words:** heel, peel, feel, feet **Decodable reader: "Read a USA Time Line"** Use decodable reader ideas (p. 23)	**Introduce prefixes un-, re-** — Routine 18 **Model:** unreal, reheat **Practice:** unkind, unlike, repeat, reread **Extra practice:** unpack, replay Explain to students that a prefix is added to the beginning of a word to change its meaning. The prefix -un means "not," and the prefix -re means "again." Demonstrate with clip: clip, unclip, reclip. Note that prefix -re is an open syllable, meaning it is not closed in with a consonant.
Word Families	Distribute letter cards to student pairs, and instruct them to form words in the -eat word family. Have them write their words on their workmats. **Letter cards:** a, b, e, h, m, n, s, t	Guide students to draw a five-branch tree, and write -eat in the trunk and an -eat word on each branch.	Distribute picture and letter cards (pages 268–269) to student pairs. Have them spell each -eet, -eed word using the letter cards and write each word on their workmats. **Picture cards:** feed, feet, seeds, tweet **Letter cards:** d, e, e, f, s, s, t, t, w
High-Frequency Words	**Introduce high-frequency words** all, people — Routine 20	**Practice high-frequency words** all, people — Routine 21 **Decodable reader: "Read a USA Time Line"** Use decodable reader ideas (p. 23)	**Introduce high-frequency words** where, draw — Routine 20
Writing	Have student pairs work together to form another word using the letter cards from the word families activity and write a sentence using the word.	Have student pairs work together to write a sentence using one of the -eat words they made in the word families activity.	Have student pairs work together to write a sentence using one of the words they wrote in the word families activity.
Spelling	**Introduce spelling words** — Routines 20, 22 all, treat, seed, bleed	**Spell words in context** — Routines 21, 23 all, treat, seed, bleed	**Introduce spelling words** — Routines 20, 22 people, street, reheat, unleash
Shared Reading	**"The U.S. in Space"** Review long o vowel teams and single letters (o, ow): go, showing Have students read the word aloud emphasizing the phonics element. As you read aloud, review long o vowel team ow and single letter o: go, showing.	**"The U.S. in Space"** Introduce long e vowel teams (ee, ea) As you read aloud, point out the long a vowel team (ee, ea) words three, team. Have students read the words aloud with you, and invite volunteers to use one of the words in an original sentence.	**"The U.S. in Space"** Review long a vowel team (ay) As you read aloud, point out the ay vowel team in way, today, day. Have students use one of the words in an original sentence.

High-Frequency Words:	Spelling:	Word Families:
all, people, where, draw	Words with -eat, -eet, -eed	-eat, -eet, -eed

Day 4	Day 5	Collaborative Learning and Independent Practice*
Phoneme Substitution `Routine 14` **Model:** beat/heat, bee/see **Practice:** meat/seat, neat/feat **Extra practice:** reach/teach, niece/piece		• Phonemic Word Sort: Words with Long e Sounds Days 1–5 • Phonemic Concentration: Words with Long e Sounds; Prefixes un-, re- Days 3–5
Blend words with prefixes un-, re- `Routine 18` **Model:** unripe, repaint **Practice:** unchain, reteach **Extra practice:** reuse, untuck **Build words with prefixes un-, re-** `Routine 19` **Model:** pack, unpack, repack **Practice:** stack, unstack, restack **Extra practice:** lock, unlock, relock, relocking	**Decodable reader: "Read a USA Time Line"** Use decodable reader ideas (p. 23).	• Phonics Crossword: Words with Long e Vowel Teams and Single Letters (e, ee, ea, ie) Days 1–5 • Picture Word Matching: Words with Long e Vowel Teams and Single Letters (e, ee, ea, ie) Days 3–5 • Read/Draw/Label: "Bedtime Reading": Long e Sounds Days 3–5
Distribute the following letter cards to student pairs, and instruct them to form words in the -eat, -eed word families. Have them write the words on their workmats. **Letter cards:** a, b, d, e, f, h, s, t	**Review -eat, -eet, -eed words** Distribute picture cards (page 269) to student pairs. Have them sort the words by word family. **Picture cards:** feed, feet, beans, tweet, seat, seeds, beet, sleep	• Word Family Picture Labels: -eat Days 1–5 • Word Family Tic-Tac-Toe: -eet, -eed Days 3–5 • Word Family Spinners/Sliders: -eat, -eet, -eed Days 3–5
Practice high-frequency words `Routine 21` all, people, where, draw	**Decodable reader: "Read a USA Time Line"** Use decodable reader ideas (p. 23).	• High-Frequency Words Beanbag Toss Days 1–5 • High-Frequency Words Bug Catch Days 3–5
Have student pairs work together to write a sentence using one of the -eat, -eed words they made in the word families activity.	**Interactive writing** (see p. 22) **Story starter:** She picked a peach. **Word bank:** tree, see, eat, field, be, seat, treat	• Reading/Writing: Respond to the Story "What to Eat?" Days 1–5 • Reading/Writing: Respond to the Poem "The Grass" Days 3–5
Spell words in context `Routines 21, 23` people, street, reheat, unleash	**Test words in dictation** Read out the spelling words for students to write. Then review their work.	• Spelling Homework: BLM 1 Days 1–5
"But Children Had Fun Anyway" **Review long a vowel teams (ai, ay)** As you read aloud, review phonics element long a vowel teams (ai, ay). Point out *play, anyway, pail.*	**"But Children Had Fun Anyway"** **Review long e vowel team (ee)** As you read aloud, point out the word with long e vowel team (ee): *seek.* Have student volunteers use one of the words in an original sentence.	

* Use this menu to plan extra practice and center activities for use through the week. All the skills needed for an activity have been introduced by the first day of the range shown. See pages 260–261 for full descriptions.

© Benchmark Education Company, LLC   Grade 1 • Advancing Phonics Skills   259

Collaborative Learning and Independent Practice

Phonological/Phonemic Awareness Activities

Phonemic Word Sort:
Words with Long e Sounds
Use on Days 1–5

Distribute copies of the week's twelve picture cards (page 269). Have pairs of students work together to sort the cards by initial sound:

- feed / feet
- beans / beet
- seat / seeds / sleep

Elicit from students that all of the words contain the long e sound.

Phonemic Concentration:
Words with Long e Sounds; Prefixes un-, re-
Use on Days 3–5

Provide students with a set of the week's picture cards (page 269), two of each card, for a total of twenty-four cards. Instruct partners to arrange the cards face down to form a 6 x 4 grid to play a concentration game. The partners should alternate turning over two cards per turn. When a student uncovers a matching pair, he/she should use the word in an oral sentence and keep the pair of cards. The student who collects the most pairs wins the game.

Phonics Activities

Phonics Crossword:
Words with Long e Vowel Teams and Single Letters (e, ee, ea, ie)
Use on Days 1–5

Provide students with BLM 2 (page 263) and have them complete the crossword activity.

Picture Word Matching:
Words with Long e Vowel Teams and Single Letters (e, ee, ea, ie)
Use on Days 3–5

Provide students with the week's twenty-four picture and word cards (pages 268–269). Have students match each picture to its word and then sort all the cards by long e spelling. (*feed/feet/seeds/beet/sheep/tweet/sleep, beans/seat, shield*)

Read/Draw/Label:
"Bedtime Reading":
Long e Sounds
Use on Days 3–5

Place copies of BLM 5 (page 266) in a center. Have student pairs take turns reading the story. Then have students complete the drawing and labeling activity.

 Word Family Activities

Word Family Picture Labels: -eat
Use on Days 1–5

Provide students with BLM 4 (page 265) and a word slider (BLM C) for the *–eat* word family. Have students use the slider to form word family words and complete the activity.

Word Family Tic-Tac-Toe: -eet, -eed
Use on Days 3–5

Provide or have students draw a tic-tac-toe board. Have partners play tic-tac-toe using words belonging to the *–eet* and *–eed* word families. One partner will use *–eet* words instead of an X to mark his/her spots on the board. The other partner will use *–eed* words instead of an O.

Word Family Spinners/Sliders: -eat, -eet, -eed
Use on Days 3–5

Construct three word spinners (BLM B), one for each of the week's word families. Write the word family on the long rectangular piece and initial letters around the circle. Provide copies of the phonics house (BLM A) and have students label the houses *-eat*, *-eet*, and *-eed*. Ask students to form words using the spinners and to list each word they form in the appropriate word family house. (This activity may also use word sliders [BLM C] instead of spinners.)

 High-Frequency Word Activities

High-Frequency Words Beanbag Toss
Use on Days 1–5

Gather Benchmark Advance high-frequency word cards for a beanbag toss. Use review words from previous weeks as well as the current week's words.

- **all / always / because / call / do / found / give / know / look / now / people / your**

Have one student choose a word to read aloud, and another to toss the bag to cover the matching card.

High-Frequency Words Bug Catch
Use on Days 3–5

Write a series of high-frequency words, from this week and previous weeks, on index cards, and place the index cards on the floor or on a table. Then provide a pair of students with plastic fly swatters. Instruct students to take turns: One student should read a high-frequency word aloud, and then the other student should "swat" it.

Writing Activities

Reading/Writing: Respond to the Story "What to Eat?"
Use on Days 1–5

Provide copies of BLM 3 (page 264) and have students write a sentence about what they like to eat.

Reading/Writing: Respond to the Poem "The Grass"
Use on Days 3–5

Provide copies of BLM 6 (page 267) and have students write about someplace they like to go.

Spelling Homework

Read each spelling word aloud with your child. Spell it aloud together. Then ask your child to write each spelling word and say it in a sentence.

all _____   people _____

treat _____   street _____

seed _____   reheat _____

bleed _____   unleash _____

Choose a different activity every day to practice this week's spelling words at home with your child.

Trace the word	Two-toned words	Write it	Letter tiles	Circle the word
Write the word with dotted lines on a sheet of paper, and then trace the dots with a different color.	Write the spelling words with crayons or colored markers. Use one color for consonants and another for vowels.	Write the word on a sheet of paper, saying aloud each letter as you write it.	Use letter tiles to spell the words and then write the words on a sheet of paper.	Write one sentence for each word and circle the spelling words.

Phonics Crossword

Complete the crossword puzzle. Fill in the words for the pictures shown.

Word Bank
field
feed
seeds
heat

What to Eat?

Read the story. Write a sentence about what you like to eat.

My dog Chief likes to eat meat.

Chief eats beef when it's time for a meal.

He gets treats for doing tricks like a seal.

My rabbit Bree does not eat meat.

She likes peaches, peas, and beets.

She likes seeds the least.

What do you like to eat?

I like

Word Family Picture Labels

Say the name of the picture aloud.
Write the beginning of the word below each picture.

_ _ _ _ _ _ _ eat

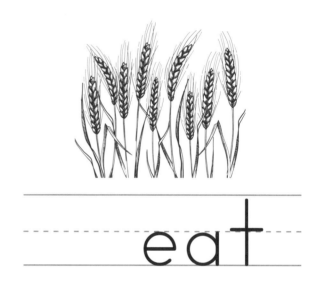

_ _ _ _ _ _ _ eat

_ _ _ _ _ _ _ eat

_ _ _ _ _ _ _ eat

Bedtime Reading

Read the story. Then draw a picture to show a part of the story.
Label anything in your picture that has a long e sound.

"Read to us, please," said Dee.

She wanted to go to sleep.

Bea was brushing her teeth.

"What will it be?" asked Mom.

"The Three Pigs? The Cheese Thief?"

"No, those give us bad dreams!" said Dee.

So they asked Mom to reread

The tales from last week.

The Grass

Read the story.
Then write a sentence about someplace you like to go.

I unzip my coat

and sit by the stream.

I take off my socks

and feel the grass under my feet.

It is so green and smells so sweet.

This is a feeling I would like to repeat!

_____

- -

_____

- -

_____

- -

_____

feed	seat
feet	seeds
sheep	tweet
beans	sleep
beet	unzip
refill	shield

Grade 1 • Advancing Phonics Skills   269

Word Cards/Picture Cards

Advancing Phonics Every Day

Letters/sounds: long i vowel teams and single letters (i, y, igh)

	Day 1	Day 2	Day 3
Phonological/ Phonemic Awareness	**Syllable Segmentation** `Routine 3` **Model:** pilot, lightning, crying **Practice:** idea, drying, delight **Extra practice:** final, mighty, cycle	**Rhyme Recognition** `Routine 5` Model: dry, cry, try Practice: bright, slight, fright Extra practice: magnify, multiply	**Phoneme Recognition** `Routine 9` Model: item/ivy/idea, fight/fries/fine **Practice:** by/cry/fly, plight/fright/tight **Extra practice:** silent/pilot/tiger, bright/sight/night
Phonics	**Review previous week's sound/symbol focus (ee, ea, ie)** `Routine 17` **Model:** piece, sea **Practice:** steam, field, fee, greet **Extra practice:** niece, chief **Introduce sound/symbol correspondence (i, y, igh)** `Routine 17` **Model:** why, sight **Practice:** by, thigh, bright **Extra practice:** spying, retry	**Blend words with i, y, igh** `Routine 18` **Model:** high, by **Practice:** sky, flight, why, tie **Extra practice:** cry, right **Build words with i, y, igh** `Routine 19` **Model:** sigh, sight, slight **Other words:** try, retry, retrying **Decodable reader: "High in the Sky"** Use decodable reader ideas (p. 23).	**Introduce open syllables** `Routine 18` **Model:** robot, item **Practice:** silent, hotel, July **Extra practice:** giant, relax Explain to students that an open syllable ends in a vowel. It is not closed in by a consonant. That means the vowel sound is long. Use these examples: *sill* (closed), *silent* (open/closed).
Word Families	Distribute letter cards to student pairs, and instruct them to form words in the *-ight* word family. Have them write their words on their workmats. **Letter cards:** b, g, h, i, m, r, s, t	Guide students to draw a simple word web, and write *-ight* in the center circle and an *-ight* word on each satellite circle.	Distribute picture cards (page 281) and letter cards to student pairs. Have students spell each *-ice, -ile* word with letter cards and write each word on their workmats. **Picture cards:** dice, mice, smile **Letter cards:** c, d, e, i, l, m, s
High-Frequency Words	**Introduce high-frequency words** `Routine 20` again, round	**Practice high-frequency words** again, round `Routine 21` **Decodable reader: "High in the Sky"** Use decodable reader ideas (p. 23).	**Introduce high-frequency words** `Routine 20` they, country
Writing	Have student pairs work together to form another word using the letter cards from the word families activity and write a sentence using the word.	Have student pairs work together to write a sentence using one of the *-ight* words they made in the word families activity.	Have student pairs work together to write a sentence using one of the words they wrote in the word families activity.
Spelling	**Introduce spelling words** `Routines 20, 22` again, bright, item, fright	**Spell words in context** `Routines 21, 23` again, bright, item, fright	**Introduce spelling words** `Routines 20, 22` round, mice, mile, smile
Shared Reading	**"The Washington Monument"** **Review long e vowel team (ea)** As you read aloud, review phonics elements, long e vowel team (ea): *reaches, each*. Have students read the word aloud with you, and emphasize the phonics elements.	**"The Washington Monument"** **Review high-frequency words: people, year** As you read aloud, point out high-frequency words *people, year*. Have students read the words aloud with you, and invite volunteers to use them in an original sentence.	**"The Washington Monument"** **Introduce high-frequency word: country's** As you read aloud, point out the high-frequency word *country* and its possessive form. Ask student volunteers to use the possessive form of the word in an original sentence.

High-Frequency Words:	Spelling:	Word Families:
again, round, they, country	Words with -ight, -ice, -ile	-ight, -ice, -ile

Day 4	Day 5	Collaborative Learning and Independent Practice*
Phoneme Categorization `Routine 13` **Model:** item/evil/idol, pry/fry/free **Practice:** sight/sit/size, Tim/tight/time **Extra practice:** giant/lion/peacock, fin/fight/fine		• Elkonin Boxes: Words with Long i Sounds Days 1–5 • Phonemic Picnic: Words with Long i Sounds Days 3–5
Blend words with open syllables `Routine 18` Model: student **Practice:** minus, pilot, locate **Extra practice:** cider, virus **Build words with i, y, igh** `Routine 19` **Model:** high, thigh **Practice:** right, fright, frighten **Extra practice:** wild, wildlife	**Decodable reader: "High in the Sky"** Use decodable reader ideas (p. 23).	• Phonics Word Builder: Words with Long i Vowel Teams and Single Letters (i, ie, y, igh) Days 1–5 • Phonics Concentration: Words with Open Syllables; Long i Vowel Teams and Single Letters (i, ie, y, igh) Days 3–5 • Read/Draw/Label: "Night Light": Long i Sounds Days 3–5
Guide students to fold their papers into four squares. Have them write an -ice word in each square. Repeat with -ile words.	**Review -ight, -ice, -ile words** Distribute letter cards to student pairs. Have partners take turns building -ight, -ice, -ile words, and writing them on their workmats. **Letter cards:** c, d, e, f, g, h, i, l, m, r, s, t	• Word Family Scramble: -ight Days 1–5 • Word Family Towers: -ice Days 3–5 • Word Family Books: -ile Days 3–5
Practice high-frequency words `Routine 21` again, round, they, country	**Decodable reader: "High in the Sky"** Use decodable reader ideas (p. 23).	• High-Frequency Words Yoga Days 1–5 • High-Frequency Words Board Game Days 3–5
Have student pairs work together to write a sentence using one of the -ice or -ile words they made in the word families activity.	**Interactive writing** (see p. 22) **Story starter:** The sun was bright. **Word bank:** light, nice, mile, while, slice	• Reading/Writing: Respond to the Story "Twilight" Days 1–5 • Reading/Writing: Respond to the Poem "Shy Mike" Days 3–5
Spell words in context `Routines 21, 23` round, mice, mile, smile	**Test words in dictation** Read out the spelling words for students to write. Then review their work.	• Spelling Homework: BLM 1 Days 1–5
"An Amazing Sight" **Review word family: ight** As you read aloud, review the word family -ight. Point out sight and right. Have students read the word aloud with you, and invite volunteers to use the word in an original sentence.	**"An Amazing Sight"** **Review long e vowel team (ee)** As you read aloud, point out the words with long e vowel team (ee): Lee, feet, sneezed. Have student volunteers use one of the words in an original sentence.	

* Use this menu to plan extra practice and center activities for use through the week. All the skills needed for an activity have been introduced by the first day of the range shown. See pages 272–273 for full descriptions.

Collaborative Learning and Independent Practice

Phonological/Phonemic Awareness Activities

Elkonin Boxes:
Words with Long i Sounds
Use on Days 1–5

Provide ten of the week's picture cards (page 281). For each card, have students sound out the word, sliding a counter into a cell of an Elkonin box for each individual phoneme. Students can do this individually, or partners can take turns choosing from the picture cards.

Phonemic Picnic:
Words with Long i
Use on Days 3–5

Fill a picnic basket (or lunch box) with toy foods. Each food should have the long i sound (for example: *pie, fries, limes, ice cream, rice*). Have partners sit on the floor as if ready for a picnic. They should take turns choosing a food, saying the name of the food, and passing it to their partner to "eat."

Phonics Activities

Phonics Word Builder:
Words with Long i Vowel Teams and Single Letters (i, ie, y, igh)
Use on Days 1–5

Distribute BLM 2 (page 275) and have students complete the activity.

Phonics Concentration:
Words with Open Syllables; Long i Vowel Teams and Single Letters (i, ie, y, igh)
Use on Days 3–5

Provide students with a set of the week's picture and word cards (pages 280–281). Instruct partners to arrange the cards face down to form a 6 x 4 grid to play a concentration game. The partners should alternate turning over two cards per turn. When a student uncovers a matching pair (a picture and its corresponding word card), he/she should use the word in an oral sentence and keep the pair of cards. The student who collects the most pairs wins the game.

Read/Draw/Label:
"Night Light": Long i Sounds
Use on Days 3–5

Place copies of BLM 5 (page 278) in a center. Have student pairs take turns reading the poem. Then have students complete the drawing activity.

 ## Word Family Activities

 ## High-Frequency Word Activities

Writing Activities

Word Family Scramble: -ight
Use on Days 1–5

Distribute BLM 4 (page 277) and have students complete the –ight word family activity.

Word Family Towers: -ice
Use on Days 3–5

Provide partners with interlocking blocks. On each block, place a piece of masking tape. Write –ice words on half of the blocks, and other decodable words on the rest of the blocks. Have students find and stack the –ice word blocks into a word family tower, pronouncing each word as they add it to the tower.

(This activity can be adapted for the –ile or -ight word family.)

Word Family Books: -ile
Use on Days 3–5

For each student, cut two index cards in half. Stack these four pieces of index cards, and then staple them to a single index card to form a "book" with four narrow pages and a final full-width page. Instruct students to write ile on the final index card so that those letters are always visible. Then have students form different word family words by writing a letter on each of the first four pages of their books, such as f, m, p, and t. (If necessary, support students by providing a bank of letters that will form real words: f, m, p, r, st, t, v.) When finished, students can flip through the first four pages to form and read aloud different word family words (such as file, mile, pile, tile).

High-Frequency Words Yoga
Use on Days 1–5

Form groups of five students. Provide each group with a five-letter HFW on an index card: again, round, where, found, brown. Instruct students to sound out each letter and read the word aloud. Then encourage students to pose in order to form the letters in the word with their bodies. Each student can then say his or her letter in order so that the group says the word.

High-Frequency Words Board Game
Use on Days 3–5

Place copies of BLM D, a spinner (BLM B), and disks or coins for playing pieces in the center. Students use the spinner to advance on the board. When they land on a space with a high-frequency word, they read the word aloud and use it in an oral sentence. Students also follow directions on the squares that have them.

Label the squares with words and directions, making a path from the START square to the FINISH square (words and directions can be repeated, as necessary). Examples of words and directions include:

- **they, country, again, round, your, know, always, all, people, draw, work, year, live, large, off, small, give, after, far, under, how, their, start**
- **"Move back two spaces"**
- **"Move forward five spaces"**
- **"Spin again"**
- **"Skip your next turn"**
- **"Switch squares with the player to your left"**

Reading/Writing: Respond to the Story "Twilight"
Use on Days 1–5

Provide copies of BLM 3 (page 276) and have students write a sentence about a time of day they like.

Reading/Writing: Respond to the Poem "Shy Mike"
Use on Days 3–5

Provide copies of BLM 6 (page 279) and have students write about a time they felt shy.

Spelling Homework

Read each spelling word aloud with your child. Spell it aloud together. Then ask your child to write each spelling word and say it in a sentence.

fright _____

bright _____

item _____

again _____

smile _____

mice _____

dry _____

round _____

Choose a different activity every day to practice this week's spelling words at home with your child.

Flashlight writing	Magnetic letters	Two-toned words	Letter tiles	Circle the word
Turn out the lights. Use a flashlight to spell each word on the wall.	Spell the words on a cookie sheet using magnetic letters and then write the words on a sheet of paper.	Write the spelling words with crayons or colored markers on a sheet of paper. Use one color for consonants and another for vowels.	Use letter tiles to spell the words and then write the words on a sheet of paper.	Write one sentence for each word and circle the spelling words.

Phonics Word Builder

**Write a letter or letters in each box to make a word.
Read the word aloud. Be sure that you make real words.**

fl ⬜

sk ⬜

m ⬜ t

f ⬜ nd

cr ⬜ ing

Twilight

Read the story.
Write a sentence about a time of day you like.

I like twilight. It is the best time.

It is not quite day, but not quite night.

It can be called dusk.

The sun is not too bright.

It is setting in the sky.

Yes, I like twilight. It is a delight!

Word Family Scramble

Cut out the tiles.
Arrange the tiles to spell the word.

igh | n | t

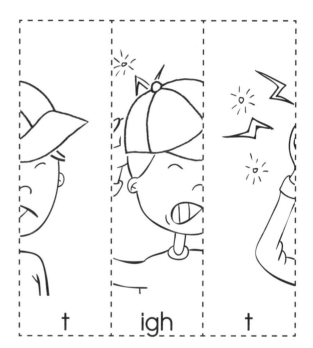

t | igh | t

t | igh | l

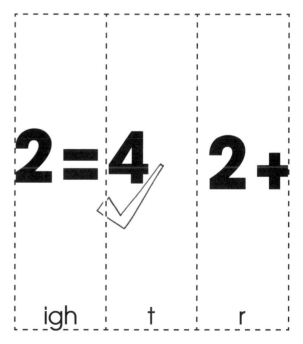

igh | t | r

Night Light

Read the poem.

When I am in bed

and the sheets are pulled tight,

the blinds are closed,

and it's late at night,

I wish I had a night light.

Not too dim, but not too bright.

Just a little bit of light!

Draw a picture of a night light you would like in your room.

Shy Mike

Read the poem. Then write about a time you have felt shy.

Little Mike is shy. I don't know why.

Meeting people makes him cry.

He holds on to his mom's hand tight.

He won't let her out of his sight.

It is too bad that Mike is so shy.

But in time, he will be fine.

_____

_____

_____

_____

_____

_____

cry	mice
dice	night
fry	lion
light	pie
kite	smile
pilot	thigh

Advancing Phonics Every Day

Letters/sounds: /är/ (farm), compound words

	Day 1	Day 2	Day 3
Phonological/ Phonemic Awareness	**Sentence Awareness** — Routine 2 **Model:** The dog barks./We will walk far. **Practice:** I sent him a card./The car is red. **Extra practice:** The room is dark./The game starts soon.	**Rhyme Production** — Routine 6 **Model:** car/far, chart/dart **Practice:** far/star, hard/card, charm/alarm **Extra practice:** dark/park, harp/carp	**Phoneme Isolation** — Routine 10 **Model:** mark, farm **Practice:** harm, dart, part **Extra practice:** argue, army
Phonics	**Review i, y, igh** — Routine 17 **Model:** bright, pilot **Practice:** item, sight, final, try **Extra practice:** light, shy **Introduce sound/symbol correspondence /är/** — Routine 17 **Model:** barn, jar **Practice:** part, farm, scarf, march **Extra practice:** charge, market	**Blend words with /är/** — Routine 18 **Model:** bark, sharp **Practice:** cart, start, barn, dark **Extra practice:** arch, harp **Dictation with /är/** — Routine 24 **Model:** car, mark **Other words:** tart, farm, star, arm **Decodable reader: "Mark Sees the Stars"** Use decodable reader ideas (p. 23).	**Blend words with /är/** — Routine 18 **Model:** armrest, backyard **Practice:** landmark, farmland, cartwheel **Extra practice:** barbell, artwork
Word Families	Distribute letter cards to student pairs, and instruct them to form words in the -ar word family. Have them write their words on their workmats. **Letter cards:** a, b, c, f, j, r, s, t	Guide students to fold their papers into four rows and to write an -ar word on each row.	Distribute picture cards (page 293) and letter cards to student pairs. Have students spell each word using the letter cards and write each word on their workmats. **Picture cards:** ball, wall **Letter cards:** a, b, l, l, w
High-Frequency Words	**Introduce high-frequency words** — Routine 20 four, great	**Practice high-frequency words** — Routine 21 four, great **Decodable reader: "Mark Sees the Stars"** Use decodable reader ideas (p. 23).	**Introduce high-frequency words** — Routine 20 boy, city
Writing	Have student pairs work together to form another word using the letter cards from the word families activity and write a sentence using the word.	Have student pairs work together to write a sentence using one of the -ar words they made in the word families activity.	Have student pairs work together to write a sentence using one of the words they wrote in the word families activity.
Spelling	**Introduce spelling words** — Routines 20, 22 scar, star, far, four	**Spell words in context** — Routines 21, 23 scar, star, far, four	**Introduce spelling words** — Routines 20, 22 stall, small, wall, great
Shared Reading	**"A Star Party"** **Review long i vowel teams and single letters (i, igh)** As you read aloud, review phonics elements, long i vowel teams and single letters (i, igh): lights, sky, bright. Have students read the words, and invite volunteers to use them in an original sentence.	**"A Star Party"** **Introduce /är/ words** As you read aloud, point out the /är/ words star, party, dark, start, Karla, farm, far, Mars. Have students read each word aloud with you, and emphasize the phonics elements.	**"The Washington Monument"** **Introduce high-frequency word: city** As you read aloud, point out the high-frequency word city. Ask student volunteers to use the word in an original sentence.

High-Frequency Words:	Spelling:	Word Families:
four, great, boy, city	Words with -ar, -all	-ar, -all

Day 4	Day 5	Collaborative Learning and Independent Practice*
Phoneme Addition Routine 15 Model: car/cart Practice: art/part, art/chart Extra practice: arm/harm, ark/park		• Elkonin Boxes: Words with /är/ Sounds Days 1–5 • Phonemic Concentration: Compound Words and Words with /är/ and Other Variant Vowel-a Sounds Days 3–5
Blend words with /är/ Routine 18 Model: armhole, barking Practice: barnyard, armpit, hardhat Extra practice: carload, ballpark **Build words with /är/** Routine 19 Model: tar, star, starfish Practice: mark, market, marketplace Extra practice: art, part, partway	**Decodable reader: "Mark Sees the Stars"** Use decodable reader ideas (p. 23).	• Word Rainbows: Words with /är/ Sounds Days 1–5 • Phonics Beanbag Toss: Compound Words and Words with /är/ and Other Variant Vowel-a Sounds Days 3–5 • Read and Label: "To the Market": Words with /är/ Sounds Days 3–5
Distribute letter cards a, b, c, f, h, l, l, m, s, t, w. Have partners take turns building -all words. Have them write the words on their workmats.	**Review -ar, -all words** Distribute the following letter cards to student pairs. Have partners build -ar and -all words and write them on their workmats. **Letter cards:** a, b, c, f, h, l, l, m, r, s, t, w	• Word Family Cube: -ar Days 1–5 • Word Family Sort: -ar, -all Days 3–5 • Word Family Board Game: -ar, -all Days 3–5
Practice high-frequency words Routine 21 four, great, boy, city	**Decodable reader: "Mark Sees the Stars"** Use decodable reader ideas (p. 23).	• High-Frequency Words "Go Fish" Days 1–5 • High-Frequency Words Bug Catch Days 3–5
Have student pairs work together to write a sentence using one of the -all words they made in the word families activity.	**Interactive writing** (see p. 22) **Story starter:** We went to the market. **Word bank:** far, car, park, farm, garden, cart	• Reading/Writing: Respond to the Story "From Farm to Scarf" Days 1–5 • Reading/Writing: Respond to the Poem "In the Box" Days 3–5
Spell words in context Routines 21, 23 stall, small, wall, great	**Test words in dictation** Read out the spelling words for students to write. Then review their work.	• Spelling Homework: BLM 1 Days 1–5
"On Mars" **Introduce words with /är/** As you read aloud, point out /är/ words: *Mars, arm, parts.* Have students read each word aloud with you, and invite volunteers to use the word in an original sentence.	**"On Mars"** **Review long i (final e)** As you read aloud, point out the words with long i (final e): *miles, like, alive.* Have student volunteers use one of the words in an original sentence.	

* Use this menu to plan extra practice and center activities for use through the week. All the skills needed for an activity have been introduced by the first day of the range shown. See pages 284–285 for full descriptions.

Collaborative Learning and Independent Practice

Phonological/Phonemic Awareness Activities

Elkonin Boxes:
Words with /är/ Sounds
Use on Days 1–5

Provide the ten picture cards for words with /är/ sounds (page 293). For each card, have students sound out the word, sliding a counter into a cell of an Elkonin box for each individual phoneme. Students can do this individually, or partners can take turns choosing from the picture cards.

Phonemic Concentration:
Compound Words and Words with /är/ and Other Variant Vowel-a Sounds
Use on Days 3–5

Provide students with a set of the week's picture cards (page 293), two of each card, for a total of twenty-four cards. Instruct partners to arrange the cards face down to form a 6 x 4 grid to play a concentration game. The partners should alternate turning over two cards per turn. When a student uncovers a matching pair, he/she should use the word in an oral sentence and keep the pair of cards. The student who collects the most pairs wins the game.

ᴬᴮ𝒞 ﹚) Phonics Activities

Word Rainbows:
Words with /är/ Sounds
Use on Days 1–5

Provide the ten picture cards for words with /är/ sounds (page 293). Instruct students to write each word, spelling each sound in the word with an individual color. You might suggest that students choose rainbow colors and use them in that order. Remind students that *ar* makes one sound, so both letters should be the same color.

Phonics Beanbag Toss:
Compound Words and Words with /är/ and Other Variant Vowel-a Sounds
Use on Days 3–5

Arrange the twelve picture cards (page 293) for a beanbag toss. Provide the word cards, and have students take turns reading a word aloud and tossing the beanbag to the corresponding picture.

Read and Write About a Poem:
"To the Market":
Words with /är/ Sounds
Use on Days 3–5

Distribute copies of BLM 5 (page 290) and have student pairs take turns reading the poem. Then have them write about a place they like to go.

 # Word Family Activities

Word Family Picture Labels: –ar, –all
Use on Days 1–5

Distribute BLM 2 (page 287) and have students write the missing letter or letters.

Word Family Sort: -ar, -all
Use on Days 3–5

Provide students with BLM 4 (page 289) and have them complete the activity.

Board Game: -ar, -all
Use on Days 3–5

Label the squares of BLM D with words and directions, making a path from START to FINISH. (Repeat words and directions as necessary.) Words and directions might include:

- **barn, park, spark, star, chart, call, fall, hall, mall, wall, back, bank, jail, male, pail, rail, sale, tack, tail, tale**
- **"Move back two spaces"**
- **"Move forward five spaces"**
- **"Spin again"**
- **"Skip your next turn"**
- **"Switch squares with another player"**

Place the prepared BLM D, a spinner (BLM B), and disks or coins for playing pieces in the center. Students take turns spinning the spinner to advance. When they land on a word, they read the word aloud and use it in an oral sentence. When they land on directions, they follow them.

High-Frequency Word Activities

High-Frequency Words "Go Fish"
Use on Days 1–5

Pick 25 high-frequency words (do not include *boy* and *city*), and write each word on two index cards to create fifty cards. Students might be instructed to draw fish on the other sides of the cards. Have groups of 2–4 students play "Go Fish" using this deck.

High-Frequency Words Bug Catch
Use on Days 3–5

Write a series of high-frequency words, from this week and previous weeks, on index cards, and place the index cards on the floor or on a table. Then provide a pair of students with plastic fly swatters. Instruct students to take turns: One student should read a high-frequency word aloud, and then the other student should "swat" it.

Writing Activities

Reading/Writing: Respond to the Story "From Farm to Scarf"
Use on Days 1–5

Provide copies of BLM 3 (page 288) and have students complete the writing activity.

Reading/Writing: Respond to the Poem "In the Box"
Use on Days 3–5

Provide copies of BLM 6 (page 291) and have students complete the drawing activity.

Spelling Homework

Read each spelling word aloud with your child. Spell it aloud together. Then ask your child to write each spelling word and use it in a sentence.

scar _____   stall _____

star _____   small _____

far _____   wall _____

four _____   great _____

Choose a different activity every day to practice this week's spelling words at home with your child.

Magnetic Letters	Write it	Flashlight writing	Circle the Word	Remember the word
Cut letters out of a magazine or newspaper, and paste them on a piece of colored paper to form each spelling word.	Write the word with dotted lines, and then trace the dots with a different color.	Turn out the lights. Use a flashlight to spell each word on the wall.	Work with your child to write a sentence for each word on a sheet of paper and circle the spelling words.	Turn the paper over and write the word from memory.

Word Family Picture Labels

Say the name of the picture aloud.
Write the beginning of the word below each picture.

_____ ar

_____ all

_____ ar

_____ all

From Farm to Scarf

Read the story.
Write a sentence about something you might find on a farm.

If you go to a farm

And see sheep in the barn,

You are not too far

From seeing yarn.

A sheep's coat is cut off each year

Then spun into yarn

for a coat, hat, or scarf!

BLM
4

Word Family Sort

Cut out the words.
Place each word in the basket for its word family.

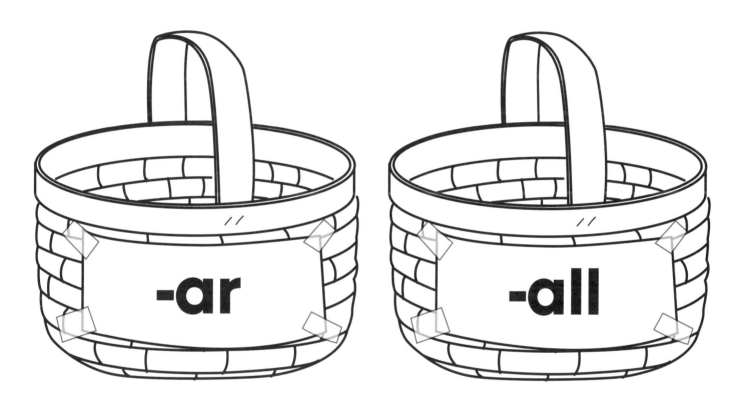

car	ball	wall	tall	far
tar	hall	bar	call	fall

To the Market

Read the poem. Then write a sentence about where you like to go.

My dad drives the car

to the market with me.

He parks in the lot

under the shade of a tree.

We pick the best cart

from the carts in the row.

Then comes the best part--

inside we go!

© Benchmark Education Company, LLC

In the Box

Read the poem.

In a big box I found

a little red car,

and a homemade star,

and a set of planes,

and a green and white train.

Such great things, one and all,

but all I wanted to find was my baseball.

Draw two toys you like.

hardhat	jar
ball	harvest
bark	park
card	shark
farm	scarf
armpit	wall

Advancing Phonics Every Day

	Day 1	Day 2	Day 3
Phonological/ Phonemic Awareness	**Syllable Segmentation** — Routine 3 **Model:** before, story **Practice:** morning, skateboarding, forget, explore **Extra practice:** more, onboard	**Phoneme Isolation** — Routine 10 **Model:** tore, chore **Practice:** soar, more, roar **Extra practice:** store, board	**Phoneme Segmentation** — Routine 11 **Model:** score, form **Practice:** worn, soar, chore, storm **Extra practice:** stork, snore
Phonics	**Review previous week's sound/symbol focus /är/** — Routine 17 **Model:** scar, carpet **Practice:** charm, march, garden **Extra practice:** cart, shark **Introduce sound/symbol correspondence /ôr/** — Routine 17 **Model:** snore, corn **Practice:** fork, born, roar, core **Extra practice:** before, morn	**Blend words with /ôr/** — Routine 18 **Model:** store, bore **Practice:** more, shore, torn **Extra practice:** billboard, hornet **Dictation with /ôr/** — Routine 24 **Model:** morn, corner **Other words:** forget, snored **Decodable reader: "Night Hunt for Food"** Use decodable reader ideas (p. 23).	**Blend words with /ôr/** — Routine 18 **Model:** order, horn **Practice:** before, form, north **Extra practice:** forest, coarse
Word Families	Distribute letter cards to student pairs, and instruct them to form words in the -orn, -ore word families. Have them write their words on their workmats. **Letter cards:** b, c, e, h, o, n, r, s, t, w	Distribute picture cards (page 305) and letter cards to student pairs. Have students spell each word using the letter cards and write each word on their workmats. **Picture cards:** corn, horn, store, snore **Letter cards:** c, e, h, n, o, r, s, t	Distribute the following letter cards to student pairs. Have students form -oar words and write each word on their workmats. **Letter cards:** a, b, o, r, r, s
High-Frequency Words	**Introduce high-frequency words** — Routine 20 laugh, move	**Practice high-frequency words** — Routine 21 laugh, move **Decodable reader: "Night Hunt for Food"** Use decodable reader ideas (p. 23).	**Introduce high-frequency words** — Routine 20 change, away
Writing	Have student pairs work together to write a sentence using one of the -orn or -ore words they wrote on their workmats.	Have student pairs work together to write a sentence using one of the -orn or -ore words they spelled in the word families activity.	Have student pairs work together to write a sentence using one of the -oar words they wrote in the word families activity.
Spelling	**Introduce spelling words** — Routines 20, 22 corn, horn, shore, laugh	**Spell words in context** — Routines 21, 23 corn, horn, shore, laugh	**Introduce spelling words** — Routines 20, 22 boar, soar, roar, move
Shared Reading	**"It's a Comet!"** **Review /är/ words** As you read aloud, review the phonics element /är/: large, far. Have students read the words aloud with you, and emphasize the phonics element.	**"It's a Comet!"** **Introduce /ôr/ words** As you read aloud, point out the /ôr/ words orbits, core, form. Have students read each word aloud with you, and emphasize the phonics element.	**"It's a Comet!"** **Review high-frequency word: move** As you read aloud, point out the high-frequency word move. Ask student volunteers to use the word in an original sentence.

High-Frequency Words:	Spelling:	Word Families:
laugh, move, change, away	Words with -orn, -ore, -oar	-orn, -ore, -oar

Day 4	Day 5	Collaborative Learning and Independent Practice*
Phoneme Addition `Routine 15` Model: or/for, ore/more Practice: oar/soar, ore/bore, ore/pore Extra practice: oar/roar, ore/core		• Phonemic Picnic: Words with /ôr/ Sounds Days 1–5 • Phoneme Cubes: Words with /ôr/ Sounds Days 3–5
Blend words with /ôr/ `Routine 18` Model: storm, reform Practice: cornered, dartboard, pork Extra practice: ordering, oars **Build words with /ôr/** `Routine 19` Model: sore, snore, spore Practice: form, fort, forth Extra practice: roar, boar, board	**Decodable reader: "Night Hunt for Food"** Use decodable reader ideas (p. 23).	• Letter Cup Substitution: Words with /ôr/ (or, ore) Days 1–5 • Picture Word Cards: Words with /ôr/ (oar, or, ore) Days 3–5 • Read/Draw/Label: "At the Store": Words with /ôr/ (oar, or, ore) Days 3–5
Guide students to fold their papers into three rows. Have them write an -oar word on each row.	**Review -orn, -ore, -oar words** Distribute the following letter cards to student pairs. Have partners build -orn, -ore, -oar words and write them on their workmats. **Letter cards:** a, b, c, e, m, n, o, r, s, t, w	• Word Family Ice Cream Cones: -orn, -ore Days 1–5 • Word Family Towers: -oar Days 3–5 • Feed the Creatures: -orn, -ore, -oar Days 3–5
Practice high-frequency words `Routine 21` change, away	**Decodable reader: "Night Hunt for Food"** Use decodable reader ideas (p. 23).	• High-Frequency Words Board Game Days 1–5 • High-Frequency Words Parking Lot Days 3–5
Have student pairs work together to write a sentence using one of the -oar words they made in the word families activity.	**Interactive writing** (see p. 22) **Story starter:** A storm is coming. **Word bank:** store, more, shore, form, for, or, roar	• Reading/Writing: Respond to the Poem "Chore Day" Days 1–5 • Reading/Writing: Respond to the Poem "Shorts?" Days 3–5
Spell words in context `Routines 21, 23` boar, soar, roar, move	**Test words in dictation** Read aloud each of the week's spelling words for students to write. Then collect and review student work.	• Spelling Homework: BLM 1 Days 1–5
"The Moon's the North Wind's Cookie" **Review /ôr/ words** As you read aloud, point out the /ôr/ word North. Have students read the word aloud with you, and emphasize the phonics element.	**"The Moon's the North Wind's Cookie"** **Review high-frequency word away** As you read aloud, point out the high-frequency word away. Have student volunteers use the word in an original sentence.	

* Use this menu to plan extra practice and center activities for use through the week. All the skills needed for an activity have been introduced by the first day of the range shown. See pages 296–297 for full descriptions.

Collaborative Learning and Independent Practice

Phonological/Phonemic Awareness Activities

Phonemic Picnic:
Words with /ôr/ Sounds
Use on Days 1–5

Fill a picnic basket (or lunch box) with toy foods. Each food should contain the phoneme from this week (and, if desired, previous weeks). (For example: *acorn squash, corn, s'mores, popcorn, oranges, pork chops*.) Have partners sit on the floor as if ready for a picnic. They should take turns choosing a food, saying the name of the food, and passing it to their partner to "eat."

Phoneme Cubes:
Words with /ôr/ Sounds
Use on Days 3–5

Gather multiple pairs of cubes (such as empty cube-shaped tissue boxes). Paste the week's twelve picture cards (page 305) on the boxes, six per box. Students can take turns rolling the cubes, saying the two words that face up, identifying the middle vowel sounds, and noting which sounds in the words are not the same.

ᴬᴮ꜀)) Phonics Activities

Letter Cup Substitution:
Words with /ôr/ (or, ore)
Use on Days 1–5

Provide plastic cups with a letter, digraph, or /ôr/ spelling written on the outside of each. Place upside-down cups in a row to spell a word. Have partners take turns fitting other cups over one of the original cups, making a new word. Students should read each word aloud and record it on a phonics house (BLM A) before continuing. Examples:

- **starting word: bore**
- **substitutions of initial letter: c, ch, l, m, s, t, w**
- **starting word: born**
- **substitutions of initial letter: c, h, t, w**

Picture Word Cards:
Words with /ôr/ (oar, or, ore)
Use on Days 3–5

Distribute the following picture word cards:

- **boar, corn, fork, roar, store, horn, stork, torn, snore, popcorn, acorn, boards**

Have partners take turns. Student 1 holds a card with the picture-only side facing student 2. Student 1 reads aloud the word on the card. Student 2 spells the word orally. If student 2 needs a clue, student 1 provides the first letter, blend, or digraph, and allows student 2 to indicate the /ôr/ spelling.

Read/Draw/Label a Story:
"At the Store":
Words with /ôr/ (oar, or, ore)
Use on Days 3–5

Place copies of BLM 5 (page 302) in a center. Have student pairs take turns reading the story. Then have them complete the activity by circling the words with the *–or* sound.

Word Family Activities

Word Family Ice Cream Cones: –orn, –ore
Use on Days 1–5

Provide students with BLM 2 (page 299) and have them complete the activity.

Word Family Towers: -oar
Use on Days 3–5

Provide partners with interlocking blocks. On each block, place a piece of masking tape. Write –oar words on half of the blocks and other decodable words on the rest of the blocks. Have students find and stack the –oar word blocks into a word family tower, pronouncing each word as they add it to the tower.

(This activity can be adapted for the –orn or –ore word family.)

Feed the Creatures: –orn, –ore, –oar
Use on Days 3–5

Provide three small plastic bins. Label each with a word family, –orn, –ore, or –oar. Use a marker to make eyes or a face on each bin to turn the bins into creatures. Provide partners with the following –orn, –ore, and –oar picture cards, and have them take turns "feeding" the creatures the appropriate cards:

- corn / chore / score / snore / store / boar / oar / roar / soar / torn

High-Frequency Word Activities

High-Frequency Words Board Game
Use on Days 1–5

Place copies of BLM D, a spinner (BLM B), and disks or coins for playing pieces in the center. Students use the spinner to advance on the board. When they land on a space with a high-frequency word, they read the word aloud and use it in an oral sentence. Students also follow directions on the squares that have them.

Label the squares with words and directions, making a path from the START square to the FINISH square (words and directions can be repeated, as necessary). Examples of words and directions include:

- laugh, move, four, great, boy, city, again, round, they, country, all, people, where, draw, found, your, know, always, brown, work, year, live
- "Move back two spaces"
- "Move forward five spaces"
- "Spin again"
- "Skip your next turn"
- "Switch squares with the player to your left"

High-Frequency Words Parking Lot
Use on Days 3–5

Provide partners with BLM 4 (page 301) and toy cars, and have them complete the activity. Students should take turns: One student should read a high-frequency word aloud, and the other student should "park" a toy car in that spot and say a sentence using the word.

Writing Activities

Reading/Writing: Respond to the Poem "Chore Day"
Use on Days 1–5

Provide copies of BLM 3 (page 300) and have students complete the writing activity.

Reading/Writing: Respond to the Poem "Shorts?"
Use on Days 3–5

Provide copies of BLM 6 (page 303) and have students complete the writing activity.

Spelling Homework

Read each spelling word aloud with your child. Spell it aloud together. Then ask your child to write each spelling word and use it in a sentence.

corn _____   boar _____

horn _____   soar _____

shore _____   roar _____

laugh _____   move _____

Choose a different activity every day to practice this week's spelling words at home with your child.

Write it	Flashlight writing	Multi-colored words	Trace your words	Letter tiles
Work with your child to write the word, saying aloud each letter as you write it.	Turn out the lights. Use a flashlight to spell each word on the wall.	Write the spelling words with crayons or colored pencils, using a different color for each letter.	Use your finger to write each spelling word in sand, flour, or a similar material.	Use letter tiles to spell the words and then write the words on a sheet of paper.

Word Family Ice Cream Cones

Place the scoops of ice cream on the correct word family cones.

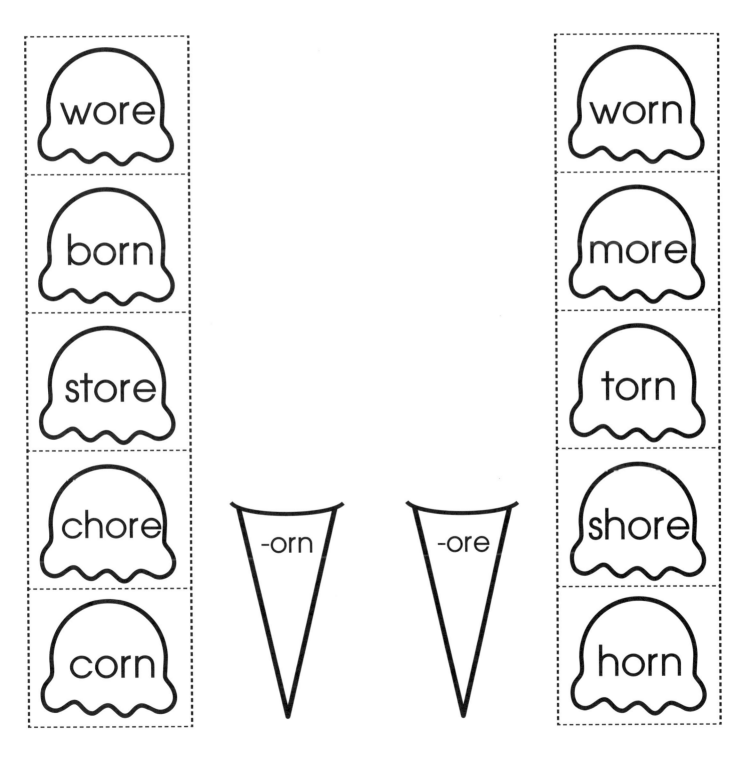

Chore Day

Read the poem. Write a sentence about a chore you are asked to do.

On a weekend morning

we know Mom will say,

"Do all your chores

by the end of the day!"

We stop reading, or eating,

or playing French horn.

We all work to help

on a weekend morn.

Name _____ Date_____

High-Frequency Words Parking Lot

Listen to the directions from your teacher.

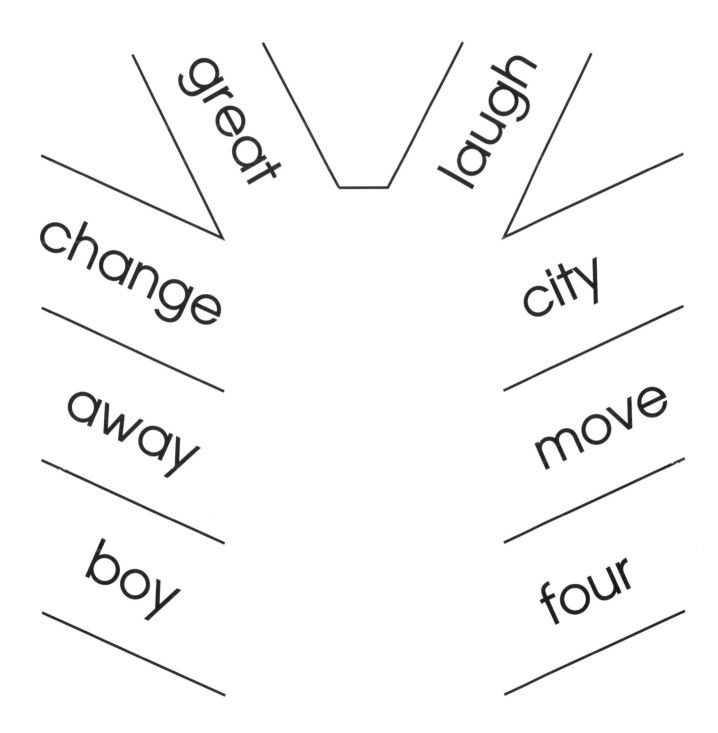

At the Store

Read the story.
Circle the words that make the *-or* sound.

We have fun when we go to the store.

Dad likes corn.

He always wants more!

Dad likes corn down to the core!

Mom likes roses but not their thorns.

Before she takes a rose, the thorns must be shorn.

I like mushrooms, right to their spores.

We have fun when we go to the store.

Shorts?

**Read the poem. Have you ever fallen off a bike?
Write a sentence to tell how.**

I wore my best jeans and rode my bike

down to the store to buy some corn.

When a car roared by and honked its horn,

I fell and saw my jeans had torn!

What could I do?

I rolled them up and made shorts.

One time, I

boar	popcorn
horn	snore
corn	acorn
fork	store
boards	stork
roar	torn

 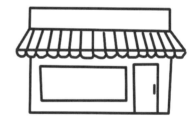

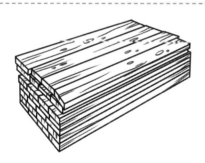 

Advancing Phonics Every Day

	Day 1	Day 2	Day 3
Phonological/ Phonemic Awareness	**Syllable Segmentation** `Routine 3` **Model:** curtain, turkey **Practice:** Saturday, thirteen, circus **Extra practice:** purple, verdict	**Syllable Blending** `Routine 4` **Model:** person, burger **Practice:** gurgle, turnip **Extra practice:** circle, purple	**Phoneme Isolation** `Routine 10` **Model:** fir, sir **Practice:** curve, bird, purse **Extra practice:** curl, swerve
Phonics	**Review previous week's sound/symbol focus /ôr/** `Routine 17` **Model:** horn, fork **Practice:** store, billboard, torn **Extra practice:** reorder, burning **Introduce sound/symbol correspondence /ûr/** `Routine 17` **Model:** bird, germ **Practice:** herd, turn, curl, shirt **Extra practice:** surf, church Explain that the *er* sound can be spelled three ways: *er* as in *germ*, *ir* as in *bird*, and *ur* as in *hurt*.	**Blend words with /ûr/** `Routine 18` **Model:** firm, swirl **Practice:** burger, spur, third **Extra practice:** person, birthday **Dictation with /ûr/** `Routine 24` **Model:** burn, girl **Other words:** turnip, dirt, hermit **Decodable reader: "Red Bird Chirps"** Use decodable reader ideas (p. 23).	**Blend words with /ûr/** `Routine 18` **Model:** further, thirst **Practice:** churning, better, swerving **Extra practice:** turning, thirteen
Word Families	Distribute letter cards to student pairs, and instruct them to form words in the -ern word family: *fern, stern, modern, pattern, western.* Have them write their words on workmats. **Letter cards:** a, d, e, f, m, n, o, r, s, t, w, p	Guide students to fold a sheet of paper into four squares. Have them write a word with *ir* in each square.	Distribute the following letter cards and have students use a phonics house (BLM A) to write words for the word family -urn. (burn, turn, churn) **Letter cards:** b, c, h, n, r, t, u
High-Frequency Words	**Introduce high-frequency words** `Routine 20` every, near	**Practice high-frequency words** `Routine 21` every, near **Decodable reader: "Red Bird Chirps"** Use decodable reader ideas (p. 23).	**Introduce high-frequency words** `Routine 20` school, earth
Writing	Have student pairs work together to write a sentence using one of the -ern words they formed on their workmats.	Have students write a sentence using each one of the *ir* words they wrote in the word families activity. Then have them share one of their four sentences with a partner.	Have student pairs work together to write a sentence using one of the -urn words they wrote in the word families activity.
Spelling	**Introduce spelling words** `Routines 20, 22` stern, fern, pattern, every	`Routines 21, 23` **Spell words in context** stern, fern, pattern, every	**Introduce spelling words** `Routines 20, 22` burn, churn, turn, near
Shared Reading	**"Shapes in the Clouds"** **Review /ôr/ words** As you read aloud, review phonics element /ôr/: *oars.* Have students read the word aloud and emphasize the phonics element.	**"Shapes in the Clouds"** **Introduce /ûr/ words** As you read aloud, point out the /ûr/ words *Kurt, bird, turning, better.* Have students read a word aloud and use it in an original sentence.	**"Shapes in the Clouds"** **Review high-frequency word: near** As you read aloud, point out the high-frequency word *near.* Ask student volunteers to use the word in an original sentence.

High-Frequency Words:	Spelling:	Word Families:
every, near, school, earth	Words with -ern, -urn	-ern, -urn

Day 4	Day 5	Collaborative Learning and Independent Practice*
Phoneme Blending Routine 12 **Model:** first, germ **Practice:** herd, turn, burn, skirt **Extra practice:** stir, term		• Elkonin Boxes: Words with /ûr/ Sounds Days 1–5 • Phonemic Word Sort: Words with Vowel-r Sounds Days 3–5
Blend words with vowel /ûr/ Routine 18 **Model:** dirt, burst **Practice:** lantern, birthday, zipper **Extra practice:** turnip, person **Build words with /ûr/** Routine 18 **Model:** urn, burn, burner **Practice:** turn, return, returning **Extra practice:** ham, hammer, hammered	**Decodable reader: "Red Bird Chirps"** Use decodable reader ideas (p. 23).	• Craft Stick Chains: Words with /ûr/ Sounds Days 1–5 • Phonics Word Builder: Words with /ûr/ Sounds Days 1–5 • Read/Draw/Label: "Robert the Nurse": Words with /ûr/ Sounds Days 3–5
Guide students to think of words with -ur. Have them say a sentence using two of the words.	**Review –ern and -urn words** Distribute the following letter cards to student pairs. Have partners build –ern and -urn words. Have them write the words on their workmats. **Letter cards:** b, c, e, f, h, n, r, s, t, u	• Word Family Books: -ern Days 1–5 • Word Family Cube: -urn Days 3–5
Practice high-frequency words Routine 21 school, earth	**Decodable reader: "Red Bird Chirps"** Use decodable reader ideas (p. 23).	• High-Frequency Words Beanbag Toss Days 1–5 • High-Frequency Words Concentration Days 3–5
Display the bird, fern, lantern, lobster, butter, curl, and hornet word cards. Have students read the words and then write a sentence using two of the words.	**Interactive writing** (see p. 22) **Story starter:** The new girl took her turn at bat. **Word bank:** burn, return, curb, shirt, curve, curl	• Reading/Writing: Respond to the Poem "The New Shirt" Days 1–5 • Reading/Writing: Continue the Poem "The Girl and the Birds" Days 3–5
Spell words in context Routines 21, 23 burn, churn, turn, near	**Test words in dictation** Read aloud each of the week's spelling words for students to write. Then collect and review the work.	• Spelling Homework: BLM 1 Days 1–5
"The Sun" **Review /ûr/ words** As you read aloud, point out the /ûr/ words other, energy. Have students read the words aloud with you, and emphasize the phonics element.	**"The Sun"** **Review high-frequency word: earth** As you read aloud, point out the high-frequency word earth. Have student volunteers use the word in an original sentence.	

* Use this menu to plan extra practice and center activities for use through the week. All the skills needed for an activity have been introduced by the first day of the range shown. See pages 308–309 for full descriptions.

Collaborative Learning and Independent Practice

🕪 Phonological/Phonemic Awareness Activities

Elkonin Boxes:
Words with /ûr/ Sounds
Use on Days 1–5

Provide copies of the following picture cards: *bird, curl, fern, girl* and *skirt* (page 317). For each card, have students sound out the word, sliding a counter into a cell of an Elkonin box for each individual phoneme. Students can do this individually, or partners can take turns choosing from the picture cards.

Phonemic Word Sort:
Words with /ûr/ and Vowel-r Sounds
Use on Days 3–5

Distribute copies of the week's twelve picture cards (page 317). Have pairs of students work together to sort the cards by vowel sound:

- **bird / butter / fern / girl / lantern / lobster / skirt**

ᴬᴮᴄ🕪 Phonics Activities

Craft Stick Chains:
Words with /ûr/ Sounds
Use on Days 1–5

Use tongue depressors or craft sticks. On each end of a stick, write decodable words with the /ûr/ sound, alternating between the three spellings *ir, er,* and *ur*. Have partners take turns choosing a stick and placing it end-to-end with another stick, matching words with the same sound and spelling.

Phonics Word Builder:
Words with /ûr/ Sounds
Use on Days 1–5

Set up a spinner with the vowels *e, i,* and *u*, and have letter tiles/cards available. Distribute BLM 2 (page 311) and have students complete the activity.

Read/Draw/Label:
"Robert the Nurse":
Words with /ûr/ Sounds
Use on Days 3–5

Place copies of BLM 5 (page 314) in a center. Have student partners read the story. Then have them complete the drawing activity and label the words with the /ûr/ sound.

 **Word Family Activities**

 **High-Frequency Word Activities**

Writing Activities

Word Family Books: -ern
Use on Days 1–5

For each student, cut two index cards in half. Stack these four pieces of index cards, and then staple them to a single index card to form a "book" with four narrow pages and a final full-width page. Instruct students to write *ern* on the final index card so that those letters are always visible. Then have students form different words by writing a letter or letters on each of the first four pages of their books. If necessary, support students by providing a bank of letters that will form real words, such as: *f, st, cav, gov, lant*. When finished, students can flip through the first four pages to form and read aloud different word family words.

Word Family Cube: -urn
Use on Days 3–5

Distribute BLM 4 (page 313) and have students form *–urn* word family words by rolling the cube and adding the letter(s) facing up to the *–urn* ending. Have students record the words they form on a word family house (BLM A).

High-Frequency Words Beanbag Toss
Use on Days 1–5

Gather Benchmark Advance high-frequency word cards for a beanbag toss. Use review words from previous weeks as well as the current week's words.

- **and / away / change / every / go / laugh / little / move / near / play / see / she / the / with / you**

Have one student choose a word to read aloud, and another to toss the bag to cover the matching card.

High-Frequency Words Concentration
Use on Days 3–5

Distribute to partners the following Benchmark Advance high-frequency word cards. Each set should contain two copies of each word, for a total of twenty-eight cards per pair of students. Have students take turns finding the matching high-frequency words.

- **again / boy / city / country / earth / every / four / great / near / people / round / school / they / where**

Reading/Writing: Respond to the Poem "The New Shirt"
Use on Days 1–5

Provide copies of BLM 3 (page 312) and have students complete the writing activity.

Reading/Writing: Continue the Poem "The Girl and the Birds"
Use on Days 3–5

Provide copies of BLM 6 (page 315) and have students read the poem and write to tell what happens next.

Spelling Homework

Read each spelling word aloud with your child. Spell it aloud together. Then ask your child to write each spelling word and use it in a sentence.

stern _____

burn _____

fern _____

churn _____

pattern _____

turn _____

every _____

near _____

Choose a different activity every day to practice this week's spelling words at home with your child.

Trace the word	Multi-colored words	Two-toned words	Remember the word	Circle the word
Write the words with dotted lines on a sheet of paper, and then trace the dots with a different color.	Write the spelling words with crayons or colored pencils, using a different color for each letter.	Write the spelling words with crayons or colored markers on a sheet of paper. Use one color for consonants and another for vowels.	Turn the paper over and write the word from memory.	Work with your child to write a sentence for each word on a sheet of paper and circle the spelling words.

Phonics Word Builder

Use a spinner to select a vowel.
Place a letter tile in the box to form a word. Read each word aloud.
Make sure that each word you form is a real word.

f ☐ r   v ☐ rb

s t ☐ r   s ☐ r

h ☐ r   sp ☐ r

The New Shirt

Read the poem. Write a sentence about a gift someone gave you.

Thursday was my birthday.

I got a purple shirt.

I wore it to dinner

with my black and purple skirt.

First Dad served us burgers,

then Mom served us cake.

I had such a great birthday,

and that is no mistake!

_____

- -

_____

- -

_____

- -

_____

BLM
4

Word Family Sort

Cut out the words.
Place each word in the basket for its word family.

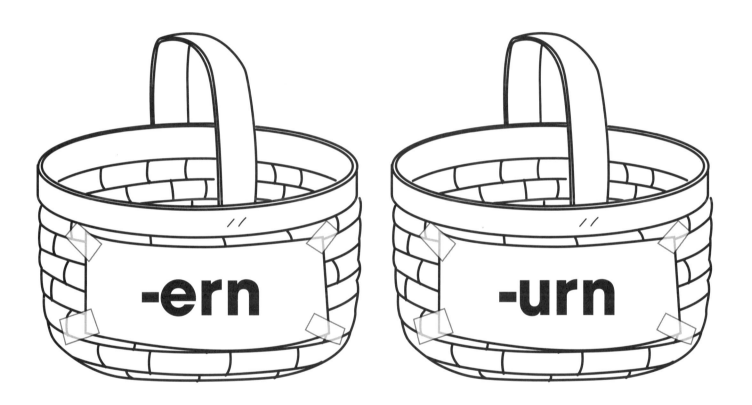

fern	churn	return
burn	turn	stern

Robert the Nurse

Read the story. Draw a picture of a nurse helping people.
Label any part of your picture that has the /ûr/ sound as in *nurse*.

Robert is a nurse.

He helps people who are hurt.

He helps people who get sick.

It can be hard work.

There are lots of germs.

But Robert returns every day.

Let's say thanks to Robert.

The Girl and the Birds

Read the poem. Write a sentence to tell what happens next.

The girl sits on her porch,

as birds fly all around.

She's ready to toss

the seeds to the ground.

First the birds turn away.

They don't have the nerve.

Then all of a sudden, they turn back and swerve!

stir	hornet
bird	girl
lantern	butter
barn	lobster
curl	horn
fern	skirt

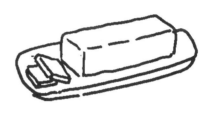

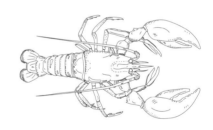

Advancing Phonics Every Day

Letters/sounds: /ou/ (house, clown); comparative inflectional endings -er, -est

	Day 1	Day 2	Day 3
Phonological/ Phonemic Awareness	**Rhyme Production** Routine 6 **Model:** house/mouse **Practice:** crown/town/down **Extra practice:** mound/sound/round	**Onset Rhyme Blending** Routine 8 **Model:** mouse/house **Practice:** shout/pout **Extra practice:** town/crown	**Phoneme Segmentation** Routine 11 **Model:** south, drown **Practice:** sour, plow, brown **Extra practice:** foul, now
Phonics	**Review /ûr/** Routine 17 **Model:** third, twirl **Practice:** bird, burn, fern, chirp **Extra practice:** birthday, first **Introduce sound/symbol correspondence: /ou/** Routine 17 **Model:** spout, frown **Practice:** pout, found, cow **Extra practice:** mouth, down	**Blend words with /ou/** Routine 18 **Model:** round, owl **Practice:** pound, bow, bound **Extra practice:** shout, scowl **Dictation with /ou/** Routine 24 **Model:** sprout, crown **Other words:** sound, how, growl **Decodable reader: "In Our Town"** Use decodable reader ideas (p. 23).	**Word Building with inflectional endings -er, -est** Routine 19 **Model:** tall, taller, tallest **Practice:** short, shorter, shortest, big, bigger, biggest **Extra practice:** small, smaller, smallest Explain to students that adding the ending -er to a word means "more," and -est means "most."
Word Families	Guide students to draw a house, with a triangle roof and square base. Have them write -out in the roof and list three -out words in the square base. Repeat for the -ouse word family. (pout, snout, scout, spout) (house, mouse, blouse, spouse)	Distribute the following letter cards to student pairs. Have students form -out and -ouse words and write each word on their workmats. **Letter cards:** e, h, m, o, p, s, t, u	Distribute letter cards to student pairs. Have them build -own words and write the words on their workmats. **Letter cards:** b, c, d, f, g, n, o, r, t, w
High-Frequency Words	**Introduce high-frequency words** Routine 20 before, done	**Practice high-frequency words** Routine 21 before, done **Decodable reader: "In Our Town"** Use decodable reader ideas (p. 23).	**Introduce high-frequency words** Routine 20 about, even
Writing	Have student pairs work together to write a sentence using one of the -out or -ouse words they wrote in the word families activity.	Have student pairs work together to write a sentence using one of the -out or -ouse words they wrote on their workmats.	Have student pairs work together to write a sentence using one of the -own words they wrote in the word families activity.
Spelling	**Introduce spelling words** Routines 20, 22 shout, house, pout, before	**Spell words in context** Routines 21, 23 shout, house, pout, before	**Introduce spelling words** Routines 20, 22 down, gown, crown, even
Shared Reading	**"Almond Milk"** **Review /ûr/ words** As you read aloud, review phonics element /ûr/: *first, water*. Have students read the words aloud with you, and emphasize the phonics element.	**"Almond Milk"** **Introduce /ou/ words** As you read aloud, point out the /ou/ word *cow's*. Have students read the word aloud with you, and have student volunteers use the word in an original sentence.	**"Almond Milk"** **Review high-frequency words** As you read aloud, point out the words *many, people* and *good*. Have students read each word to you. Then ask student volunteers to use the word in an original sentence.

High-Frequency Words:	Spelling:	Word Families:
before, done, about, even	Words with -out, -ouse, -own	-out, -ouse, -own

Day 4	Day 5	Collaborative Learning and Independent Practice*
Phoneme Blending Routine 12 **Model:** loud, louder, loudest **Practice:** proud, prouder, proudest **Extra practice:** brown, browner, brownest		• Elkonin Boxes: Words with /ou/ Sounds Days 1–5 • Phonemic Concentration: Words with /ou/ Sounds; Comparative Inflectional Endings –er, –est Days 3–5
Blend words with comparative inflectional endings -er, -est Routine 18 **Model:** high, higher, highest **Practice:** kind, kinder, kindest; sad, sadder, saddest **Extra practice:** round, rounder, roundest **Build words with comparative inflectional endings -er, -est** Routine 19 **Model:** cold, colder, coldest **Practice:** fast, faster, fastest; smart, smarter, smartest **Extra practice:** low, lower, lowest	**Decodable reader: "In Our Town"** Use decodable reader ideas (p. 23).	• Phonics Crossword Puzzle: Words with /ou/ Sounds Days 1–5 • Phonics Board Game: Words with /ou/ Sounds; Comparative Inflectional Endings –er, –est Days 3–5 • Read/Draw/Label: "A Cow in Town": Words with /ou/ Sounds Days 3–5
Distribute picture cards (page 329) and letter cards to student pairs. Have students spell each word using the letter cards and write each word on their workmats. **Picture cards:** clown, frown **Letter cards:** c, f, l, n, o, r, w	**Review -out, -ouse, -own words** Distribute the following letter cards to student pairs. Have partners build -out, -ouse, and -own words and write them on their workmats. **Letter cards:** b, c, e, f, h, m, o, p, r, s, t, u, w	• Word Family Spinners/Sliders: –out, –ouse Days 1–5 • Word Family Tic-Tac-Toe: –out, –ouse Days 1–5 • Word Family Towers: –own Days 3–5
Practice high-frequency words Routine 21 before, done, about, even	**Decodable reader: "In Our Town"** Use decodable reader ideas (p. 23).	• High-Frequency Words Yoga Days 1–5 • High-Frequency Words Chatterboxes Days 3–5
Have student pairs work together to write a sentence using one of the -own words they made in the word families activity.	**Interactive writing** (see p. 22) **Story starter:** The mouse ran out of its house. **Word bank:** brown, loud, found, down, crowd, shout	• Reading/Writing: Respond to the Story "The Brown Mouse" Days 1–5 • Reading/Writing: Respond to the Poem "How Loud Now?" Days 3–5
Spell words in context Routines 21, 23 down, gown, crown, even	**Test words in dictation** Read out the spelling words for students to write. Then review their work.	• Spelling Homework: BLM 1 Days 1–5
"A Farmer's Boy" **Introduce /ou/ words** As you read aloud, point out the /ou/ words *how, cow*. Have students read the words aloud with you, and emphasize the phonics element.	**"A Farmer's Boy"** **Review /ûr/ words** As you read aloud, point out the /ûr/ words *together, Farmer's, Jersey*. Have student volunteers use each word in an original sentence.	

* Use this menu to plan extra practice and center activities for use through the week. All the skills needed for an activity have been introduced by the first day of the range shown. See pages 320–321 for full descriptions.

Collaborative Learning and Independent Practice

ᗰᐪ)) Phonological/Phonemic Awareness Activities

Elkonin Boxes:
Words with /ou/ Sounds
Use on Days 1–5

Provide the week's picture cards for words with /ou/ sounds (page 329). For each card, have students sound out the word, sliding a counter into a cell of an Elkonin box for each individual phoneme. Students can do this individually, or partners can take turns choosing from the picture cards.

Phonemic Concentration:
Words with /ou/ Sounds; Comparative Inflectional Endings –er, –est
Use on Days 3–5

Provide students with a set of the week's picture cards (page 329), two of each card, for a total of twenty-four cards. Instruct partners to arrange the cards face down to form a 6 x 4 grid to play a concentration game. The partners should alternate turning over two cards per turn. When a student uncovers a matching pair, he/she should use the word in an oral sentence and keep the pair of cards. The student who collects the most pairs wins the game.

ᴬᴮ)) Phonics Activities
C

Phonics Crossword Puzzle:
Words with /ou/ Sounds
Use on Days 1–5

Provide students with BLM 2 (page 323) and have them complete the crossword activity.

Phonics Board Game:
Words with /ou/ Sounds; Comparative Inflectional Endings –er, –est
Use on Days 3–5

Place copies of BLM D, a spinner (BLM B), and disks or coins for playing pieces in the center. Students use the spinner to advance on the board. If they land on a space that has a word with an /ou/ sound or the inflectional ending –er or –est, they use it an oral sentence and spin again. If the word does not have an /ou/ sound or the inflectional ending –er or –est, the next player spins. Students also follow directions on the squares that have them.

Label the squares with words and directions, making a path from the START square to the FINISH square (words and directions can be repeated, as necessary). Examples of words and directions include:

- **bow, brown, clown, couch, crown, down, frown, house, mound, mouse, pout, shout, softer, softest, taller, tallest, harder, hardest, box, brand, crop, dog, frog, mend, mash, pond, rind, send; soft, tall, hard**
- **"Move back two spaces"**
- **"Move forward five spaces"**
- **"Spin again"**
- **"Skip your next turn"**
- **"Switch squares with the player across from you"**

Read/Draw/Label a Poem:
"A Cow in Town":
Words with /ou/ Sounds
Use on Days 3–5

Distribute copies of BLM 5 (page 326) and have student pairs take turns reading the poem. Then have them complete the activity by circling the words as instructed.

Word Family Activities

Word Family Spinners/Sliders: –out, –ouse
Use on Days 1–5

Construct two word spinners (BLM B), one for each of the week's word families. Write the word family on the long rectangular piece and initial letters around the circle. Provide copies of the phonics house (BLM A) and have students label the houses -out and -ouse. Ask students to form words using the spinners and to list each word they form in the appropriate word family house. (This activity may also use word sliders [BLM C] instead of spinners.)

Word Family Tic-Tac-Toe: –out, –ouse
Use on Days 1–5

Provide or have students draw a tic-tac-toe board. Have partners play tic-tac-toe using words belonging to the –out and –ouse word families. One partner will use –out words instead of an X to mark his/her spots on the board. The other partner will use –ouse words instead of an O.

Word Family Towers: –own
Use on Days 3–5

Provide partners with interlocking blocks. On each block, place a piece of masking tape. Write –own words on half of the blocks, and other decodable words on the rest of the blocks. Have students find and stack the –own word blocks into a word family tower, pronouncing each word as they add it to the tower.

(This activity can be adapted for the –out or –ouse word family.)

High-Frequency Word Activities

High-Frequency Words Yoga
Use on Days 1–5

Form groups of four and six students. Provide each group with a four- or six-letter HFW on an index card (*done, near, away; before, school, change*). Instruct students to read the word aloud. Then encourage students to pose in order to form the letters in the word with their bodies. Each student can then say his or her letter in order so that the group says the word.

High-Frequency Words Chatterbox
Use on Days 3–5

Fold BLM 4 (page 325) to form a "chatterbox." Instruct students to play with a partner. One student chooses a word on an outside flap, says the word, and spells it aloud while the other student opens and closes the chatterbox for each letter in the word. Then the other student should pick a word on an inside flap, says the word, and spells it aloud. Finally, the first student should open that flap and form an oral sentence using the word that is found there.

Writing Activities

Reading/Writing: Respond to the Story "The Brown Mouse"
Use on Days 1–5

Provide copies of BLM 3 (page 324) and have students complete the writing activity.

Reading/Writing: Respond to the Poem "How Loud Now?"
Use on Days 3–5

Provide copies of BLM 6 (page 327) and have students complete the writing activity.

Spelling Homework

Read each spelling word aloud with your child. Spell it aloud together. Then ask your child to write each spelling word and say it in a sentence.

shout _____   louder _____

house _____   loudest _____

pout _____   crown _____

before _____   even _____

Choose a different activity every day to practice this week's spelling words at home with your child.

Trace your words	Letter tiles	Magnetic letters	Two-toned words	Circle the word
Use your finger to write each spelling word in sand, flour, or a similar material.	Use letter tiles to spell the words and then write the words on a sheet of paper.	Spell the words on a cookie sheet using magnetic letters and then write the words on a sheet of paper.	Write the spelling words with crayons or colored markers on a sheet of paper. Use one color for consonants and another for vowels.	Work with your child to write a sentence for each word on a sheet of paper and circle the spelling words.

Phonics Crossword

Complete the crossword puzzle.
Fill in the words for the pictures shown.

Word Bank
couch
house
shout
clown

The Brown Mouse

Read the story.
Write a sentence to tell why the mouse is not brown at the end.

A little brown mouse came down

into the kitchen of a house.

He did not make a sound.

Before the mouse could eat,

he saw a cat prowling by.

So the mouse jumped into a cup and crouched down.

But the cup was full of flour.

Now the mouse is not brown!

High-Frequency Words Chatterbox

Listen to the directions from your teacher.

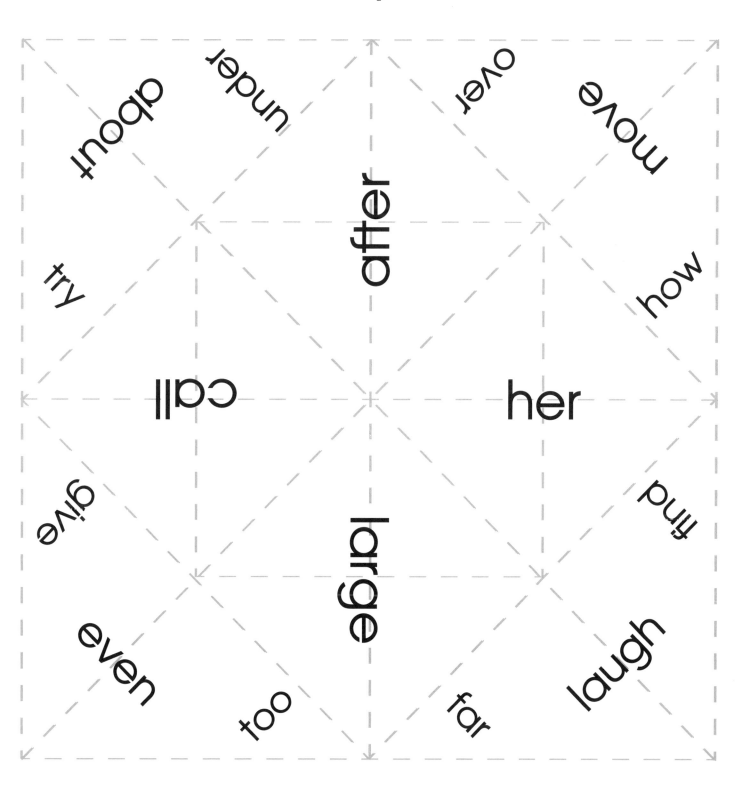

A Cow in Town

Read the poem. Then circle each *ow* word.
Underline each *ou* word.

A cow came right into town

and people shouted out,

"Why is this cow around?"

They scowled and they frowned,

they yelled and they howled.

The cow bowed her head down.

She just wanted the grass on the ground.

How Loud Now?

Read the poem. Then write a sentence about things that are loud.

My mom asked me how

I can shout so loud.

She can hear me

Even in a crowd!

But when she asks for help

with cleaning the house,

it seems that I'm as quiet

as a little baby mouse.

_____

- -

_____

_____

- -

_____

_____

- -

_____

clown	shorter
couch	shortest
frown	shout
house	taller
mouse	tallest
pouch	crowd

Advancing Phonics Every Day

Letters/sounds:
/oi/ (join, boy), suffix -ly

	Day 1	**Day 2**	**Day 3**
Phonological/ Phonemic Awareness	**Syllable Segmentation** `Routine 3` **Model:** avoid, cowboy **Practice:** annoy, poison, enjoy, moisture **Extra practice:** noisy, royal	**Syllable Blending** `Routine 4` **Model:** oyster, voices **Practice:** rejoin, destroy, boiling **Extra practice:** employ, moisture	**Phoneme Recognition** `Routine 9` **Model:** toy/joy/boy **Practice:** boil/soil/spoil **Extra practice:** boil/coil/foil
Phonics	**Review previous week's sound/symbol focus /ou/** `Routine 17` **Model:** round, drown **Practice:** found, shout, plow, crown **Extra practice:** proudest, how **Introduce sound/symbol correspondence /oi/** `Routine 17` **Model:** joy, oink **Practice:** boy, joint, soil, toy **Extra practice:** noise, ploy	**Blend words with /oi/** `Routine 18` **Model:** coin, toy **Practice:** soy, foil, coil **Extra practice:** moist, joint **Dictation with /oi/** **Model:** enjoy, spoil `Routine 24` **Other words:** destroy, points, noise **Decodable reader: "Roy Makes a Choice"** Use decodable reader ideas (p. 23).	**Introduce sound/symbol correspondence: suffix –ly** `Routine 18` **Model:** slowly, kindly **Practice:** nicely, silently, yearly **Extra practice:** quickly, finally Explain to students that the suffix -*ly* is added to make an adjective into an adverb. Say: *The turtle is slow. The turtle moves slowly.* Adding -*ly* to *slow* tells how the turtle moves slowly.
Word Families	Guide students to fold their papers into four rows. Have them write –*oil* at the top of their papers and an –*oil* word in each row.	Distribute the following letter cards to student pairs. Have students form –*oil* words and write each word on their workmats. **Letter cards:** b, c, f, i, l, o, s, t	Distribute letter cards to student pairs. Have them build –*oin* words and write the words on their workmats. **Letter cards:** c, e, i, j, l, m, n, o, p, s, t
High-Frequency Words	**Introduce high-frequency words** `Routine 20` walk, buy	**Practice high-frequency words** `Routine 21` walk, buy **Decodable reader: "Roy Makes a Choice"** Use reader ideas (p. 23).	**Introduce high-frequency words** `Routine 20` only, through
Writing	Have student pairs work together to write a sentence using one of the –*oil* words they wrote in the word families activity.	Have student pairs work together to write a sentence using one of the –*oil* words they wrote on their workmats.	Have student pairs work together to write a sentence using one of the –*oin* words they wrote in the word families activity.
Spelling	**Introduce spelling words** `Routines 20, 22` boil, spoil, foil, walk	**Spell words in context** `Routines 21, 23` boil, spoil, foil, walk	**Introduce spelling words** `Routines 20, 22` join, coin, rejoin, buy
Shared Reading	**"Animal Dentists"** **Review /ou/ words** As you read aloud, review phonics element /ou/: *however, how*. Have students read the words aloud with you, clapping out the syllables.	**"Animal Dentists"** **Introduce /oi/ words** As you read aloud, point out the /oi/ word *pointy*. Have students read the word aloud with you, and have student volunteers use the word in an original sentence.	**"Animal Dentists"** **Introduce high-frequency word: only** As you read aloud, point out the high-frequency word *only*. Have student volunteers use the word in an original sentence.

High-Frequency Words:	Spelling:	Word Families:
walk, buy, only, through	Words with -oil, -oin	-oil, -oin

Day 4	Day 5	Collaborative Learning and Independent Practice*
Phoneme Substitution Routine 14 **Model:** coil/boil, toy/boy **Practice:** foil/soil, joy/soy **Extra practice:** spoil/toil		• Phoneme Cubes: Words with /oi/ Sounds Days 1–5 • Phonemic Word Sort: Words with /oi/ Sounds; Suffix –ly Days 3–5
Blend words with suffix –ly Routine 18 **Model:** sadly, gladly **Practice:** weekly, sharply, sweetly **Extra practice:** brightly, darkly **Build words with suffix –ly** Routine 19 **Model:** silent, silently **Practice:** short, shortly, quick, quickly **Extra practice:** near, nearly, brave, bravely	**Decodable reader: "Roy Makes a Choice"** Use decodable reader ideas (p. 23).	• Letter Cup Substitution: Words with /oi/ Sounds Days 1–5 • Phonics Concentration: Words with /oi/ Sounds; Suffix –ly Days 3–5 • Read/Draw/Label: "The Boys Made Noise": Words with /oi/ Sounds Days 3–5
Distribute picture cards (page 341) and letter cards to student pairs. Have students spell each word using the letter cards and write each word on their workmats. **Picture cards:** coins, point **Letter cards:** c, i, n, o, p, s, t	**Review –oil, –oin words** Distribute the following letter cards to student pairs. Have partners build –oil and –oin words. Have them write the words on their workmats. **Letter cards:** b, c, i, j, l, n, o, p, s, t	• Word Family Picture Labels: –oil Days 1–5 • Word Family Board Game: –oil, –oin Days 3–5 • Feed the Creatures: –oil, –oin Days 3–5
Practice high-frequency words Routine 21 walk, buy, only, through	**Decodable Reader: "Roy Makes a Choice"** Use decodable reader ideas (p. 23).	• High-Frequency Words Graph Days 1–5 • High-Frequency Words "Go Fish" Days 3–5
Have student pairs work together to write a sentence using one of the –oin words they made in the word families activity.	**Interactive writing** (see p. 22) **Story starter:** The boy picked out a toy. **Word bank:** joy, coin, soil, voice, enjoy, noisy	• Reading/Writing: Respond to the Story "Joy and Roy" Days 1–5 • Reading/Writing: Continue the Story "Floyd's Toy" Days 3–5
Spell words in context Routines 21, 23 join, coin, rejoin, buy	**Test words in dictation** Read aloud each of the week's spelling words for students to write. Then collect and review student work.	• Spelling Homework: BLM 1 Days 1–5
"Double Trouble" **Review /oi/ words** As you read aloud, point out the /oi/ word *noisy.* Have students read the word aloud with you, clapping out the syllables.	**"Double Trouble"** **Review long i vowel team (igh)** As you read aloud, point out the words with *igh, bright, light.* Have student volunteers use each word in an original sentence.	

* Use this menu to plan extra practice and center activities for use through the week. All the skills needed for an activity have been introduced by the first day of the range shown. See pages 323–333 for full descriptions.

Collaborative Learning and Independent Practice

 Phonological/Phonemic Awareness Activities

Phoneme Cubes:
Words with /oi/ Sounds
Use on Days 1–5

Gather multiple pairs of cubes (such as empty cube-shaped tissue boxes). Paste the picture cards for words with /oi/ sounds (page 341) on the boxes, five per box. Students can take turns rolling the pair of cubes, saying the two words that face up, and identifying which sounds are the same and which sounds are different.

Phonemic Word Sort:
Words with /oi/ Sounds; Suffix –ly
Use on Days 3–5

Distribute copies of the week's picture cards, excluding the suffixes (page 341). Have pairs of students work together to sort the cards by sound spelling:

- boil / foil / oil /oink / point / coins / voice / soil
- boy / toys

^A_C^B)) Phonics Activities

Letter Cup Substitution:
Words with /oi/ Sounds
Use on Days 1–5

Provide plastic cups with a letter, blend, or vowel team written on the outside of each. Place upside-down cups in a row to spell a word. Have partners take turns fitting other cups over one of the original cups, making a new word. Students should read each word aloud and record it on a phonics house (BLM A) before continuing. Examples:

- starting word: boy
- substitutions of initial letter: j, pl, s, t
- starting word: boil
- substitutions of initial letter: br, c, f, s, sp, t

Phonics Concentration:
Words with /oi/ Sounds; Suffix -ly
Use on Days 3–5

Provide students with a set of the week's picture and word cards (pages 340–341). Instruct partners to arrange the cards face down to form a 6 x 4 grid to play a concentration game. The partners should alternate turning over two cards per turn. When a student uncovers a matching pair (a picture and its corresponding word card), he/she should use the word in an oral sentence and keep the pair of cards. The student who collects the most pairs wins the game.

Read/Draw/Label a Story:
"The Boys Made Noise": Words with /oi/ Sounds
Use on Days 3–5

Distribute copies of BLM 5 (page 338) and have student pairs take turns reading the story. Then have them complete the activity by circling and underlining the words as instructed.

Word Family Activities

Picture Labels: –oil
Use on Days 1–5

Provide students with BLM 2 (page 335) and a word slider (BLM C) for the –oil word family. Have students use the slider to form word family words and complete the activity.

Board Game: –oil, –oin
Use on Days 3–5

Label the squares of BLM D with words and directions, making a path from START to FINISH. Words and directions might include:

- boil, broil, coil, foil, soil, coin, join, joint, loin, point, book, brown, can, cot, found, jug
- "Move back two spaces"
- "Move forward five spaces"
- "Spin again"
- "Skip your next turn"

Place the prepared BLM D, a spinner (BLM B), and disks or coins for playing pieces in the center. Students play by spinning the spinner to advance. If they land on a space that has an –oil or –oin word, they use it in an oral sentence and spin again. If the word is not an –oil or –oin word, the next player spins.

Feed the Creatures: –oil, –oin
Use on Days 3–5

Label each of two small plastic bins with a word family, –oil or –oin. Use a marker to make eyes or a face on each bin to turn the bins into creatures. Provide partners with the following –oil and –oin picture cards and have them take turns "feeding" the creatures the appropriate cards:

- boil / coil / coin / foil / join / point / soil

High-Frequency Word Activities

High-Frequency Words Graph
Use on Days 1–5

Provide students with BLM 4 (page 337) and have them complete the activity.

High-Frequency Words "Go Fish"
Use on Days 3–5

Pick twenty-five high-frequency words, and write each word on two index cards to create fifty cards. Students might be instructed to draw fish on the other sides of the cards. Have groups of 2–4 students play "Go Fish" using this deck.

Writing Activities

Reading/Writing: Respond to the Story "Joy and Roy"
Use on Days 1–5

Provide copies of BLM 3 (page 336) and have students complete the writing activity.

Reading/Writing: Continue the Story "Floyd's Toy"
Use on Days 3–5

Provide copies of BLM 6 (page 339) and have students complete the story as instructed.

Spelling Homework

Read each spelling word aloud with your child. Spell it aloud together. Then ask your child to write each spelling word and say it in a sentence.

boil _____

join _____

spoil _____

coin _____

foil _____

rejoin _____

walk _____

buy _____

Choose a different activity every day to practice this week's spelling words at home with your child.

Trace the word	Multi-colored words	Write it	Write it again	Remember the word
Write the word with dotted lines on a sheet of paper, and then trace the dots with a different color.	Write the spelling words with crayons or colored pencils, using a different color for each letter.	Work with your child to write the word, saying aloud each letter as you write it.	Have your child write the word three times on a sheet of paper and circle the vowels.	Turn the paper over and write the word from memory.

Word Family Picture Labels

Say the name of the picture aloud.
Write the word below each picture.

c _ _ _ _ _ _ _ _ _ _ _ _

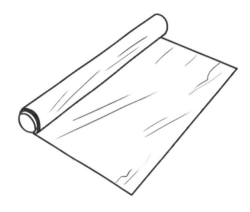

f _ _ _ _ _ _ _ _ _ _ _ _

s _ _ _ _ _ _ _ _ _ _ _ _

b _ _ _ _ _ _ _ _ _ _ _ _

Joy and Roy

Read the story. Write a sentence about something you enjoy doing.

Roy and Joy dug in the soil.

The soil was moist because of the rain.

Then Roy pointed!

He saw a bright thing!

"It's just some foil," said Joy.

But it was an old coin.

What do you think it was worth?

_____

- -

_____

- -

_____

- -

_____

High-Frequency Words Graph

How many letters are in each word? Write the words below the graph.
Color in the graph for each word.

	walk	buy	only	through
7				
6				
5				
4				
3				
2				
1				

The Boys Made Noise

Read the story. Circle all the *oi* words. Underline all the *oy* words.

The four boys were making

a lot of noise.

They shouted at the top

of their voices.

They banged and clanged their toys.

The boys were filled with so much joy

that Mom and Dad didn't want to spoil their fun.

Floyd's Toy

Read the story. Then write a sentence about what Floyd does next.

Floyd wanted a toy.

He walked with his dad to the toy store.

He went through the racks and

pointed to the one he wanted.

"How many coins do you have, Floyd?" asked Dad.

"I have ten dimes," Floyd said in a strong voice.

"Well, ten dimes will buy that toy," Dad said.

Floyd was filled with joy!

oink	point
boy	quickly
boil	oil
coins	toys
foil	voice
loudly	soil

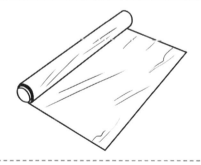

Advancing Phonics Every Day

Letters/sounds:
/o͞o/ (broom) vowel team syllables,
/o͝o/ (book) vowel team syllables

	Day 1	Day 2	Day 3
Phonological/ Phonemic Awareness	**Rhyme Recognition** Routine 5 **Model:** zoo/boo **Practice:** moon/spoon **Extra practice:** soon/noon	**Rhyme Production** Routine 6 **Model:** bloom/gloom, tool/stool **Practice:** root/loot, pool/spool **Extra practice:** shoot/boot, room/groom	**Phoneme Substitution** Routine 14 **Model:** good/hood **Practice:** book/look/cook **Extra practice:** wood/stood
Phonics	**Review previous week's sound/symbol focus:** /oi/ Routine 17 **Model:** toy, point **Practice:** choice, joy, noise **Extra practice:** cowboy, spoil **Introduce sound/symbol correspondence:** /o͞o/ Routine 17 **Model:** bloom, zoom **Practice:** room, soon, noon **Extra practice:** smooth, choose	**Blend words with /o͞o/** Routine 18 **Model:** croon, moose **Practice:** soon, shoot, boo **Extra practice:** doom, boom **Dictation with /o͞o/** Routine 24 **Model:** spoon, room **Other words:** choose, moon, root **Decodable reader: "A Room for Moose"** Use decodable reader ideas (p. 23).	**Introduce sound/symbol correspondence:** /o͝o/ Routine 17 **Model:** took, foot **Practice:** cook, hook, look **Extra practice:** stood, brook
Word Families	Guide students to draw a simple five-petal flower. Have them write –oom in the center and an –oom word in each petal.	Distribute the following letter cards to student pairs. Have students form –oom words and write each word on their workmats. **Letter cards:** b, d, l, m, o, o, r	Distribute picture cards (page 353) and letter cards to student pairs. Have students spell each word using the letter cards and write each word on their workmats. **Picture cards:** hood, wood **Letter cards:** d, h, o, o, w
High-Frequency Words	**Introduce high-frequency words** Routine 20 does, another	**Practice high-frequency words does, another** Routine 21 **Decodable reader: "A Room for Moose"** Use decodable reader ideas (p. 23).	**Introduce high-frequency words** Routine 20 wash, some
Writing	Have student pairs work together to write a sentence using one of the –oom words they wrote in the word families activity.	Have student pairs work together to write a sentence using one of the –oom words they wrote on their workmats.	Have student pairs work together to write a sentence using one of the –ood words they wrote on their workmats.
Spelling	**Introduce spelling words** Routines 20, 22 bloom, room, broom, does	**Spell words in context** Routines 21, 23 bloom, room, broom, does	**Introduce spelling words** Routines 20, 22 stood, wood, good, another
Shared Reading	**"Field Trip Funds"** **Review /oi/ words** As you read aloud, review phonics element /oi/: *enjoy* Have students read the word aloud with you, clapping out the syllables.	**"Field Trip Funds"** **Introduce /o͞o/ words** As you read aloud, point out the /o͞o/ word *zoo*. Have students read the word aloud with you, emphasizing the phonics element.	**"Field Trip Funds"** **Introduce /o͝o/ words** As you read aloud, point out the /o͝o/ words *book, books, neighborhood.* Have students read the words aloud with you, emphasizing the phonics element.

High-Frequency Words:	Spelling:	Word Families:
does, another, wash, some	Words with -oom, -ood	-oom, -ood

Day 4	Day 5	Collaborative Learning and Independent Practice*
Phoneme Deletion `Routine 16` **Model:** brook/book **Practice:** hoodie, hood **Extra practice:** cookie, cook		• Phonemic Picnic: Words with /oo͞/ Sounds Days 1–5 • Phonemic Classroom Clean-Up: Words with /oo͞/, /oo͝/ Sounds Days 3–5
Blend words with /oo͝/ `Routine 18` **Model:** book, crook **Practice:** shook, stood, wood **Extra practice:** hood, foot **Build words with /oo͝/** `Routine 19` **Model:** hook, cook **Practice:** cook, book, look **Extra practice:** hood, hook, shook	**Decodable reader: "A Room for Moose"** Use decodable reader ideas (p. 23).	• Word Rainbows: Words with /oo͞/ Sounds Days 1–5 • Phonics Ice Cream Cones: Words with /oo͞/, /oo͝/ Sounds Days 3–5 • Read/Draw/Label: "The Real Moon?": Words with /oo/ Sounds Days 3–5
Distribute the following letter cards to student pairs. Have students form –ood words and write each word on their workmats. **Letter cards:** d, g, h, o, o, s, t, w	Distribute picture cards (page 353) and letter cards to student pairs. Have students spell each word using letter cards. **Picture cards:** broom, groom, hood, wood **Letter cards:** b, d, g, h, l, m, o, o, r, r, w	• Word Family Books: –oom Days 1–5 • Word Family Sort: –oom, –ood Days 3–5 • Word Family Tic-Tac-Toe: –oom, –ood Days 3–5
Practice high-frequency words `Routine 21` does, another, wash, some	**Decodable reader: "A Room for Moose"** Use decodable reader ideas (p. 23).	• High-Frequency Words Beanbag Toss Days 1–5 • High-Frequency Words Bug Catch Days 3–5
Have student pairs work together to write a sentence using one of the –ood words they made in the word families activity.	**Interactive writing** (see p. 22) **Story starter:** Tom and Molly walked through the woods. **Word bank:** look, took, gloom, bloom, good, wood	• Reading/Writing: Continue the Story "Loose Tooth" Days 1–5 • Days 3–5 Reading/Writing: Respond to the Poem "No Fish" Days 3–5
Spell words in context `Routines 21, 23` stood, wood, good, another	**Test words in dictation** Read out the spelling words for students to write. Then review their work.	• Spelling Homework: BLM 1 Days 1–5
"A New Kind of Eggs" **Review /oo͞/ words** As you read aloud, point out the /oo͞/ word cool. Have students read the word aloud with you, emphasizing the phonics element.	**"Double Trouble"** **Review contractions with not** As you read aloud, point out the contractions not, weren't, don't, can't. Have student volunteers use one of the words in an original sentence.	

*Use this menu to plan extra practice and center activities for use through the week. All the skills needed for an activity have been introduced by the first day of the range shown. See pages 344–345 for full descriptions.

Collaborative Learning and Independent Practice

 Phonological/Phonemic Awareness Activities

Phonemic Picnic:
Words with /o͞o/ Sounds
Use on Days 1–5

Fill a picnic basket (or lunch box) with toy foods. Each food should contain the /o͞o/ sound (for example: *bamboo shoots, noodles, mushrooms, soup*). Have partners sit on the floor as if ready for a picnic. They should take turns choosing a food, saying the name of the food, and passing it to their partner to "eat."

Phonemic Classroom Clean-Up:
Words with /o͞o/, /o͝o/ Sounds
Use on Days 3–5

Set up two bins, one with the *broom* picture card taped to it, and the other with the *wood* picture card taped to it (page 353). Have partners pronounce each word, pointing out the middle /o͞o/ sound in *broom* and the middle /o͝o/ sound in *wood*. Scatter around the classroom the other ten picture cards. Instruct partners to find the cards and place words with the middle /o͞o/ sound in the *broom* bin, and words with the middle /o͝o/ sound in the *wood* bin.

A B C))) Phonics Activities

Word Rainbows:
Words with /o͞o/ Sounds
Use on Days 1–5

Provide students with the week's six picture cards for words with the /o͞o/ sound (page 353). Instruct students to write each word, spelling each sound in the word with an individual color. You might suggest that students choose rainbow colors and use them in that order. Remind students that the two *o*'s in each word should be the same color because together they make one sound.

Phonics Ice Cream Cones:
Words with /o͞o/, /o͝o/ Sounds
Use on Days 3–5

Provide students with BLM 2 (page 347) and have them complete the activity.

Read/Draw/Label a Poem:
"The Real Moon?":
Words with /oo/ Sounds
Use on Days 3–5

Distribute copies of BLM 5 (page 350) and have student pairs take turns reading the poem. Then have them complete the activity by circling and underlining the words as instructed.

 # Word Family Activities

 # High-Frequency Word Activities

 # Writing Activities

Word Family Books: –oom
Use on Days 1–5

For each student, cut two index cards in half. Stack these four pieces of index cards, and then staple them to a single index card to form a "book" with four narrow pages and a final full-width page. Instruct students to write *oom* on the final index card so that those letters are always visible. Then have students form different word family words by writing a letter on each of the first four pages of their books, such as *br, gl, r,* and *z*. (If necessary, support students by providing a bank of letters that will form real words: *b, bl, br, d, gl, l, r, z*.) When finished, students can flip through the first four pages to form and read aloud different word family words (such as *broom, gloom, room, zoom*).

Word Family Sort: –oom, –ood
Use on Days 3–5

Provide students with BLM 4 (page 349) and have them complete the activity.

Word Family Tic-Tac-Toe: –oom, –ood
Use on Days 3–5

Provide or have students draw a tic-tac-toe board. Have partners play tic-tac-toe using words belonging to the *–oom* and *–ood* (as in *good*) word families. One partner will use *–oom* words instead of an X to mark his/her spots on the board. The other partner will use *–ood* words instead of an O.

High-Frequency Words Beanbag Toss
Use on Days 1–5

Gather Benchmark Advance high-frequency word cards for a beanbag toss. Use review words from previous weeks as well as the current week's words.

- **about / another / before / does / every / four / great / laugh / move / some / walk / wash**

Have one student choose a word to read aloud and another student toss the bag to cover the matching card.

High-Frequency Words Bug Catch
Use on Days 3–5

Write a series of high-frequency words, from this week and previous weeks, on index cards, and place the index cards on the floor or on a table. Then provide a pair of students with plastic fly swatters. Instruct students to take turns: One student should read a high-frequency word aloud, and then the other student should "swat" it.

Reading/Writing: Continue the Story "Loose Tooth"
Use on Days 1–5

Provide copies of BLM 3 (page 348) and have students end the story with an original sentence.

Reading/Writing: Respond to the Poem "No Fish"
Use on Days 3–5

Provide copies of BLM 6 (page 351) and have students complete the activity as instructed.

Spelling Homework

Read each spelling word aloud with your child. Spell it aloud together. Then ask your child to write each spelling word and say it in a sentence.

bloom _____

room _____

broom _____

does _____

stood _____

wood _____

good _____

another _____

Choose a different activity every day to practice this week's spelling words at home with your child.

Flashlight writing	Magnetic letters	Multi-colored words	Trace your words	Two-toned words
Turn out the lights. Use a flashlight to spell each word on the wall.	Spell the words on a cookie sheet using magnetic letters and then write the words on a sheet of paper.	Write the spelling words with crayons or colored pencils, using a different color for each letter.	Use your finger to write each spelling word in sand, flour, or a similar material.	Write the spelling words with crayons or colored markers on a sheet of paper. Use one color for consonants and another for vowels.

Phonics Ice Cream Cones

Place the scoops of ice cream on the cones with the same sound.

Loose Tooth

Read the story. Write a sentence to finish the story.

Phil was in a bad mood.

He had a loose tooth.

He could not eat much food.

Phil went to his room.

He sat on a stool, filled with gloom.

Then his mom came in with a big spoon.

What food do you think she made?

_____

_____

_____

_____

_____

Word Family Sort

Cut out the words.
Place each word in the room for its word family.

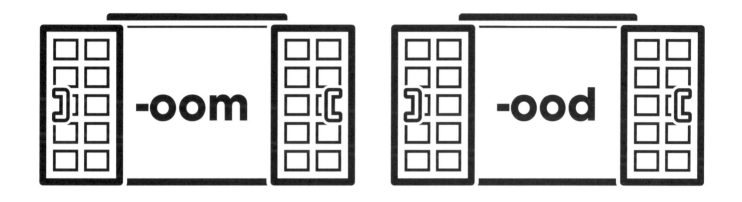

wood	zoom	room	stood	groom
hood	doom	bloom	good	boom

The Real Moon?

**Read the poem. If a word has the same *oo* sound as *good*, circle it.
If a word has the same *oo* sound as *too*, underline it.**

I went to my room to read a book,

It was about the moon.

I looked out my window and saw

what looked like the real moon!

It was round, and it was smooth,

and it was as white as a goose.

I felt like a goof when Dad took it down—

it was just a balloon that got loose!

No Fish

Read the poem. Write why you think the kid did not catch a fish.

I took a fishing rod and a hook

to catch a fish down at the brook.

I got here at ten, but it is past noon.

I hope I catch a fish—and soon.

I want to take the fish home to cook.

Dad can show me how in his book.

But look at my hook! No fish to cook!

Could it be my hook isn't good?

The hook

balloon	scoop
broom	bloom
cookie	rooster
hook	scooter
foot	wood
hood	brook

Advancing Phonics Every Day

Letters/sounds:
silent letters (wr, kn, gn)

	Day 1	Day 2	Day 3
Phonological/ Phonemic Awareness	**Onset and Rime Segmentation** `Routine 7` **Model:** wrap, wreck **Practice:** wrist, wrong, wrote **Extra practice:** wren, write	**Phoneme Segmentation** `Routine 11` **Model:** write, wreath **Practice:** wrong, wreck, writer **Extra practice:** wrapping, wrist	**Onset and Rime Blending** `Routine 8` **Model:** knee, gnaw **Practice:** knit, gnat, gnarl **Extra practice:** knead, kneel
Phonics	**Review previous week's sound/symbol focus:** /oo/, /ŏŏ/ `Routine 17` **Model:** broom, book **Practice:** spoon, noon, wood, took **Extra practice:** moon, hood **Introduce sound/symbol correspondence: silent letters (wr)** `Routine 17` **Model:** wrist, wrap **Practice:** wrong, wrench **Extra practice:** wreck, writer	**Blend words with silent letters (wr)** `Routine 18` **Model:** wristband, wrote **Practice:** wrapper, wreck, wreath **Extra practice:** wrong, written **Dictation with silent letters (wr)** `Routine 24` **Model:** wrench, wrist **Other words:** wry, wring, wren **Decodable reader: "Know About Storms"** Use reader ideas (p. 23).	**Introduce sound/symbol correspondence: silent letters (kn, gn)** `Routine 17` **Model:** knife, gnat **Practice:** knot, gnome, knee **Extra practice:** kneecap, sign
Word Families	Guide students to draw a word web. Have them write -oon in the center circle and an -oon word in each satellite circle.	Distribute the following letter cards to student pairs. Have students form -oon words and write each word on their workmats. **Letter cards:** m, n, o, o, p, s	Distribute picture cards (page 365) and letter cards to student pairs. Have students spell each word using the letter cards and write each word on their workmats. **Picture cards:** pool, spool **Letter cards:** l, o, o, p, s
High-Frequency Words	**Introduce high-frequency words** `Routine 20` better, carry	**Practice high-frequency words** `Routine 21` better, carry **Decodable reader: "Know About Storms"** Use reader ideas (p. 23).	**Introduce high-frequency words** `Routine 20` learn, very
Writing	Have student pairs work together to write a sentence using one of the -oon words they wrote in the word families activity.	Have student pairs work together to write a sentence using one of the -oon words they wrote on their workmats.	Have student pairs work together to write a sentence using one of the -ool words they wrote on their workmats.
Spelling	**Introduce spelling words** `Routines 20, 22` noon, write, soon, better	**Spell words in context** `Routines 21, 23` noon, write, soon, better	**Introduce spelling words** `Routines 20, 22` stool, gnat, knee, carry
Shared Reading	**"Dogs Help the Deaf"** **Review /oo/, /ŏŏ/ words** As you read aloud, review phonics element /oo/, /ŏŏ/, *look, too.* Have students read them aloud, emphasizing the phonics element.	**"Dogs Help the Deaf"** **Introduce silent letters (kn)** As you read aloud, point out the word with silent letters (kn) *know.* Have students read the word aloud with you, emphasizing the phonics element.	**"Dogs Help the Deaf"** **Review /ûr/** As you read aloud, point out the words with /ûr/, *turn, turns.* Have students read them aloud, emphasizing the phonics element.

High-Frequency Words:	Spelling:	Word Families:
better, carry, learn, very	Words with -oon, -ool	-oon, -ool

Day 4	Day 5	Collaborative Learning and Independent Practice*
Phoneme Blending — Routine 12 **Model:** sign, knife **Practice:** knob, knot, gnat **Extra practice:** know, gnaw		• Elkonin Boxes: Words with Silent Letters (wr) Days 1–5 • Phonemic Concentration: Words with Silent Letters (wr, kn, gn) Days 3–5
Blend words with silent letters (kn, gn) — Routine 18 **Model:** knew, gnaw **Practice:** knit, gnat, gnarl **Extra practice:** knead, gnaw **Dictiation with silent letters (kn, gn)** — Routine 24 **Model:** knee, design **Practice:** gnawing, kneeling, knight **Extra practice:** resign, knowing	**Decodable Reader: "Know About Storms"** Use decodable reader ideas (p. 23).	• Phonics Board Game: Words with wr/r/ Days 1–5 • Picture Word Matching: Words with Silent Letters (wr, kn, gn) Days 3–5 • Read/Draw/Label: "Oh, Gnats!": Words with Silent Letters (wr, kn, gn) Days 3–5
Distribute the following letter cards to student pairs. Have students form *-ool* words and write each word on their workmats. **Letter cards:** d, f, l, o, o, p, r, s, t	**Review -oon, -ool words** Distribute picture cards (page 365) and letter cards to student pairs. Have students spell each word using the letter cards. **Picture cards:** moon, pool, spool, spoon **Letter cards:** l, m, n, o, o, p, s	• Word Family Towers: –oon Days 1–5 • Word Family Crossword: –oon, –ool Days 3–5 • Word Family Ice Cream Cones: –oon, –ool Days 3–5
Practice high-frequency words — Routine 21 better, carry, learn, very	**Decodable reader: "Know About Storms"** Use decodable reader ideas (p. 23).	• High-Frequency Words Yoga Days 1–5 • High-Frequency Words "Go Fish" Days 3–5
Have student pairs work together to write a sentence using one of the *-ool* words they made in the word families activity.	**Interactive writing** (see p. 22) **Story starter:** Mark and Jill jumped in the pool. **Word bank:** soon, cool, knew, sign, wrung	• Reading/Writing: Continue the Story "The Secret Pal" Days 1–5 • Reading/Writing: Respond to the Poem "Knox Knits" Days 3–5
Spell words in context — Routines 21, 23 stool, gnat, knee, carry	**Test words in dictation** Read out the spelling words for students to write. Then review their work.	• Spelling Homework: BLM 1 Days 1–5
"I Know All the Sounds That the Animals Make" **Review silent letters /kn/** As you read aloud, point out the word with silent letters (*kn*), *know*. Have students read the word aloud, and have student volunteers use the word in a sentence.	**"Dogs Help the Deaf"** **Review /oo/ words** As you read aloud, point out the words with /oo/, *moose, hoot, moo, goose*. Have student volunteers use one of the words in an original sentence.	

* Use this menu to plan extra practice and center activities for use through the week. All the skills needed for an activity have been introduced by the first day of the range shown. See pages 356–357 for full descriptions.

Collaborative Learning and Independent Practice

Phonological/Phonemic Awareness Activities

Elkonin Boxes:
Words with Silent Letters (wr)
Use on Days 1–5

Provide the week's three picture cards for words with *wr* (page 365). For each card, have students sound out the word, sliding a counter into a cell of an Elkonin box for each individual phoneme. Students can do this individually, or partners can take turns choosing from the picture cards. Remind students that *wr* is just one phoneme.

Phonemic Concentration:
Words with Silent Letters (wr, kn, gn)
Use on Days 3–5

Provide students with a set of the week's picture cards (page 365), two of each card, for a total of twenty-four cards. Instruct partners to arrange the cards face down to form a 6 x 4 grid to play a concentration game. The partners should alternate turning over two cards per turn. When a student uncovers a matching pair, he/she should use the word in an oral sentence and keep the pair of cards. The student who collects the most pairs wins the game.

Phonics Activities

Phonics Board Game:
Words with wr/r/
Use on Days 1–5

Place copies of BLM D, a spinner (BLM B), and disks or coins for playing pieces in the center. Students use the spinner to advance on the board. If they land on a space that has a word with *wr*/r/, they use it an oral sentence and spin again. If the word does not have *wr*/r/, the next player spins. Students also follow directions on the squares that have them.

Label the squares with words and directions, making a path from the START square to the FINISH square (words and directions can be repeated, as necessary). Examples of words and directions include:

- write, wrap, wreath, wrist, wrench, wrong, wrote, wring, wrung, wristwatch, rate, ripe, rich, rise, went, wound, right, wing, rung, wait
- "Move back two spaces"
- "Move forward five spaces"
- "Spin again"
- "Skip your next turn"
- "Switch squares with the player across from you"

Picture Word Matching:
Words with Silent Letters (wr, kn, gn)
Use on Days 3–5

Provide students with the week's picture and word cards for words with silent letters (pages 364–365). Have students match each picture to its word and then sort all the pairs by initial sound (*wreath/wrench/wrist, knife/knit*).

Read/Draw/Label a Poem:
"Oh, Gnats!": Words with Silent Letters
(wr, kn, gn)
Use on Days 3–5

Distribute copies of BLM 5 (page 362) and have student pairs take turns reading the poem. Then have them complete the activity as instructed.

 Word Family Activities

Word Family Towers: –oon
Use on Days 1–5

Provide partners with interlocking blocks. On each block, place a piece of masking tape. Write *–oon* words on half of the blocks, and other decodable words on the rest of the blocks. Have students find and stack the *–oon* word blocks into a word family tower, pronouncing each word as they add it to the tower.

(This activity can be adapted for the *–ool* word family.)

Word Family Crossword: –oon, –ool
Use on Days 3–5

Provide students with BLM 2 (page 359) and have them complete the crossword activity.

Word Family Ice Cream Cones: –oon, –ool
Use on Days 3–5

Provide students with BLM 4 (page 361) and have them complete the activity.

 High-Frequency Word Activities

High-Frequency Words Yoga
Use on Days 1–5

Form groups of five and six students. Provide each group with a five- or six-letter HFW on an index card (*carry, about, every, better, before, school*). Instruct students to sound out each letter and read the word aloud. Then encourage students to pose in order to form the letters in the word with their bodies. Each student can then say his or her letter in order so that the group says the word.

High-Frequency Words "Go Fish"
Use on Days 3–5

Pick twenty-five high-frequency words, and write each word on two index cards to create fifty cards. Students might be instructed to draw fish on the other sides of the cards. Have groups of 2–4 students play "Go Fish" using this deck.

Writing Activities

Reading/Writing: Continue the Story "The Secret Pal"
Use on Days 1–5

Provide copies of BLM 3 (page 360) and have students write to tell about the idea of a secret pal.

Reading/Writing: Respond to the Poem "Knox Knits"
Use on Days 3–5

Provide copies of BLM 6 (page 363) and have students complete the activity as instructed.

Spelling Homework

**Read each spelling word aloud with your child. Spell it aloud together.
Then ask your child to write each spelling word and say it in a sentence.**

noon _____   stool _____

write _____   gnat _____

soon _____   knee _____

better _____   carry _____

**Choose a different activity every day to practice
this week's spelling words at home with your child.**

Write it	Flashlight writing	Multi-colored words	Trace your words	Letter tiles
Work with your child to write the word, saying aloud each letter as you write it.	Turn out the lights. Use a flashlight to spell each word on the wall.	Write the spelling words with crayons or colored pencils, using a different color for each letter.	Use your finger to write each spelling word in sand, flour, or a similar material.	Use letter tiles to spell the words and then write the words on a sheet of paper.

Word Family Crossword

Complete the crossword puzzle. Fill in the words for the pictures shown.

Word Bank

pool

spool

spoon

noon

moon

The Secret Pal

Read the poem. Write to tell about the idea of a secret pal.

I wrapped up a little gift for my good friend Hal.

I wrote a note signed, "From your secret pal."

Then I went to Hal's home and knocked on the door.

I put the gift on the porch next to his garden gnome.

When Hal opened the door, I ran quickly and hid.

I jumped out and Hal said, "It was you! I knew it!"

_____

- -

_____

- -

_____

- -

_____

Word Family Ice Cream Cones

Place the scoops of ice cream on the correct word family cones.

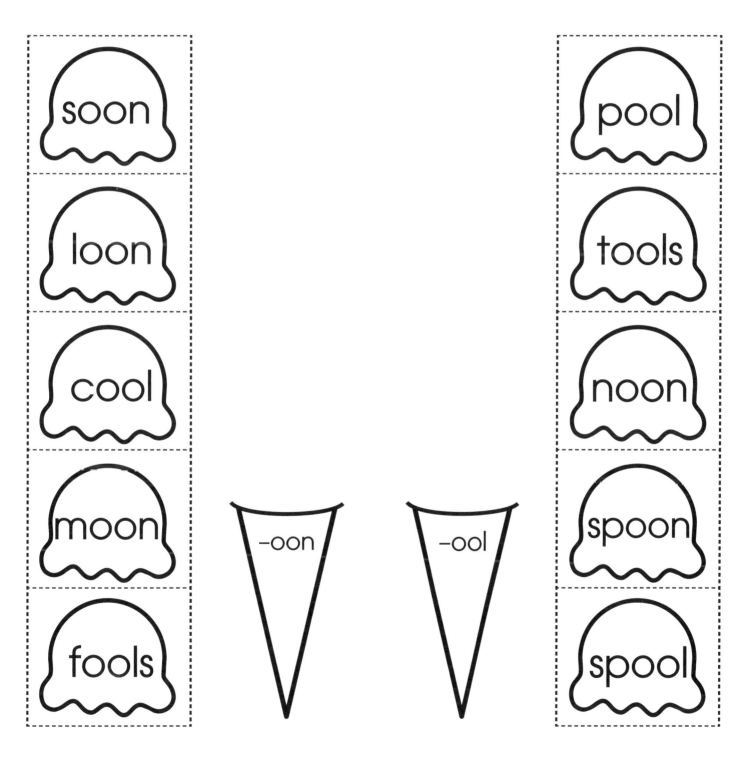

Oh, Gnats!

**Read the poem. Underline all the words with *g* in them.
Then circle the word with a silent *g*.**

Slap! Slap!

I slap at my wrists and my knees.

What kind of bugs are these?

They do not bite or sting.

They just fly all around me.

They're not moths, hornets, or bees.

They're gnats! Oh, go away please!

Knox Knits

Read the poem.
Then write a sentence about something you do very well.

Knox has a knack for knitting.

He knits night and day.

In fact, if you ask him,

this is what Knox will say:

"I can knit kneepads and knotted hats.

I can knit wrist wrappers, too.

You can ask for anything

and I can knit that for you!"

I _____

_____

signs	raccoon
gnome	spool
knife	spoon
knit	wreath
moon	wrench
pool	wrist

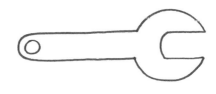

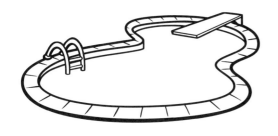

Advancing Phonics Every Day

	Day 1	Day 2	Day 3
Phonological/ Phonemic Awareness	**Rhyme Recognition** `Routine 5` **Model:** paw/raw, stalk/talk **Practice:** straw/saw, salt/malt **Extra practice:** caught/taught, halt/fault	**Rhyme Production** `Routine 6` **Model:** caught/taught, law/saw **Practice:** jaw/paw, cause/pause **Extra practice:** walk/talk	**Phoneme Categorization** `Routine 13` **Model:** dawn/fawn/down **Practice:** crawl/growl/ball, bale/ball/mall **Extra practice:** after/also/almost
Phonics	**Review silent letters (wr, kn, gn)** `Routine 17` **Model:** wrench, knife **Practice:** sign, writer, knob **Introduce sound/symbol correspondence: /ô/** `Routine 17` **Model:** yawn, also **Practice:** walk, awful, crawl	**Blend words with /ô/** `Routine 18` **Model:** straw, auto **Practice:** draw, always, talking **Dictation with /ô/** `Routine 24` **Model:** straw, taught **Other words:** jaw, August, also, salt **Decodable reader: "Paul Takes a Walk"** Use decodable reader ideas (p. 23).	**Introduce sound/symbol correspondence: suffixes (ful, less)** `Routine 19` **Model:** help, helpful, helpless **Practice:** hope, hopeful, hopeless; care, careful, careless **Extra practice:** fear, fearful, fearless Explain that the suffix -*ful* means "full of" and the suffix -*less* means "without." Adding these suffixes to words changes their meaning.
Word Families	Guide students to draw a simple cup and straw. Have them write –*aw* in the straw and four –*aw* words in the cup.	Distribute the following letter cards to student pairs. Have students form –*aw* words and write each word on their workmats. **Letter cards:** a, d, j, p, r, s, w	Distribute picture cards (page 377) and letter cards to student pairs. Have students spell each word using the letter cards and write each word on their workmats. **Picture cards:** fawn, yawn **Letter cards:** a, f, n, w, y
High-Frequency Words	**Introduce high-frequency words** `Routine 20` mother, father	**Practice high-frequency words** `Routine 21` mother, father **Decodable reader: "Paul Takes a Walk"** Use decodable reader ideas (p. 23).	**Introduce high-frequency words** `Routine 20` never, below
Writing	Have student pairs work together to write a sentence using one of the –*aw* words they wrote in the word families activity.	Have student pairs work together to write a sentence using one of the –*aw* words they wrote on their workmats.	Have student pairs work together to write a sentence using one of the –*awn* words they wrote on their workmats.
Spelling	**Introduce spelling words** cause, claw, stalk, mother	**Spell words in context** cause, claw, stalk, mother	**Introduce spelling words** yawn, caught, dawn, father
Shared Reading	**"Rainbow"** `Routines 20, 22` **Review silent letters (kn)** As you read aloud, review phonics element, silent letters (*kn*): *know* Have students read the word aloud with you, emphasizing the phonics element.	**"Rainbow"** `Routines 21, 23` **Introduce /ô/ words** As you read aloud, point out the word with /ô/: *fall* Have students read the word aloud with you, emphasizing the phonics element.	**"Rainbow"** `Routines 20, 22` **Introduce high-frequency word: below** As you read aloud, point out the high-frequency word *below*. Have students read the word aloud with you, clapping out the syllables.

High-Frequency Words:	Spelling:	Word Families:
mother, father, never, below	Words with -aw, -awn	-aw, -awn

Day 4	Day 5	Collaborative Learning and Independent Practice*
Phoneme Addition `Routine 15` **Model:** raw/draw, law/claw **Practice:** talk/stalk, law/slaw **Extra practice:** saw/straw		• Phonemic Picnic: Words with /ô/ Sounds Days 1–5 • Phoneme Cubes: Words with /ô/ Sounds Days 3–5
Blend words with suffixes (ful, less) `Routine 18` **Model:** needless, grateful **Practice:** lifeless, harmless, harmful **Build words with suffixes (ful, less)** `Routine 19` **Model:** pain, painful, painless **Practice:** power, powerful, powerless; use, useful, useless	**Decodable reader: "Paul Takes a Walk"** Use decodable reader ideas (p. 23).	• Phonics Word Builder: Words with /ô/ Sounds Days 1–5 • Phonics Beanbag Toss: Words with /ô/ Sounds; Suffixes –ful, –less Days 3–5 • Read/Draw/Label a Story: "Walk in the Woods": Words with /ô/ Sounds Days 3–5
Distribute the following letter cards to student pairs. Have students form –awn words and write each word on their workmats. **Letter cards:** a, d, f, l, n, w	**Review –aw, –awn words** Distribute picture cards (page 377) and letter cards to student pairs. Have students spell each word using the letter cards. **Picture cards:** draw, fawn, yawn, straw **Letter cards:** a, d, f, n, r, s, t, w, y	• Word Family Picture Labels: –aw Days 1–5 • Word Family Spinners/Sliders: –aw, –awn Days 3–5 • Feed the Creatures: –aw, –awn Days 3–5
Practice high-frequency words `Routine 21` mother, father, never, below	**Decodable reader: "Paul Takes a Walk"** Use decodable reader ideas (p. 23).	• High-Frequency Words Concentration Days 1–5 • High-Frequency Words Board Game Days 3–5
Have student pairs work together to write a sentence using one of the –awn words they made in the word families activity.	**Interactive writing** (see p. 22) **Story starter:** I just saw something crawl in the house. **Word bank:** awful, caught, paw, claw, walk	• Reading/Writing: Continue the Story "Claude and the Ball" Days 1–5 • Reading/Writing: Respond to the Poem "Paul the Lobster" Days 3–5
Spell words in context yawn, caught, dawn, father	**Test words in dictation** Read out the spelling words for students to write. Then review their work.	• Spelling Homework: BLM 1 Days 1–5
"My Homemade Band" `Routines 21, 23` **Introduce /ô/** As you read aloud, point out the words with /ô/: saw, called. Have students read the words aloud with you, and have volunteers use each word in a sentence.	**"My Homemade Band"** **Review /o͞o/ words** As you read aloud, point out the word with /o͞o/: good. Have student volunteers use the word in an original sentence.	

* Use this menu to plan extra practice and center activities for use through the week. All the skills needed for an activity have been introduced by the first day of the range shown. See pages 368–369 for full descriptions.

Collaborative Learning and Independent Practice

𝄞)) Phonological/Phonemic Awareness Activities

Phonemic Picnic:
Words with /ô/ Sounds
Use on Days 1–5

Fill a picnic basket (or lunch box) with toy foods. Each food should contain the phoneme from this week (and, if desired, previous weeks). (For example: *coleslaw, cauliflower, strawberries, meatballs*.) Have partners sit on the floor as if ready for a picnic. They should take turns choosing a food, saying the name of the food, and passing it to their partner to "eat."

Phoneme Cubes:
Words with /ô/ Sounds
Use on Days 3–5

Gather multiple pairs of cubes (such as empty cube-shaped tissue boxes). Paste the week's eight picture cards for words with the /ô/ sound (page 377) on the boxes. Students can take turns rolling the cubes, saying the two words that face up, and identifying the sounds that are the same and the sounds that are different in each pair.

ᴬᴮ)) Phonics Activities
C

Phonics Word Builder:
Words with /ô/ Sounds
Use on Days 1–5

Label a spinner (BLM B) with the letters *c, h, l, p*, and *t*, and provide students with letter tiles (or cutouts) of each letter. Have students use the spinner and letter tiles to complete the activity on BLM 2 (page 371). Note that student answers may vary.

Phonics Beanbag Toss:
Words with /ô/ Sounds; Suffixes –ful, –less
Use on Days 3–5

Arrange the twelve picture cards (page 377) for a beanbag toss. Provide the word cards (page 376), and have students take turns reading a word aloud and tossing the beanbag to the corresponding picture.

Read/Draw/Label a Story:
"Walk in the Woods":
Words with /ô/ Sounds
Use on Days 3–5

Distribute copies of BLM 5 (page 374) and have student pairs take turns reading the story. Then have them complete the activity as instructed.

Word Family Activities

Word Family Picture Labels: –aw
Use on Days 1–5

Provide students with BLM 4 (page 373) and a word slider (BLM C) for the –aw word family. Have students use the slider to form word family words and complete the activity.

Word Family Spinners/Sliders: –aw, –awn
Use on Days 3–5

Construct two word spinners (BLM B), one for each of the week's word families. Write the word family on the long rectangular piece and initial letters around the circle. Provide copies of the phonics house (BLM A) and have students label the houses -aw and -awn. Ask students to form words using the spinners and to list each word they form in the appropriate word family house. (This activity may also use word sliders [BLM C] instead of spinners.)

Feed the Creatures: –aw, –awn
Use on Days 3–5

Provide two small plastic bins. Label each with a word family, –aw or –awn. Use a marker to make eyes or a face on each bin to turn the bins into creatures. Provide partners with the following –aw and –awn picture cards, and have them take turns "feeding" the creatures the appropriate cards:

- draw / hawk / straw / fawn / yawn

High-Frequency Word Activities

High-Frequency Words Concentration
Use on Days 1–5

Distribute to partners the high-frequency word cards. Each set should contain two copies of each word, or twenty-eight cards. Instruct partners to arrange the cards face down to form a 7 x 4 grid to play a concentration game. The partners should alternate turning over two cards per turn. When a student uncovers a matching pair, he/she should use the word in an oral sentence and keep the cards. The student who collects the most pairs wins the game.

- another / better / buy / carry / does / father / learn / mother / only / some / through / very / walk / wash

High-Frequency Words Board Game
Use on Days 3–5

Label the squares of BLM D with words and directions, making a path from START to FINISH. (Repeat words and directions as necessary.) Words and directions might include:

- never, below, once, upon, hurt, that, because, from, their, when, why, many, right, start, find, how, over, under, try, give, far, too
- "Move back two spaces"
- "Move forward five spaces"
- "Spin again"
- "Lose next turn"

Place the prepared BLM D, a spinner (BLM B), and disks or coins for playing pieces in the center. Students play by spinning the spinner to advance. When they land on a high-frequency word, they read the word aloud and use it in an oral sentence. Then the next player spins.

Writing Activities

Reading/Writing:
Continue the Story "Claude and the Bell"
Use on Days 1–5

Provide copies of BLM 3 (page 372) and have students write a sentence to end the story.

Reading/Writing:
Respond to the Poem "Paul the Lobster"
Use on Days 3–5

Provide copies of BLM 6 (page 375) and have students complete the activity as instructed.

Spelling Homework

Read each spelling word aloud with your child. Spell it aloud together. Then ask your child to write each spelling word and say it in a sentence.

cause _____

yawn _____

claw _____

caught _____

stalk _____

mother _____

dawn _____

father _____

Choose a different activity every day to practice this week's spelling words at home with your child.

Trace the word	Flashlight writing	Remember the word	Circle the word	Magnetic letters
Write the word with dotted lines on a sheet of paper, and then trace the dots with a different color.	Turn out the lights. Use a flashlight to spell each word on the wall.	Turn the paper over and write the word from memory.	Work with your child to write a sentence for each word on a sheet of paper and circle the spelling words.	Spell the words on a cookie sheet using magnetic letters and then write the words on a sheet of paper.

Phonics Word Builder

Place a letter tile in each box to make a word.
Read the word aloud.
Be sure that you make real words.

☐ aw   ☐ awn

☐ aunch   ☐ aunt

☐ all   ☐ alk

☐ aught   ☐ awk

Claude and the Ball

Read the story. Write a sentence about how you think the story will end.

It's a hot day in August.

Laura and Austin play ball on the lawn.

Laura tosses the ball to Austin.

He almost catches it,

but it falls to the ground.

Here comes their dog Claude!

He grabs the ball in his jaws.

_____

- -

_____

- -

_____

- -

_____

- -

Word Family Picture Labels

Say the name of the picture out loud. Write the first letters of the word below each picture.

awk

Walk in the Woods

Read the story. Draw a picture to show part of the story.
Label anything in your picture that has the same sound as *law*.

We took a walk in the woods on a fall day.

We saw lots of awesome things.

We saw prints from a raccoon's paws.

We saw small bugs crawling on the ground.

We saw claw marks from a wild animal.

Then we saw a hawk in the sky!

There are always things to see in the woods.

Paul the Lobster

Read the poem. Write a sentence to tell about a thing you have drawn.

Paul is a lobster.

He likes to draw with chalk.

He holds it in his claw

as he draws on the sidewalk.

When Paul is finished drawing

he quickly crawls away.

People are always shocked

a lobster can draw that way.

caught	launch
priceless	yawn
draw	helpful
fawn	chalk
painful	straw
hawk	toothless

Advancing Phonics Every Day

Letters/sounds:
long e (y, ey), consonant-le syllables

	Day 1	Day 2	Day 3
Phonological/ Phonemic Awareness	**Rhyme Recognition** Routine 6 **Model:** honey, sunny, money **Practice:** pulley, wooly, bully **Extra practice:** jockey, hockey	**Rhyme Production** Routine 6 **Model:** funny/sunny **Practice:** volley/trolley, honey/money **Extra practice:** Sidney/kidney	**Phoneme Recognition** Routine 9 **Model:** lady, tiny **Practice:** very, valley **Extra practice:** silly, city
Phonics	**Review previous week's sound/symbol focus: /ô/** Routine 17 **Model:** lawn, caught **Practice:** claw, talk, always **Extra practice:** awful, almost **Introduce sound/symbol correspondence: long e (y, ey)** Routine 17 **Model:** key, quickly **Practice:** turkey, pulley, minty **Extra practice:** valley, story	**Blend words with long e (y, ey)** Routine 18 **Model:** jockey, bunny **Practice:** turkey, runny, story **Extra practice:** penny, thirty **Dictation with long e (y, ey)** Routine 24 **Model:** chimney, sixty **Other words:** pulley, teary, sticky **Decodable reader: "City Lights"** Use decodable reader ideas (p. 23).	**Introduce sound/symbol correspondence: consonant-le syllables** Routine 18 **Model:** little, beagle **Practice:** dribble, fiddle, bubble **Extra practice:** circle, turtle
Word Families	Guide students to draw a word web. Have them write –eep in the center circle and an –eep word in each satellite circle.	Distribute the following letter cards to student pairs. Have students form –eep words and write each word on their workmats. **Letter cards:** b, d, k, e, e, p, w	Distribute picture cards (page 389) and letter cards to student pairs. Have students spell each word using the letter cards. **Picture cards:** hockey, key, turkey **Letter cards:** a, c, e, h, k, l, l, o, r, t, u
High-Frequency Words	**Introduce high-frequency words** Routine 20 blue, answer	**Practice high-frequency words** Routine 21 blue, answer **Decodable reader: "City Lights"** Use decodable reader ideas (p. 23).	**Introduce high-frequency words** Routine 20 eight, any
Writing	Have student pairs work together to write a sentence using one of the –eep words they wrote in the word families activity.	Have student pairs work together to write a sentence using one of the –eep words they wrote on their workmats.	Have student pairs work together to write a sentence using one of the –ey words they made in the word families activity.
Spelling	**Introduce spelling words** Routines 20, 22 deep, chimney, valley, blue	**Spell words in context** Routines 21, 23 deep, chimney, valley, blue	**Introduce spelling words** Routines 20, 22 purple, dazzle, pulley, answer
Shared Reading	**"Day or Night?"** **Review /ô/** As you read aloud, review phonics element /ô/: *fall, all.* Have students read each word aloud with you, emphasizing the phonics element.	**"Day or Night?"** **Introduce long e (y)** As you read aloud, point out the word with long e (*y*): *many.* Have students read the word aloud with you, clapping out the syllables.	**"Day or Night?"** **Introduce consonant-le syllables** As you read aloud, point out the word with consonant-le syllable *simple.* Have students read the word aloud with you, emphasizing the phonics element.

High-Frequency Words:	Spelling:	Word Families:
blue, answer, eight, any	Words with -eep, -ey	-eep, -ey

Day 4	Day 5	Collaborative Learning and Independent Practice*
Phoneme Categorization `Routine 13` **Model:** cable, stable, staying **Practice:** paddle, dangle, pattern **Extra practice:** little, fiddle, listen		• Phonemic Word Sort: Words with Long e Sounds Days 1–5 • Phonemic Classroom Clean-Up: Words with Long e Sounds; Consonant-le Syllables Days 3–5
Blend words with consonant-le syllables `Routine 18` **Model:** middle, cuddle **Practice:** simple, maple, humble **Extra practice:** candle, drizzle **Dictation with consonant-le syllables** `Routine 24` **Model:** jungle, handle **Practice:** paddle, cable **Extra practice:** stable, puzzle	**Decodable reader: "City Lights"** Use decodable reader ideas (p. 23).	• Phonics Concentration: Words with Long e Sounds Days 1–5 • Phonics Crossword: Words with Long e (y, ey); Consonant-le Syllables Days 3–5 • Read/Draw/Label a Poem: "Turkey and Turtle": Words with Long e (y, ey); Consonant-le Syllables Days 3–5
Distribute the following letter cards to student pairs. Have students form –ey words and write each word on their workmats. **Letter cards:** c, e, h, k, m n, o, y	**Review –eep, –ey words** Distribute picture cards (page 389) and letter cards to student pairs. Have students spell each word using the letter cards. **Picture cards:** beep, sheep, key, hockey **Letter cards:** b, c, e, e, h, k, o, p, s, y	• Word Family Books: –eep Days 1–5 • Word Family Tic-Tac-Toe: –eep, –ey Days 3–5
Practice high-frequency words `Routine 21` blue, answer, eight, any	**Decodable reader: "City Lights"** Use decodable reader ideas (p. 23).	• High-Frequency Words Parking Lot Days 1–5 • High-Frequency Words Beanbag Toss Days 3–5
Have student pairs work together to write a sentence using one of the –ey words they made in the word families activity.	**Interactive writing** (see p. 22) **Story starter:** Molly found a key. **Word bank:** journey, funny, very, keep, deep	• Reading/Writing: Respond to the Poem "Trolley Time" Days 1–5 • Reading/Writing: Respond to the Poem "Monkey Keys?" Days 3–5
Spell words in context `Routines 21, 23` purple, dazzle, pulley, answer	**Test words in dictation** Read out the spelling words for students to write. Then review their work.	• Spelling Homework: BLM 1 Days 1–5
"My Shadow" **Introduce consonant-le syllables** As you read aloud, point out the word with consonant-le syllables *little*. Have students read the word aloud with you, and have student volunteers use the word in a sentence.	**"My Shadow"** **Introduce long e (y)** As you read aloud, point out the word with long e (*y*): *very*. Have student volunteers read the word aloud with you, clapping out the syllables.	

* Use this menu to plan extra practice and center activities for use through the week. All the skills needed for an activity have been introduced by the first day of the range shown. See pages 380–381 for full descriptions.

Collaborative Learning and Independent Practice

 Phonological/Phonemic Awareness Activities

Phonemic Word Sort:
Words with Long e Sounds
Use on Days 1–5

Distribute copies of the week's picture cards for words with long e (page 389). Have pairs of students work together to sort the cards by the location of the long e sound (middle or final):

- beep / sheep
- candy / dirty / hockey / key / turkey / money

Phonemic Classroom Clean-Up:
Words with Long e Sounds; Consonant-le Syllables
Use on Days 3–5

Set up two bins, one with the *beep* picture card taped to it, and the other with the *circle* picture card taped to it (page 389). Have partners pronounce each word, pointing out the long e sound in *beep* and the final consonant-le sound in *circle*. Scatter around the classroom the other ten picture cards. Instruct partners to find the cards and place words with the long e sound in the *beep* bin, and words with the final consonant-le sound in the *circle* bin.

ᴬBᴄ)) Phonics Activities

Phonics Concentration:
Words with Long e Sounds
Use on Days 1–5

Provide students with two sets of the week's eight long e picture and word cards (pages 388–389). Instruct partners to arrange the cards face down to form a 4 x 4 grid to play a concentration game. The partners should alternate turning over two cards per turn. When a student uncovers a matching pair (a picture and its corresponding word card), he/she should use the word in an oral sentence and keep the pair of cards. The student who collects the most pairs wins the game.

Phonics Crossword:
Words with Long e (y, ey); Consonant-le Syllables
Use on Days 3–5

Provide students with BLM 2 (page 383) and have them complete the crossword activity.

Read/Draw/Label a Poem:
"Turkey and Turtle": Words with Long e (y, ey); Consonant-le Syllables
Use on Days 3–5

Distribute copies of BLM 5 (page 386) and have student pairs take turns reading the poem. Then have them complete the activity as instructed.

Word Family Activities

Word Family Books: –eep
Use on Days 1–5

For each student, cut two index cards in half. Stack these four pieces, and then staple them to a whole index card to form a "book" with four narrow pages and a final full-width page. Instruct students to write -eep on the final index card so that those letters are always visible. Then have students form different word family words by writing a letter on each of the first four pages of their books, such as *d, p, sl,* and *w* (options: *b, cr, d, p, s, sh, sl, w*). When finished, students can flip through the first four pages to form and read aloud different word family words (such as *deep, peep, sleep, weep*).

Word Family Tic-Tac-Toe: –eep, –ey
Use on Days 3–5

Provide or have students draw a tic-tac-toe board. Have partners play tic-tac-toe using words belonging to the *–eep* and *–ey* word families. One partner will use *–eep* words instead of an X to mark his/her spots on the board. The other partner will use *–ey* words instead of an O.

High-Frequency Word Activities

High-Frequency Words Parking Lot
Use on Days 1–5

Provide partners with BLM 4 (page 385) and toy cars, and have them complete the activity. Students should take turns: One student should read a high-frequency word aloud, and the other student should "park" a toy car in that spot and say a sentence using the word.

High-Frequency Words Beanbag Toss
Use on Days 3–5

Gather Benchmark Advance high-frequency word cards for a beanbag toss. Use review words from previous weeks as well as the current week's words.

- answer / any / blue / call / could / draw / eight / found / great / long / many / near

Have one student choose a word to read aloud, and another toss the bag to cover the matching card.

Writing Activities

Reading/Writing:
Respond to the Poem "Trolley Time"
Use on Days 1–5

Provide copies of BLM 3 (page 384) and have students complete the activity as instructed.

Reading/Writing:
Respond to the Poem "Monkey Keys?"
Use on Days 3–5

Provide copies of BLM 6 (page 387) and have students complete the activity as instructed.

Spelling Homework

Read each spelling word aloud with your child. Spell it aloud together. Then ask your child to write each spelling word and say it in a sentence.

deep _____

purple _____

chimney _____

dazzle _____

valley _____

pulley _____

blue _____

answer _____

Choose a different activity every day to practice this week's spelling words at home with your child.

Trace the word	Write it	Remember the word	Letter tiles	Flashlight writing
Write the word with dotted lines on a sheet of paper, and then trace the dots with a different color.	Write the word on a sheet of paper, saying aloud each letter as you write it.	Turn the paper over and write the word from memory.	Use letter tiles to spell the word and then write the word on a sheet of paper.	Turn out the lights. Use a flashlight to spell each word on the wall.

Phonics Crossword

Complete the crossword puzzle. Fill in the words for the pictures shown.

Word Bank

candy

circle

dirty

donkey

uncle

Trolley Time

**Read the poem. Write a sentence about a trip you
have taken with your family.**

My family took a trolley ride

way down a mountainside.

We slowly went far down

into a deep valley with a town.

It was a fine and pretty trip,

and we were happy not to slip.

But then my sister started to cry,

and we had to say goodbye.

_____

- -

_____

- -

_____

High-Frequency Words Parking Lot

Listen to the directions from your teacher.

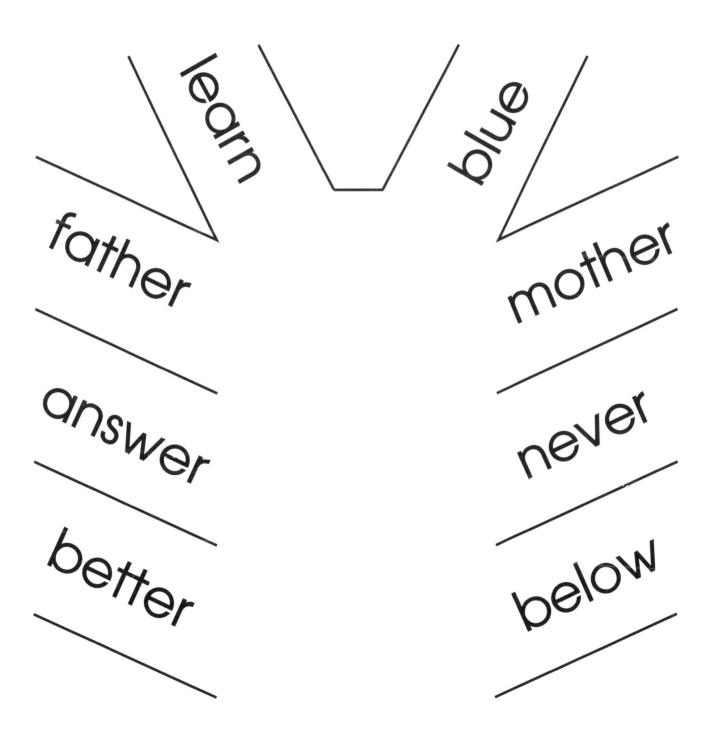

Turkey and Turtle

**Read the poem. Draw a picture to show any part of the poem.
Label any part of your picture that makes a long e sound using *-y* or *-ey*.**

A turkey and a turtle wanted to have a race.

They lined up carefully at the starting place.

The turkey gobbled and wobbled.

He knew he would win.

The turtle shuffled and struggled.

He knew the odds were slim.

Then the turkey fell in a puddle!

His feathers got all wet.

The turtle kept on going, and then he won the bet.

Monkey Keys?

Read the poem. Write a sentence to tell if you think the story at the end of the poem is true.

Tell me, please, if you are able,

Is my house key on the table?

I just can't tell my dad and mom

about that little monkey, Tom.

Did he take my keys at the zoo?

Who would think that is true? Would you?

beep	**key**
candy	**pickles**
circle	**sheep**
dirty	**table**
freckles	**turkey**
hockey	**money**

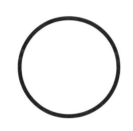

How to Make a Chatterbox

There are many short videos online that show how to make a chatterbox. Please locate one of them if you'd like step-by-step instructions with visual support.

NOTE: If you make the chatterbox starting with a printed blackline master from *Advancing Phonics Skills*, be sure to start Step 4 with the printed side FACE DOWN.

Materials Needed

• Paper

• Scissors

• Pencil or pen

Steps

1. Start with a square piece of paper. If using a 8½" x 11" piece of paper, fold the short side so that it aligns with the long side. Then use scissors to cut the paper to form a square.

2. Fold the paper diagonally to create a crease. Then unfold.

3. Fold the paper along the opposite diagonal to create another crease. Then unfold.

4. Fold each corner so that the point of the corner touches the point where the creases cross. If you use a printed BLM from *Advancing Phonics Skills*, remember to complete this step with the printed side FACE DOWN. Be sure to fold all four corners.

5. Flip the paper over.

6. Fold each corner so that the point of the corner touches where the creases cross again. Be sure to fold all four corners.

7. Write words, numbers, or drawings on the flaps and inside the flaps. (This step is already complete if you use a printed blackline master from *Advancing Phonics Skills*.)

8. Fold to form a rectangle.

9. Place your fingers under the four corner flaps and use.